Trajectories of Freedom

Trajectories of FREEDOM

CARIBBEAN SOCIETIES, 1807–2007

Edited by

ALAN COBLEY AND VICTOR C. SIMPSON

UNIVERSITY OF THE WEST INDIES PRESS
Jamaica • Barbados • Trinidad and Tobago

University of the West Indies Press
7A Gibraltar Hall Road, Mona
Kingston 7, Jamaica
www.uwipress.com

© 2013 by Alan Cobley and Victor C. Simpson

All rights reserved. Published 2013

A catalogue record of this book is available from the National Library of Jamaica.

ISBN: 978-976-640-411-6

Cover photograph: Dancers performing at "Three Nights of Freedom", the cultural event accompanying the conference "Trajectories of Freedom", Barbados, 2007. At centre is the late Jolicoeur Bengi, who was among the victims of the Haitian earthquake of 2010. Photo provided by kind courtesy of the Faculty of Humanities and Education, University of the West Indies, Cave Hill, Barbados.

Book and cover design by Robert Harris.
Set in Scala 10/14 x 27
Printed in the United States of America.

CONTENTS

Introduction / **1**
VICTOR C. SIMPSON AND ALAN COBLEY

PART 1 HISTORY AND POLITICS

1   Different Trajectories of Freedom in the Anglophone Caribbean / **13**
BRIDGET BRERETON

2   Tropical Libertarians: Anarchist Networks in the Circum-Caribbean, 1900–1915 / **26**
KIRWIN R. SHAFFER

3   Eric Williams and the Labour Movement in Trinidad and Tobago / **41**
JEROME TEELUCKSINGH

PART 2 LITERATURE AND PERFORMANCE

4   Dominica as Spiritual Landscape: Representations of Nature in Jean Rhys's *Wide Sargasso Sea* and Marie-Elena John's *Unburnable* / **63**
ENA HARRIS

5   Independence or Nationalism? A Fresh Look at Andreu Iglesias's *Los derrotados* / **71**
VICTOR C. SIMPSON

| 6 | Performative Bondage: Caryl Phillips's *Dancing in the Dark* / **87**
AGNEL BARRON |

| 7 | Freedom of the Spirit and African Cultural Retentions: The Case of East Port of Spain, Trinidad and Tobago / **95**
SANDRA GIFT AND OBA KENYATTA OMOWALE KITEME |

| 8 | Myth and Ritual in Hosay, Ramleela and Carnival as Expressions of a Vibrant Caribbean Culture / **109**
EDITH PÉREZ SISTO |

PART 3 EDUCATION AND LANGUAGE

| 9 | Museum Education as a Means to Promote Equal Opportunities / **129**
HILDE NEUS VAN DER PUTTEN |

| 10 | "Can u assist me?" Help Needed with Students' Use of Standard English / **148**
KELVIN QUINTYNE |

| 11 | Language, Identity and Freedom: A Creole Perspective / **156**
HAZEL SIMMONS-MCDONALD |

PART 4 GENDER

| 12 | Exploring Representations of Gender and Sexuality in (Jamaican) Dancehall Popular Culture: The Search for a Method / **173**
AGOSTINHO M.N. PINNOCK |

| 13 | The Twenty-first-Century Caribbean Woman's Question: What Is the Meaning of Freedom? / **192**
APRIL BERNARD |

Contributors / **209**

INTRODUCTION

VICTOR C. SIMPSON AND ALAN COBLEY

IN MAY 2007 THE Faculty of Humanities and Education of the University of the West Indies, Cave Hill, in Barbados hosted a conference entitled: "Trajectories of Freedom: Caribbean Societies, 1807–2007". The theme of the conference was inspired by the two-hundredth anniversary of the abolition of the transatlantic slave trade in the British Empire, a year marked by a rash of celebrations and commemorations. The conference was also intended to problematize and interrogate shifting notions and expressions of "freedom" as they have evolved in Caribbean societies over the past two hundred years and as they were being applied in the context of the contemporary Caribbean. Submissions were invited regionally and internationally from the widest possible range of disciplinary and interdisciplinary perspectives on this theme. In the event, more than forty-five papers were presented during the three days of the conference. It is our hope that the selection of papers presented here is representative of the range and quality of the discourse that the participants enjoyed.

While this collection seeks to share aspects of the academic discourse of our "Trajectories of Freedom" conference, an important part of the proceedings occurred outside the conference rooms. In addition to the academic sessions held each day, an innovative feature of this event was a lively evening programme in which the general public was invited to join with conference participants in an exploration of the themes of the conference under the general title "Three Nights of Freedom". On each night the spotlight was turned on one of three main linguistic areas in our region: the English-speaking, the French-speaking and the Spanish-speaking Caribbean – with a keynote address on each region forming the centrepiece of each evening's programme.

On the first night, Professor Bridget Brereton of the University of the West Indies, St Augustine, delivered a paper entitled "Different Trajectories of

Freedom in the Anglophone Caribbean". This was followed on the second night by an address by Professor Jorge Duany of the University of Puerto Rico, Río Piedras, entitled "The Freedom Movement in the Spanish-Speaking Caribbean during the Twentieth Century". The series was concluded on the final evening with an address entitled "Assimilation or Emancipation: the Guadeloupean Dilemma", delivered by M. Jean-Claude Lombion, then mayor of Morne a l'Eau, Guadeloupe. The programme each night also included drama, dance and drumming performances that highlighted the culture of each subregion and reflected on the theme. We were fortunate to have the presence of three Haitian artists during these performances: acclaimed choreographer and dancer Jean-René Delsoin, who served as guest choreographer, Haitian master drummer Rodrigue Jean-Baptiste, who provided the percussive drive, and Jolicoeur Bengi, who was one of the featured dancers. By the third night, there was standing room only for latecomers among the excited and engaged audience in the theatre of the Errol Barrow Centre for Creative Imagination, where the event was held. In a very real sense, these evening performances formed a critical part of the discussions held each day and added a unique dimension to them.

The memory of this tremendous moment in the cultural life of the Cave Hill campus was tinged with sadness when news was received recently that Jolicoeur Bengi was killed during the catastrophic earthquake in Haiti on 12 January 2010, when the school in which he was teaching collapsed, burying him in the rubble. All who came into contact with Bengi (as we called him) during his brief visit to Barbados will remember his effortless ability to communicate – despite not speaking English – both through his joyous smile and with his sheer exuberant physicality as a dancer. This collection is dedicated to his memory and, more generally, to the people of Haiti, who have suffered so much over the past two centuries in their continuing struggle – against incredible odds – to be free. Haiti was the first independent black republic in the hemisphere and the first to overthrow chattel slavery. Haiti will always remain a symbol of the triumph of the human spirit and a beacon of hope and resilience – not only for Caribbean people but also for freedom-loving people everywhere.

For those familiar with the history of the former British West Indies, it need hardly be stated that the Emancipation Act implemented throughout the British Empire on 1 August 1834 fell far short of delivering complete freedom for the formerly enslaved people in those islands and territories. The very effective legislative, judicial, economic and political ploys adopted by the dominant class in the West Indies after emancipation – in collaboration with sympathetic colonial governments and the West India Lobby in the metropole – were used to retain social, economic and political control in the region and served to restrict the "freedom" of the formerly enslaved in myriad ways. As a result, the postemancipation period, arguably even to the present, has been one of struggle to assert the freedoms promised by emancipation. This is no less true in other parts of the Caribbean, where the struggle was waged against other colonial masters. And even though the historical path to ultimate freedom followed by the people of the region is marked with many victories, the process is far from complete. As Stephen Geofroy puts it, "The concept of emancipation . . . understood as an ongoing quest for the furtherance of human dignity in the Caribbean in various spheres of life is very much unfinished business" (Geofroy 2007, 1).

Freedom is a complex concept. It appears to be an absolute, yet in practice it is laden with ambiguity. If a formerly enslaved person is no longer in that condition, then that person may be said to be "free". Similarly, if a country is recognized as an independent state after having been a colony for centuries, it may be said to be a "free" country. However, if the former enslaved have little food, no jobs, no adequate housing and no access to education, can they really be considered free? To state the proposition more starkly, if the formerly enslaved remain economically dependent on their former enslavers, are they truly free? And if a country has ceased to be a colony and has become a politically independent state, yet more powerful states continue to use it as a pawn in a broader geopolitical chess game, is that country truly free? Questions such as these remain relevant in the Caribbean two hundred years after the Haitian Revolution, on the one hand, and the ending of the transatlantic slave trade by the British, on the other, sounded the death knell of slavery in the region – as well as the ending of formal colonial rule in much of the Caribbean during the last half of the twentieth century. Many people in the Caribbean still do not enjoy the personal freedom which, by Orlando Patterson's definition, "gives a person the sense that one . . . is not being coerced or restrained and . . . the conviction that one can do as he pleases within the limits of [the] other person's desire to do the same" nor the civic freedom that gives them an "opportunity to participate in the life and governance of one's society" (Patterson 1991, 3–4).

The dominance enjoyed by the imperialistic powers and the privileges which they claimed over Caribbean people during the nineteenth and twentieth centuries continued the sense of superiority and entitlement that had been characteristic of the former slave masters and owners, while the sense of inferiority and incapacity developed by the enslaved over centuries carried over and was maintained into the postcolonial period. All this conspired to maintain an unequal balance of power which was defined largely in terms of ethnicity and class: it meant a continuation of white dominance and black/brown subordination. For example, in Barbados the white oligarchy was able to maintain ownership and control of the plantations and their production while the formerly enslaved were forced to continue as labourers on the plantations of their former masters. The evidence is clear that coloured and black Barbadians "were denied the chance of competing as sugar producers by a united front of white planters and their merchant bankers" (Craton 1997, 338). Circumstances such as these contributed in great measure to the length of time and the difficulty involved in the quest for genuine freedom pursued by the formerly enslaved and their descendants. Even today, black business people in Barbados complain of being denied the credit needed to establish and maintain businesses by (white-owned) banks and finance houses. While Barbados may be seen in some ways as a particularly stark example of the interplay of ethnicity, class and power, the same broad outlines of struggle have been seen in many territories across the Caribbean over the past two hundred years.

The various slave rebellions over the centuries throughout the Caribbean demonstrated the natural yearning among the enslaved for freedom, culminating in the revolution in Santo Domingo in 1791. That seminal event remains a beacon of hope and an example for oppressed people everywhere. Indeed, it is difficult to discuss the question of freedom without acknowledging the influential role of the events in Haiti at the turn of the nineteenth century in defining what true freedom might mean for Caribbean people. To some extent the slave rebellions that broke out in Barbados, Demerara and Jamaica in the early years of the nineteenth century reflected the influence of the events in Haiti and the ideas they represented, and they attest to the longing for freedom that motivated enslaved people everywhere. The leaders of these various uprisings shared a simple desire for freedom and wished, in the words of the Barbados national anthem, to be "craftsmen of their fate". At some level they all recognized, as Michael Craton puts it, that "slavery distorts the personality and all human relationships, so that only in resistance can the self be realized and dignity restored" (Craton 1997, 305). This spirit continued to motivate the common folk in the decades after emancipation. The workers in various islands of the Caribbean in the 1860s and 1870s through their many struggles reminded the ruling class that it still stood in the way of the people's freedom. Again, during the widespread riots of the 1930s, a full century after emancipation, the yearning of the masses for the fulfilment of the promise that emancipation portended was revitalized and recast in insistent demands for their rights as members of the working class.

But bold and epoch-making though the events of the Haitian Revolution were, the history of Haiti since that time is an outstanding and painful reminder of the fact that neither liberation from enslavement nor the attainment of political sovereignty is a guarantee of genuine freedom. Some of the chapters in this work spring from a recognition of this fact and seek to identify some of the areas that need to be addressed in order for Caribbean populations at large to experience genuine freedom. The attainment of political independence, in spite of the euphoria surrounding it, has had to come face to face with the economic and political realities which see the local ruling class remain entrenched in its economic hegemony and the attendant political clout that it is consequently able to exercise. Even the freedom that political sovereignty implies is circumscribed by the influence of more powerful states. In some cases Caribbean states have aligned themselves with more powerful states on various issues in the hope of economic gain (St Vincent and the Grenadines with Japan on the issue of whaling, for example, or St Lucia's recent switch of diplomatic allegiance from China to Taiwan). Furthermore, the power of the "colossus of the north" – that is, the United States – has been strongly felt across the region over the last century through numerous military invasions and incursions into countries such as Haiti, the Dominican Republic, Cuba, Puerto Rico and Grenada, not to mention less formal but often no less invasive economic and cultural influences.

Today, many in Haiti remain oppressed by poverty, inadequate economic opportunities, political oppression and foreign interference. It is only perhaps in the area of cultural expression that one senses a flourishing which genuine freedom would be expected to facilitate. The aspiration to true freedom has to be seen also, in part, in the struggle to maintain or hold on to the legacy of Africanness. This has been one means of resistance to being overwhelmed by Western standards and other influences, particularly in the cultural sphere, which has been seen throughout the Caribbean. If Western colonial and former colonial powers can be seen as agents of enslavement – whatever form that enslavement may take – then efforts to resist the encroachment of values and norms from sources external to the region and to foreground the African cultural traditions of Caribbean people in response may be seen as part of the continuing struggle for freedom. In this case the effort is aimed at (re)claiming the right to freedom of expression. In the words of Geofroy, freedom "is a call for breaking the hold of cultural chains that hold Caribbean peoples in bondage" (2007, 6).

This collection is divided into four loose subthemes. The first section, entitled "History and Politics", begins with Bridget Brereton's fascinating overview of the historical struggles for freedom in the anglophone Caribbean. Brereton makes the crucial point, borne out in the rest of the collection, that there were myriad ways to struggle for freedom besides the obvious examples of marronage and revolt. Her examples range from masquerade to religion and from "defiant speech acts" to styles of dress. Other contributions in this section include Kirwin Shaffer's discussion on the circulation of anti-imperialist ideas of anarchism in the Caribbean. As Shaffer points out, "Anarchism is a philosophy of freedom", with a special concern for the rights of workers and the freedom of the individual from state control and economic exploitation. This presentation demonstrates clearly the anticolonial and pro-worker orientation of the movement in some Spanish-speaking areas of the Caribbean and circum-Caribbean in affirming the right of individuals and societies to be free from domination by elite groups. Theirs was an attempt at revolution through the spread of ideas of freedom. Time has shown how fragile a commodity freedom can be. In areas such as Haiti, Grenada and Cuba, governments have promised economic, social and political freedom only to descend into oppression (often with the collaboration of powerful foreign forces), provoking as a result violent reactions which themselves have had only limited success in bringing to the people the freedom they long for. In his chapter, Jerome Teelucksingh discusses the problematic relationship between Eric Williams and organized labour in Trinidad and Tobago. This is a fascinating account not least because of the irony reflected in what were indeed two parallel struggles for freedom. While the working class was struggling to establish its rights and consolidate its freedoms in the wake of the labour upheavals of the 1930s, which themselves were a sometimes violent manifestation of resistance to some aspects of the legacy of slavery, the new political forces were seeking to affirm their legitimacy as worthy successors to colonial government.

The second section of the collection, entitled "Literature and Performance", focuses on work by the novelists Jean Rhys and Marie-Elena John, as well as

César Andreu Iglesias and Caryl Phillips, as Ena Harris, Victor C. Simpson and Agnel Barron respectively grapple with the concept of freedom as differently addressed by the various authors. Harris highlights the contrast in the effect of the Dominican landscape (which she refers to as "a site of remembrance and resistance") on the descendants of the enslaved on one hand, and on the other on those of the former colonists and enslavers. Simpson brings into sharp relief the unusual Caribbean situation of Puerto Rico, where freedom from colonial domination has eluded the island for five centuries: today political freedom is considered to be a luxury that the island can ill afford, one that tends to be associated with instability and underdevelopment. Sixty years ago Puerto Rican leadership decided on the alternative of "cultural freedom" which it has vigorously pursued ever since. In the chapter, Simpson argues that Andreu Iglesias's novel anticipates this present-day reality in which the independence project, in spite of its violent manifestations of the 1930s, elicits very little interest. Barron addresses the "performative bondage" in which black performers are forced to practice their profession. This is a classic example that demonstrates the limits of freedom, or at least the limits of formal emancipation. Black people may be emancipated from slavery in a formal way, but on the mental level, they have not necessarily assimilated what freedom really is. The result is that they are still content to continue responding to the tacit demands and expectations of the former enslavers, who themselves, because they remain in a position of privilege, continue to expect the servant response from those they still consider to be inferior.

This section concludes with contributions by Edith Pérez Sisto and by Sandra Gift and Oba Kiteme. Pérez Sisto argues that the rituals associated with Hosay, Ramleela and carnival celebrations reflect, among other things, the search for understanding of self. This suggests that these rituals can also be seen as an expression of religious and cultural freedom, which was threatened and suppressed in former times of colonial dominance of both Africans and East Indians. The celebration of carnival is significant to the extent that it harks back to religious and cultural ideas and practices that are widely recognized to have been an essential part of the coping mechanism of the enslaved. In a vital sense, therefore, it must be seen as an annual celebration of freedom which its observance during the period of slavery prefigured. Gift and Kiteme address the nature and role of performing arts in the community in east Port of Spain, which as they say was once referred to as "a haven for emancipated slaves ... to practice their ancestral rituals". As the authors argue, these activities are significant in reinforcing our understanding of the extent of African retentions in this area and, by extension, in the Caribbean. Culture was used as a means of resistance to, and at the same time as an affirmation of, African influence during the postemancipation period and continues to be so used in the postcolonial period. Each chapter in this section in its own way demonstrates the vibrancy of the culture, important areas of self-expression for previously subjugated groups, brought to the Caribbean either by the indentured servants or by the enslaved.

The third section of the collection, "Education and Language", brings together contributions on aspects of two critical areas in which development is vital to the attainment of true emancipation. The concept of the pursuit and creation of freedom as a multifaceted and continuous activity is reflected in Hilde Neus van der Putten's discussion of museum education in Suriname. The assimilation of knowledge and understanding of one's past is generally seen as an integral aspect of charting a way forward for any nation. As postcolonial societies in the Caribbean engage in the business of nation building, the aspect of education provided by the museum experience can form an integral element in this process. Neus van der Putten argues for more of this kind of education for young people to promote popular knowledge of cultural heritage, which she also sees as potentially creating equal opportunity for all. Language education, especially the use of varieties of language in the Caribbean that diverge from Standard English, provides the focus for the other two chapters in this section. Kelvin Quintyne grapples with the impact on teaching English in the classroom of the new phenomenon of "e-English". In the Caribbean experience, the widely held belief that Creole languages are inferior and that the use of such languages inhibits intellectual and social development is firmly grounded in the experience of colonialism and in the neocolonialist thinking that still characterizes these societies. Addressing the need for "freedom of language" in the St Lucian context, Hazel Simmons-McDonald argues that whatever "inferiority" there may be is not inherent in the language but rather is the result of the politics surrounding the language and its use.

The final section of the collection, "Gender", brings together two novel contributions on aspects of gender in Caribbean society. Venturing into the Jamaican dancehalls to explore maleness and alternative sexualities, Agostinho Pinnock challenges the validity of the methodological concept of objectivity in conducting certain types of research in the Caribbean and argues for other criteria of assessment or validation to be recognized in the Caribbean academy.

April Bernard rounds out the collection with a discussion about the meaning of freedom for Caribbean women in the twenty-first century in which she argues for an appropriate definition of the concept that would help to integrate women fully into the development process.

Together, these essays are illustrative of the historical and continuing efforts in the various spheres of human endeavour in the Caribbean, including culture, education, language, social organization, gender and politics – notwithstanding the constraints placed on Caribbean people by the legacies of slavery and colonialism – to finish the business of emancipation. Together, we hope, they evoke the spirit of our ancestors and, by so doing, make their own small contribution to our region's continuing struggle to achieve true freedom.

References

Craton, Michael. 1997. *Empire, Enslavement and Freedom in the Caribbean*. Kingston: Ian Randle.

Geofroy, Stephen. 2007. "Freedom, Post-Modernism and Caribbean Masculine 'Redefinitions'". http://www.cavehill.uwi.edu/fhe/histphil/philosophy/chips/2007/papers/geofroy.pdf.

Patterson, Orlando. 1991. *Freedom in the Making of Western Culture*. New York: Basic Books.

PART 1

HISTORY AND POLITICS

1.

DIFFERENT TRAJECTORIES OF FREEDOM IN THE ANGLOPHONE CARIBBEAN

BRIDGET BRERETON

> I taken my pen in hand a runaway slave, to inform your exelcy of the evil of slavery. Sir slavery is a bad thing and if any man will make a slave of a man after he is born free, i should think it an outrage becose i was born free of my mother wom and after i was born the monster, in the shape of a man, made a slave of me in your dominion now Sir i ask your excelcy in the name of God and his kingdom is it wright for God created man kind equal and free so i have a writ to my freedom.
> – William Gilbert

HIS NAME WAS WILLIAM GILBERT, a formerly enslaved man from St Croix who had managed to escape to Boston, and he was writing to the king of Denmark (St Croix was one of the Danish colonies) in 1847, forty years after the abolition of the British transatlantic trade in enslaved Africans and just before Danish emancipation (Thompson 2006, 41). He expressed, in his poorly spelled but eloquent words, the universal passion for freedom among the enslaved. For Caribbean slavery was not a system which totally dehumanized its victims, however much it damaged their bodies and psyches; to equate it with "social death", with all due respect to Orlando Patterson, is a misleading exaggeration. There were always crucial areas of the enslaved's lives that were largely outside the enslavers' control: the provision ground/marketing complex was a more or less autonomous space, as were religion, some aspects of expressive culture, and family life. These areas were central to their non-stop struggles for a degree of control over the conditions of their existence, and they constituted the core of their lives after the end of formal slavery.

Historians have come to accept that there were many ways of resisting slavery and that the day-to-day actions (including so-called *petit marronage*) were not only more frequent than the violent rebellions but were in some ways more insidious and more undermining of the system. (This, of course, is in no way meant to deny the huge impact of the great rebellions, especially the Haitian Revolution, and the British Caribbean risings of 1816, 1823 and 1831.) The historiography recognizes, too, that attempting to distinguish sharply between "resistance" and "accommodation" (or "collaboration") in the behaviour of the enslaved is to construct a false dichotomy.

I want to apply these generally accepted insights to the period after the end of slavery in the anglophone Caribbean. There were many trajectories of freedom: many ways of struggling for it, many routes to self-assertion and community building, many modes of resisting efforts to negate the promise of emancipation. We know that the postemancipation nineteenth century was marked by endemic protests, risings and some large-scale rebellions. But these actions, which have been extensively studied – riots always generate a paper trail – were not the only, nor necessarily the most significant, ways in which the formerly enslaved, and others, pursued freedom. This chapter discusses some of the other ways in which people sought to defend their freedom and assert their right to autonomy and humanity.

Afro-Caribbean elation at the time of emancipation was accompanied by a deep feeling of mistrust: Was it binding, could it be snatched back? This is why so many chose to purchase their freedom in the last years of slavery, even when its end was known to be imminent, and why others would choose to buy out their remaining years or months of apprenticeship, even when it was known that it was to terminate two years early – even when they were urged not to waste their money by well-meaning magistrates and clergymen. In fact, the frequency of self-purchase out of apprenticeship seems to have increased as August 1838 drew closer. In the Bahamas, people took loans from the brand-new Friendly Societies to do this in the last months of the scheme. They did not want to be wholly dependent on Queen Victoria's freedom; they wanted a legally executed "free paper" for themselves and their relatives if they could manage it.

Rumours of re-enslavement swept the Caribbean from time to time in the decades after 1838, much as rumours of imminent freedom had done in the years before 1834. Many, perhaps most, refused to enter annual hiring contracts with employers (the norm for agricultural labour in Britain), in the belief that this would somehow forfeit their freedom: "A foolish idea has got into the negroes' head", wrote one exasperated Jamaican magistrate in March 1839, "that, to use his own words, he must not sell 'his free'". To be "bound down" was not to be free (Heuman 2006, 102; Brereton 1999, 106).

Perhaps these deep-seated and, indeed, perfectly rational fears about the permanence of emancipation were especially strong in St Lucia and Dominica, with their memories of an earlier emancipation by the revolutionary French in 1794, which had then been taken away – by the British in St Lucia and by Napoleon in Guadeloupe, Dominica's close neighbour. In Dominica, these fears sparked off a major riot in 1844, the "Guerre Negre", when many of the formerly enslaved interpreted the attempt to take a census as a prelude to re-enslavement. This is what a freedman called Saint Louis was reported to have said (no doubt his patois was translated into Standard English):

> I think that our freedom can be taken away from us, because it was once done in another country near to us; it was the French who gave their people free, and afterwards made them slaves again; my parents told me so when I was quite a child, and I have remembered it ever since; what is done once can be done again, and we all know that liberty is good; I don't know but what the English will do like the French one of these days; it is only for the Queen to send a Gazette, and say "make them slaves again", and they will be all made slaves; if a man pays money, and does not get a receipt, he can be made to pay the money again, so it is with freedom; if we have been made free and have not paper to show for it, we can be made slaves again. (Chase 1989, 130)

In St Lucia, where the earlier betrayal had also taken place, after the first emancipation was reversed following the British defeat of the "L'Armée Francaise dans les bois" ("The French Army in the Woods") in 1796–97, self-purchases during the last years of slavery and during the apprenticeship were especially numerous. Claire Robertson, reporting on her attempts to tap into oral traditions about the two emancipations (1794 and 1834–38), concludes, "St Lucians, never trustful due to repeated betrayals of liberté, and ever seeking security in a threatening present, choose the freedom their ancestors taught them: legal title to land, strategic family cooperation, hard work, migration when necessary and, above all, independence" (Robertson 2000, 118).

Perhaps no single community in the anglophone Caribbean was as vigilant to guard its freedom, to protect its special position, as the Jamaican Maroons. In his fascinating presentation and discussion of oral traditions told to him by the present-day Maroons of Moore Town and Accompong, anthropologist Ken Bilby recounts how these communities sought to defend what they understood to be their rights and immunities, long after the end of slavery in Jamaica – and even longer after the peace treaties of the 1730s (Bilby 2006). Attempts by the colonial government to send surveyors or land valuators into Maroon territory were invariably resisted as a possible prelude to land seizure or the imposition of taxes contrary to the 1739 treaty. In 1946 a land dispute in the Moore Town area led to a serious confrontation when the colonial police entered the community and tried to arrest a man without first consulting the Maroon colonel. This is how Colonel Harris described the event in a written account several years later (and note how the past, evoked by references to Nanny, the abeng and the drums, frames the account of a recent event):

> The sight of so many armed men storming their gates wrought immediate transformation on the now peaceful Maroons – their cohesion and discipline reached new heights of perfection; the spirit of Nanny lived again. Shattering the morning calm the abeng flung its urgent message across the hills, the drums beat their imperative commands, and the answering echoes brought the kinsmen with uncanny speed to the scene of potential danger. . . . But adopting certain methods which this writer is not free to reveal, the Maroons thwarted every design. And as the evening shadows began to lengthen and the clansmen repaired to their common meeting place, and the subdued roll of the drums became more and more haunting, more and more unnerving, 125 uniformed men – their duty unaccomplished through no fault of theirs – returned to their headquarters. (Bilby 2006, 344)

In 1959 the *Gleaner* reported:

> The Maroons of Scots Hall are protesting the entrance upon their property of Government land valuators who have been carrying out the new land valuation on the unimproved value basis. Recently valuators were refused entry into the district when the Colonel gave orders for the abeng to be blown summoning all Maroons in the area to block the entrance of the valuators. They are relying upon the Treaty of 1739, which allowed them hundreds of acres free of taxation, to escape the new rates. (Bilby 2006, 356)

But it was not only valuators and surveyors who felt the mistrust and hostility of the Maroons; missionaries and schoolteachers did too, especially around the time of emancipation. As a letter from clergymen of the Church Missionary Society in 1837 explained,

> When the Society's Missionaries first came to Moore Town & erected the School-House, the Maroons were very suspicious of their intentions; & would never assemble in the building for Public worship at night without placing Scouts in the skirts of the town to guard against surprise; for they were apprehensive that it was a trick of the white people to get them together in one house, in order that they might surround it, while the Maroons were engaged in prayer, take them prisoners & ship them off the Island: as had been done in the case of the Trelawney Maroons [in 1795], who surrendered on the pledge that they would be allowed to remain in the Island. (Bilby 2006, 366)

Vigilance in defence of freedom, whether through collective action inspired by a living tradition and remembered past of resistance or by individual choices and strategies, was crucial to the Afro-Caribbean people. So too were struggles to control their cultural and spiritual lives and to assert their humanity in the face of crushing racism and oppression.

Many of the collective acts of protest which took place in the decades after emancipation can best be understood as primarily assertions of the right to develop and control autonomous cultural expressions. Jamaicans rioted against attempts to ban Jonkonnu celebrations in Kingston, Afro-Trinidadians battled the police in defence of the aspects of carnival they most cherished, Grenadians came out onto the streets for their right to celebrate (improbable as it may seem) Guy Fawkes' Day (1885). In St Vincent, Christmas, pre-Lenten and crop-over carnivals were all important in the postemancipation years, and attempts by the authorities to ban them in Kingstown led to at least four riots between 1850 and 1879. Masquerading and related "play" were central to the lives of the Kingstown working class, whose members (like their counterparts all over the region) wanted to control their own cultural expression. Despite the use of police raids, legislation and the militia, a scholar has recently concluded that the St Vincent authorities failed to quell the main forms of popular culture in the nineteenth century (Boa 2005). In addition, Indian immigrants and Indo-Trinidadians collided with the local authorities in defence of their pan-Indian celebration, Hosay or Muharram, in 1884, with fatal results – and this too was part of the trajectory of freedom.

The defence of popular culture might also involve asserting a claim to live by values and standards other than those imposed by the elites, the churches or the schools. As we all know, the postemancipation period witnessed an intense campaign to transform the formerly enslaved people and their descendants by wiping out all those cultural forms that could be seen as African derived, the legacy of Afro-Creole "slave culture". This process, and the responses of the people to it, has been exhaustively studied in Jamaica in Brian Moore and Michele Johnson's fine book *Neither Led nor Driven* (2004). They show that the Afro-Jamaican people appropriated much of the dominant culture – especially Christianity and the Bible – and transformed it by a process of creolization, while often simply ignoring those aspects of it which seemed unacceptable, such as the insistence on lifelong monogamous marriage and the confinement of women to domesticity. Afro-Jamaican folk religion, their family and gender patterns, their beliefs and customs ("superstitions"), were not fundamentally transformed by the relentless efforts of the local and imperial elites. Moore and Johnson show that cultural self-determination resulted from the masses exercising their own cultural power, making creolization "expansionist, continuous and silently relentless" (Moore and Johnson 2004).

One cultural site where the determination of the Afro-Caribbean people to live by their own values was especially obvious was in the region's cities and towns. Here men and women – but the women were particularly visible – lived very public lives on the streets of towns like Kingston and Kingstown, Port of Spain and St George's, Georgetown and Bridgetown. These "loose women", "women of abandoned character" (to use a phrase in the title of an article by Swithin Wilmot [1995] on Jamaica), or "jamettes" (to use the Trinidadian Creole term), defied respectable society by living by their own standards of femininity, which had little in common with those of Victorian decency. They were out on the streets, they were highly visible, they shocked convention, and all the colonial newspapers, not to mention the travel literature of the period, were full of denunciations.

Of course religious expression was a vital part of popular culture, and many historians have noted that the right to practise religion as they chose was a critical aspect of freedom for the formerly enslaved and their descendants. For most, this involved syncretic Afro-Christian faiths, or neo-African ones, as well as African-derived magical and healing practices, and we are all familiar with the history of these struggles in the nineteenth and indeed in the twentieth centuries. I want to briefly mention two rather different religious journeys, both taking place (or ending up) in Trinidad.

Between about 1810 and 1840, Trinidad had a remarkable community of Islamic Africans, known locally (as elsewhere) as Mandingoes. But in the Trinidad case, these people, never numbering more than a few hundred and predominantly male, made themselves into a cohesive community. Under the leadership of a few men literate in Arabic, some of them former soldiers of the West India regiments, and united by religion and ethnic ties, they systematically purchased their co-religionists, and made them work for a time without wages to pay back their purchase price, then freed them. They acquired property both in Port of Spain and in the country, and held on to their Islamic faith. Two scholars who have recently re-examined this community think that the Mandingoes were responsible for about five hundred manumissions (out of a total of around three thousand) between 1808 and 1834. This was a Muslim "brotherhood" inspired by the Islamic *tariqua* as it operated in West Africa. In 1840 – and this was really at the moment this remarkable community began to fade away – the acknowledged leader was Samba Makumba, a man of Mande origins, who had been enslaved during religious and political turmoil engulfing the Senegambia area in the early 1800s, and brought to Trinidad at the age of twenty-one in 1800 or 1801. Literate in Arabic, he bore the title of Emir, a spiritual leader; his "Creole" name was Simon Boissiere. For this group, the struggle – successful for a time – was to hold on to Islam in a colonial society where all the pressures were towards Christian conversion or adherence to Afro-Christian syncretic faiths (Trotman and Lovejoy 2004).

A very different, but also remarkable, religious journey was that of Maria Jones (c. 1780–after 1860). We know about her because the Baptist Mission in Trinidad published in 1851 a short account of her life and conversion. Needless to say, this was a typical conversion narrative with all the limitations of that genre, but there is enough to reconstruct the story of a rebellious spirit who appropriated Christianity at least in part as a means of asserting a claim to full humanity. Born in West Africa around 1780, she was kidnapped, enslaved and transported to St Vincent at the age of seven. Even in the stilted language of the missionary we can sense her vibrancy: "She had a very high spirit, which was not easily subdued; and indeed, was never entirely tamed, till it was humbled by the grace of God. All through her life of slavery she showed much strength and independence of mind and would often utter sentiments and feelings which proved that she did not willingly submit to the yoke imposed upon her." Maybe because she was an "unprofitable slave", as the narrative says, but more likely because enslaved persons were worth much more in rapidly developing Trinidad than in St Vincent, she was sold to a Trinidadian and laboured as a field worker on two estates in different parts of the island. She was attached to an estate near Arima in 1838. When the Mico Charity opened a school there,

Maria Jones, nearly sixty, insisted on going – not only to the evening and Sunday classes designed for adults but also to the day school with the children. She learned to read, came under the influence of the teacher who was affiliated to the Scottish Presbyterian church which had just been established in Port of Spain, joined this church and was married to the man "with whom for years she had lived as wife, according to the Negro, or rather, slave custom". That these were empowering events for her is suggested by this passage:

> She soon informed [the Baptist minister] of the change that had recently taken place in her condition, remarking at the same time, with evident pride, that now "she called Mrs Jones, and not Maria, as before time". This she said, purposely, in the hearing of several other females present, turning to them as she spoke, as though anxious to improve the occasion by promoting them to go and do likewise. She seemed to move among them like a queen, as though conscious of some superiority over them in point of character.

Falling under the influence of George Cowen, the pioneer English Baptist missionary to Trinidad, she received baptism by total immersion and joined this church. After the ceremony she declared (according to the missionary pamphlet):

> I batize four times now, but only one time right! Fore dem tief me in Africa, dem priests dere do somtin for batize; when me come to buckra country, dem catholic priests do what dem call batism; dem put oil on my head, salt in me mout, and make cross on me face; but now me read bible for me own self, me no find dis dere. When me join Cotch church, dem take me 'gain and prinkle water in me face for batist, but neder dis right, when me come for know better; no more one way, same fashion blessed Saviour he self do.

This of course marks the triumphant end of the pamphlet, but Maria Jones entered the archival record one more time, when at the age of about eighty she met E.B. Underhill, the noted Baptist leader, during his visit to Trinidad in 1860. That she was a missionary success story is clear enough; but there is another story, that of a rebellious and strong-minded woman who survived enslavement as a child, the middle passage, and field labour in St Vincent and Trinidad, lived to a very old age despite the hardships of such a life, and appropriated Christianity in its rival forms as a source of empowerment and strength (Jones 1851).

I want to look briefly at two other ways of defending freedom in the aftermath of emancipation, which we might not generally recognize as such. Although the evidence tells us that the enslaved were never truly dehumanized, never thought of themselves as less than fully human, we know that inherent in slavery as a system – and indeed inherent in colonialism – was an attempt to deny or reduce the personhood of its victims. Seen most starkly in chattel slavery, it was a drive to commodify people, a process of "thingification". Of course, such an ideological project was not going to lie down and die with the formal end of slavery. So it was crucial to the formerly enslaved and their descendants to assert or reclaim their personhood, not for themselves but in their relations with Others, especially but not only the white "massas". Speech acts, verbal encounters, were one mode. Seen merely as annoying "insolence" by most commentators, or occasionally just as amusing, these verbal conflicts with whites were really about claims to humanity and equality at the interpersonal level.

The formerly enslaved in Antigua, wrote Frances Lanagan in 1844, "make it a constant boast, 'Me free, me no b'long to you'". C.W. Day, who lived in some of the islands for a few years around 1850, told the story of Miss Betsy of Barbados, a sixty-year-old formerly enslaved woman who was working for him during his stay there. She refused to go to market one day – "Me no feel dispose!" – because she had not gotten her stockings on: "You tink, because I wait on you, I not nobody at all!" What Day saw as amusing yet exasperating behaviour from a person whose only correct response – according to her class and ethnic status – was instant, deferential obedience, was in fact an assertion of worth and equality. Miss Betsy, elderly by mid-nineteenth-century standards, a "housekeeper", was a person of status according to Afro-Creole values. Her verbal joust with Day was a claim to equal humanity and a rejection of any relegation to being merely a unit or instrument of labour.

Civility and courtesy were important, symbolized especially by the use of titles of respect. Many postemancipation observers commented on the use of *sir, miss, ma'am* and *mister* in conversations among Afro-Creoles, often with amusement when it was the "lower orders" doing it. Day complained that in Barbados street vendors would ignore customers unless addressed politely, while addressing each other as *sir, miss* and *lady*. Sensitivity to racial terms was part of this too. *Negro* – as well as the N-word – equated with "slave", and questioning or rejecting both terms was also to claim respect and equality. Day, again, said Barbadians hated the N-word, which they used toward each other as a vile insult, but also objected to *Negro*: "we is coloured people", he reported their saying. If this was widespread, it was, perhaps a claim not only to respectability but also to middle-class identity, granted the normal use of *coloured* in the nineteenth-century Caribbean (Lanagan 1844, 17; Day 1852, 1:21–22, 1:33–34, 2:131).

In addition to defiant speech acts such as those just discussed, clothing choices might be another (nonverbal) mode of asserting personhood and equality. Nothing so annoyed (occasionally merely amused) upper-class observers as the delight shown by the formerly enslaved – above all the women – in dressing up in European finery quite inappropriate to their class and racial status. Of course, dress was a key visible marker of class identity in the nineteenth century, and the respectable in Europe complained when their own lower orders transgressed this line in their attire; but many of the descriptions of dressed-up working-class women in the Caribbean suggest that their possession of dark skins and non-Caucasian facial features and body types made the transgression far more objectionable than at home. In defying the unwritten but customary rules of dress in a deeply stratified postemancipation society by dressing in European-style clothes and hats and using expensive fabrics, Afro-Caribbean working-class women disrupted the customary social equilibrium and even threatened white privilege. It reflected a claim to be somebody, a nonverbal way of expressing, "You tink, because I wait on you, I not nobody at all!" by persons who – by ethnicity and class – were supposed to be invisible nobodies. It was expressive behaviour that destabilised the colonial codes and norms. It was in a way mimicry, which should be flattering; but, as Homi Babha has said (1997, 152–60), mimicry in the colonial context is also mockery and potentially menacing.

To defy class and racial boundaries through clothes was, indeed, menacing because it was potentially destabilizing. The vast social gulf between white and black women, between the elite and the lower orders, was supposed to be made visible in the humble dress of the labourers and peasants. So those who transgressed must be ridiculed and humiliated. A revealing case was that of "Duchess" in Barbados, an apprentice who was found guilty in 1836 of stealing cash from her former mistress and spending it on fancy clothes. The magistrate publicly scorned her, not so much for the theft as (so it appeared) for the crime of dressing above her station: "She had bought wearing apparel fine enough for a Princess. Their colours vied with those of the rainbow, first a flaming bright yellow bonnet, flashy dresses without number, necklaces and earrings without end, rose coloured silk stockings and two pairs of pink satin shoes." The magistrate ordered Duchess to try on the shoes: "This was done before a very crowded court who shouted when the pink satins were placed upon the hoofs [note the word] of Duchess. In truth I never saw anything as unsuitable as the satins to such feet" (Buckridge 2004; Boa 2005, 257; Newton 2005, 236).

In considering these different ways of struggling for freedom and asserting self-worth and humanity – and of course I could have discussed many other ways and cited many more examples – I simply want to suggest that, as students of history, we should seek to understand all these very diverse trajectories of freedom and not be seduced only or mainly by the "big events", the major collective protests, the riots and rebellions, important though these undeniably were.

Finally, I want to make a point that I think is important but which this discussion has in fact ignored, a point which resonates especially in Trinidad and Tobago, and Guyana, though it is relevant everywhere. When we consider trajectories of and struggles for freedom in the Caribbean, we ought not to leave out the people who entered the region through the post-1838 immigration schemes. We ought to find ways of integrating the story of their experiences and struggles into the mainstream narrative of the Afro-Caribbean people. Generally speaking, and I am as guilty as anyone in this, we tend to separate out the history of the Indians, the Chinese and the others to put it in a little ghetto of its own. So, for instance, one might find in Caribbean Examinations Council (CXC) history examination papers questions about the postemancipation peasantries, say in the period 1838 to 1900, which are framed so that the Indo-Caribbean people are excluded, despite their major role in peasant development in Trinidad and Guyana at least in the second half of that period. We need to accept, and to write as if we believed it, that all the people who entered the Caribbean after 1838, and all their descendants, were also an integral element in the region's struggles for freedom. I have not done so in this chapter, so let me end by recounting another Jamaican Maroon oral testimony from Bilby's book which does just that, and in my view, very movingly:

> This text relates a memory of an incident personally experienced by the narrator, Ruth Lindsay of Moore Town, who was born in 1901, early in the 20th century. It is included here because it demonstrates particularly clearly how different layers of Maroon history may be collapsed and interwoven with personal memories that continue to summon up deep emotions in the present. The Maroon elder recalls how, in her younger days, while she was on her way to Port Antonio, she hap-

pened upon a group of indentured Indian labourers assigned to Windsor Estate, just to the north of Moore Town. As she watched, a woman who badly needed to urinate broke away from the work gang and came running over in her direction to get away from the busha. But the white man noticed her absence. Catching her in the act of relieving herself, the busha began to flog the Indian woman with a bull pizzle whip, ignoring her cries for mercy. More than half a century later, with obvious feeling, the Maroon narrator remembers how the scene brought tears to her eyes, not only because of her compassion for this woman, but also because she was able to imagine right then and there the humiliations her own ancestors would have suffered at the hands of the whites if the Maroons hadn't fought for their freedom – the same kind she had just seen the "mad bakra" inflict on this "slave Coolie". (Bilby 2006, 90–91, 97–98)

Acknowledgements

This chapter has been adapted from a keynote address given at the conference "Trajectories of Freedom", held at the Faculty of Humanities and Education, University of the West Indies, Cave Hill, Barbados, May 2007.

References

Babha, Homi. 1997. "Of Mimicry and Man: The Ambivalence of Colonial Discourse". In *Tensions of Empire: Colonial Cultures in a Bourgeois World*, edited by F. Cooper and A.L. Stoler, 152–60. Berkeley: University of California Press.

Bilby, Kenneth. 2006. *True-Born Maroons*. Kingston: Ian Randle.

Boa, Sheena. 2005. "Young Ladies and Dissolute Women". In *Gender and Slave Emancipation in the Atlantic World*, edited by P. Scully and D. Paton, 247–66. Durham, NC: Duke University Press.

Brereton, Bridget. 1999. "Family Strategies, Gender, and the Shift to Wage Labour in the British Caribbean". In *The Colonial Caribbean in Transition*, edited by B. Brereton and K. Yelvington, 77–107. Kingston: University of the West Indies Press.

Buckridge, Steeve O. 2004. *The Language of Dress Resistance and Accommodation in Jamaica, 1750–1890*. Kingston: University of the West Indies Press.

Chase, R. 1989. "Protest in Post-emancipation Dominica: The 'Guerre Negre' of 1844". *Journal of Caribbean History* 23 (2): 118–41.

Day, C.W. 1852. *Five Years' Residence in the West Indies*. 2 vols. London.

Heuman, Gad. 2006. *The Caribbean*. London: Hodder and Arnold.
Jones, Maria. 1851. *Maria Jones: Her History in Africa and in the West Indies*. Port of Spain: Baptist Mission.
Lanagan, Frances. 1844. *Antigua and the Antiguans*. London.
Moore, Brian, and Johnson, Michele. 2004. *Neither Led nor Driven: Contesting British Cultural Imperialism in Jamaica, 1865–1920*. Kingston: University of the West Indies Press.
Newton, Melanie. 2005. "Philanthropy, Gender and the Production of Public Life in Barbados, ca. 1790–1850". In *Gender and Slave Emancipation in the Atlantic World*, edited by P. Scully and D. Paton, 225–46. Durham, NC: Duke University Press.
Robertson, Claire. 2000. "Claiming Freedom: Abolition and Identity in St Lucian History". *Journal of Caribbean History* 34 (1–2): 89–129.
Thompson, Alvin. 2006. *Flight to Freedom*. Kingston: Ian Randle.
Trotman, David, and Paul Lovejoy. 2004. "Community of Believers: Trinidad, Muslims and the Return to Africa, 1810–1850". In *Slavery on the Frontiers of Islam*, edited by P. Lovejoy, 219–31. Princeton, NJ: Princeton University Press.
Wilmot, Swithin. 1995. "Females of Abandoned Character"? Women and Protest in Jamaica, 1838–1865". In *Engendering History: Caribbean Women in Historical Perspective*, edited by V. Shepherd, B. Brereton and B. Bailey, 279–95. Kingston: Ian Randle.

2.

TROPICAL LIBERTARIANS
Anarchist Networks in the Circum-Caribbean, 1900–1915

KIRWIN R. SHAFFER

> La red está tendida, y en ella caerán los gordos de levita, plumíferos y coronas.
>
> [The network is stretched out, and in it will fall the fat Levites, the feathered and the crowned.]
> – R. Huerta, ¡Tierra!, 2 July 1914

ANARCHISTS ALWAYS SAW THEMSELVES as part of a larger working-class internationalist movement fighting against the forces of bourgeois internationalism. However, most scholarship has focused on the role of anarchist movements within a particular country, taking a national look at an international movement. This is not to argue that such studies are somehow "missing the boat" – my own books and articles are on anarchism in a single country, Cuba and Puerto Rico (Shaffer 2005, 2013) – but it has long struck me as odd that our studies are so localized. Thus, as I was researching and writing about anarchism in Cuba from the 1890s to the 1920s, I began to think about how anarchists interacted with one another in separate but increasingly connected zones of the Americas. This chapter, then, explores the actions and motions of Spanish-speaking anarchists who, through their labour, writings and agitation for freedom, created anarchist "spaces" in different parts of the Caribbean. These men and women saw themselves as internationalists who rejected the limiting visions of nationalism and national political struggles. As internationalists, they developed linkages between different locales in the circum-Caribbean and in doing so created a transnational anarchist network of like-minded working-class intellectuals promoting a particular anti-authoritarian version of libertarian freedom in the first two decades of the twentieth century.

Introduction: Mapping the Anarchist Anti-authoritarian Topography

The research that follows suggests that the emergence and development of this Caribbean anarchist network was linked to three particular historical developments. First, Spanish immigration into Cuba was surpassed only by Spanish immigration to Argentina in the early twentieth century. Many of these working-class migrants were either committed anarchists or had been exposed to a long tradition of anarchist activity in Spain. These Spanish anarchists sometimes dominated the embryonic anarchist movements (as in Panama) and sometimes supplemented native Caribbean anarchists (as in Cuba and Puerto Rico). Second, the spread of this anarchist network is linked (if not exclusively, then in part) to the spread of US military and economic influence throughout the Caribbean basin in the early twentieth century. The strong US military and political presence in Cuba and Puerto Rico provided an anti-imperialist foil for these anarchists. Likewise, the expansion of US-based labour unions like the American Federation of Labor and the growing proletarianization of the cigar industry by US-dominated tobacco entities were developments that anarchists both lamented and rallied against. The creation of the Panama Canal Zone in 1904 and the subsequent ten-year construction project to build the canal provided a new locale for anarchists to migrate and in which to agitate. Third, while Spanish migration and US political, military and economic influence were keys to understanding the rise of the anarchist network, it was the development of a strong anarchist presence in Cuba, especially Havana, that created the possibility for such a network. Havana became not just a stopping-off point for Spanish anarchists but more importantly the hub that linked the spokes or tentacles of the network. The key to Havana's role in the network was the long-running (1902–15) anarchist weekly newspaper ¡Tierra!, which served as a central organ of communication and fundraising. While other anarchist papers in Havana played brief roles in coordinating the network and small newspapers in Puerto Rico and Panama helped to organize the movement in those locales, it was ¡Tierra!'s longevity and the fact that the movements based in Puerto Rico and Panama were small and underfinanced that facilitated ¡Tierra!'s key role in holding the network together.

If Havana was the hub of the network, then one of the longest-running and most continuous spokes was south Florida, especially the cigar rolling factories in Tampa. Because it is a stretch to call south Florida part of the Caribbean (despite its prominent role in the Havana-based network) this chapter will not explore that locale. The next important spoke linked to the Havana hub was Puerto Rico not only because of its historical links with Cuba as Spain's last two colonies in the Americas but also because both found themselves – to different degrees, to be sure – intimately linked to the growing US presence in the Caribbean. The third spoke linked to the Cuban hub was the Panama Canal Zone, in the "liberated" former Colombian province of Panama. While Panama had little recent historical connection with Florida, Cuba or Puerto Rico, by the time the United States began its engineering marvel, the Canal Zone represented yet another US-controlled enclave in which Spanish-speaking anarchists found themselves, sometimes arriving from Cuba. An early US official in Panama was Lieutenant Colonel George W. Goethals. He had served as an officer in the low-key Puerto Rican campaign following the US invasion of the island in 1898. In 1907, he took over control of the US-run Isthmian Canal Commission just as anarchist activity in the Canal Zone was beginning to surge (Navas 1979, 128). Thus, as anarchists migrated to these new US-controlled enclaves, they frequently encountered US officials like Goethals who also migrated between these locations.

To unravel this anarchist network in the region, we need to focus especially on the few bodies of evidence in the anarchist press that help us to sketch out the network's dimension. Anarchist newspapers generally followed one of three formats: (1) strictly propaganda organs that mainly reprinted theoretical works of famous anarchists; (2) organs generally associated with a particular industry, especially anarcho-syndicalist newspapers that revolved around the tobacco or the services industries; (3) or, a combination of propaganda pieces, hard news, critical commentary of local and international issues and fundraising machines. ¡Tierra! was the third. Through the discussions of local events on pages one and two, as well as the printed correspondence from throughout the network on page three and the financial contributions and monetary flows coming into the paper from throughout the network on page four, we can trace the central themes, issues, actors and conditions which made each locale unique but which also tied these locales together into a larger transnational movement. Using this evidence, we can explore what anarchist concepts of freedom meant in the circum-Caribbean, identify the leading anarchist space

– and, thus, the hub of the network, Cuba – and, finally, use the mostly Cuban-based sources to understand the development of anarchism and anarchist antiauthoritarian critiques in Puerto Rico and Panama during anarchism's heyday in the region from 1900 to 1915.

Anarchist Concepts of Freedom in the Early Twentieth-Century Caribbean Basin

By 1900 the Spanish-speaking branch of the international anarchist movement had spread from the Iberian Peninsula to penetrate the far corners of the Western Hemisphere. Relatively large and important anarchist groups became major social and political actors in the urban areas of South America, especially Argentina, Peru, Uruguay and Brazil. These movements, largely rooted in those countries' expanding export industries, led strikes for improved living and working conditions, including the call for an eight-hour workday. Less well-known anarchist movements of differing sizes emerged in the Americas' northern hemisphere. In Cuba, Mexico, Puerto Rico, Spanish-speaking communities of the United States and the Canal Zone in Panama, these movements struggled to create their own anarchist utopian visions of society not only against oligarchic governments but also under the nose – and often the sword – of an expanding United States.

Anarchism is a philosophy of freedom. As historian Peter Marshall puts it, "anarchism holds up the bewitching ideal of personal and social freedom, both in the negative sense of being free from all external restraint and imposed authority, and in the positive sense of being free to celebrate the full harmony of being" (Marshall 1986, xv). Murray Bookchin's definition of social anarchism best reflects my vision for what anarchists believed: a philosophy that

> celebrates the thinking human mind without in any way denying passion, ecstasy, imagination, play, and art. Yet rather than reify them into hazy categories, it tries to incorporate them into everyday life. It is committed to rationality while opposing the rationalization of experience; to technology, while opposing the "megamachine"; to social institutionalization, while opposing class rule and hierarchy; to genuine politics based on the confederate coordination of municipalities or communes by the people in direct face-to-face democracy, while opposing parliamentarianism and the state. (Bookchin 1995, 56–57)

In their quest to create a free society for all regardless of race, ethnicity, nationality or gender, anarchists focused their attention on the main power structures of society – an "unholy trinity", if you will, of capital, church and state. Anarchists never completely rejected the concept of private property or even of small merchants (many were in fact restaurateurs, book sellers or print shop operators), but they did reject the growing industrialization of economic life. In the Caribbean basin, this challenge to industrial capital played out in places like the Cuban and Puerto Rican sugar or tobacco export sectors. In Panama, the massive engineering project to build the canal brought anarchists into direct conflict with those who exploited labour to build the canal. Besides this struggle against capital, anarchists found themselves struggling against fellow workers' apathy or workers inclined to support political parties rather than an anarchist movement.

While anarchists would challenge this worker apathy and the economic servitude they encountered in these locations, they focused considerable attention on governments and governmental policies as these impacted labour conditions and rights, migration, politics and broader issues of individual and collective freedom. Here, anarchists from throughout the Spanish-speaking world migrated between different parts of the circum-Caribbean, encountering both national governments and the growing influence of US foreign policy in the region – a policy that increasingly saw the region as crucial to US military, economic and political expansion. As a result, anarchists battled both domestic and international capitalists as well as local and national governmental actions that were heavily influenced or controlled by Washington. In this context, anarchists represented a growing internationalist, transnationalist movement shaped by and responding to the growing interconnectedness of transnational capital flows and expanding US foreign policy. In fact, one should recall that the anarchist network in Cuba, Puerto Rico and Panama in particular developed at the same time in countries whose recent "independence" was directly linked to US foreign policy concerns: Cuban independence came as a result of US intervention and then military occupation as US-based industrial concerns poured into the island; Puerto Rican separation from Spain resulted in the island becoming increasingly linked to the United States, which would grant US citizenship to Puerto Ricans in 1917; and Panama's independence in late 1903 was directly linked to US designs to build a canal across the isthmus, resulting in the country being sliced in two as the US came to control the ten-mile wide canal zone from the Caribbean to the Pacific that ran straight through the middle of the new country.

Unravelling the Network: Anarchist Journalism and Monetary Contributions

While anarchists in Cuba created the most developed and long-lasting anarchist movement in any Caribbean country, it is crucial to remember that anarchists never saw themselves or their goals in purely country-specific or nationalist terms. While these radicals intellectually believed in the tenets of anarchist internationalism, many of these anarchists practised internationalism when they migrated to find work, following the flows of transnational capital around the Caribbean. Because so many anarchists themselves were migratory and followed the flows of transnational capital to agitate as they looked for work, the anarchist movement in Cuba made it a key point to keep local and migrating readers informed on events in the Caribbean region and to provide a forum for small-scale, embryonic anarchist groups and individuals to describe their own local and national scenes to readers.

Anarchists throughout the network established newspapers whenever they could. In Caguas, Puerto Rico, the tobacco-working anarchists published *Voz Humana* from 1905 to 1906. From 1911 to 1912, anarchists in the Panama Canal Zone published *El Único*. The ability to publish such newspapers was no small feat. For men (and sometimes women) to find the money and time to create these propaganda organs attests to their commitment to the anarchist cause while struggling just to put food on the table. These newspapers, while shortlived, nevertheless gave a local voice to anarchism in Puerto Rico and Panama respectively. Yet, because of the scarcity of an anarchist press throughout the network's spokes, Cuban-based papers became the key communicative link. Occasionally, the Havana-based *La Voz del Dependiente* or *Vía Libre* published correspondence from the anarchist frontier, but the most important newspaper was *¡Tierra!*, published by a revolving series of mostly anarcho-communist editors.

¡Tierra! was the longest-running and most prominent anarchist newspaper in Havana, Cuba, operating from 1902 to 1915. There were more than twenty-five anarchist newspapers created in Cuba (mostly Havana) in the decades following independence. Many were "propaganda rags" that did little more

than espouse anarchist rhetoric and reprint famous writings from anarchists around the world. Some were more focused on particular industries like those aimed at printers or restaurant employees. But ¡Tierra! did all of this and more. Not only was the paper adept at reprinting famous tracts or discussing the intricacies of various union activities but also its revolving door of editors made a point of focusing on Cuban national news from an anarchist standpoint, printing letters to the editor and reporting on the various anarchist initiatives across the island. It was just as important that ¡Tierra!'s editors – unique among the island's newspapers – regularly provided one or two pages of each issue to print correspondence from the region's anarchist movements. This published correspondence provides some of the few surviving pieces of evidence concerning anarchists, anarchist ideas and anarchist responses to events in places like Puerto Rico and Panama.

This correspondence did more than just keep the international community aware of events outside of Cuba. Just as important was the distribution of ¡Tierra! to these countries, complete with the correspondence. Because anarchists in Puerto Rico and Panama could rarely afford to create their own organs, writers from throughout the network could describe events and critique reality from an anarchist perspective, they could communicate with other groups in their locale or they could announce upcoming meetings by having these published in ¡Tierra!, which was then sent back to Puerto Rico and Panama for dissemination. The paper was published weekly, so that a writer could conceivably send in his or her correspondence one week, have it published in the paper the next and then distributed back home the following week – a turnaround time of two to three weeks.

Most columns in ¡Tierra! were not about hard news but were interpretative pieces aiming to construct an international anarchist critique while localizing it for the relevant situation, that is, "Puerto Ricanizing" or "Isthmianizing" international anarchism. This is particularly evident in the writings from Puerto Rico of Pablo Vega Santos, Juan Vilar and Alfonso Torres. Likewise, the regular correspondence from Aquilino López and Braulio Hurtado from Panama reflected local reality from an internationalist perspective. These activists' correspondence critiqued working and living conditions, challenged workers to reject their apathy and join the cause, lambasted local politicians and political parties, and regularly harangued the dominating influence of Washington on local affairs. Thus, they took the standard anarchist critiques on labour, politics and colonialism and applied them to their local situations.

By sending these "nationalized" critiques to Havana for publication and dissemination to the world and back home, these writers engaged in their own internationalizing of anarchism by linking their movements to each other through Cuba. Their local analyses played out for local readers but likewise found readers everywhere in ¡Tierra!'s distribution network throughout the region. In that sense, internationalism operated on several levels: through the localizing of anarchist internationalism in analysing local circumstances, through the publication of these local critiques outside the country for return dissemination, and through the distribution of these analyses and perspectives of Puerto Rico and Panama for larger non-island, non-isthmian audiences who, for instance, had the paper's correspondence read to them by public readers (lectores) in cigar factories up and down the East Coast of the United States and throughout Cuba. Such an experience would, ideally, help those listeners of the news come to a greater international consciousness themselves.

Besides just the correspondence, ¡Tierra! published lists of financial contributors to the newspaper's coffers, as well as lists of people who donated money to various causes such as helping families of deported or imprisoned anarchists around the region or collecting money for speaking tours, newspaper deficit reduction campaigns, and events like the Mexican Revolution. Almost invariably, foreign correspondence arrived at ¡Tierra!'s offices with some form of monetary contribution and the names of the contributors attached. These international monetary flows, while never more than a small percentage of the newspaper's weekly income, were nevertheless not insignificant – especially for the sender. The first contributions from Puerto Rico arrived to ¡Tierra! in January 1905 from the Caguas-based anarchists who would soon open their own newspaper, Voz Humana. According to ¡Tierra!, 14 January 1905, Pablo Vega Santos had collected nearly three pesos from seventeen Cagueño anarchists, representing about 5 per cent of that week's newspaper income. Sometimes monthly, at times semimonthly, and occasionally weekly, Puerto Ricans contributed anywhere from 5 to 10 per cent of ¡Tierra!'s income for any particular issue during 1905, with contributions gradually arriving from other Puerto Rican towns and cities such as Río Grande, San Juan, Cayey and Mayagüez. From 1906 to 1907, Puerto Rican contributions began to wane, but more arrived from new locations such as Arecibo, Ponce and Bayamón. The famous anarchist Luisa Capetillo sent her first contributions to the Havana paper in April 1909 from Arecibo and then followed that two weeks later with more money and her first ¡Tierra! column critiquing

Spanish repression. Both were sent from San Juan, reflecting her increasingly migratory dimensions in agitating for the anarchist cause within the island's Free Federation of Labor, which was affiliated with the American Federation of Labor. By 1911, the money flows from Puerto Rico to ¡Tierra! fell to new lows, with little money coming from the island. A brief surge in subscriptions occurred in mid-1912, spearheaded by Juan Vilar in Caguas, while serving a one-year jail sentence on trumped-up public indecency charges. However, even these contributions in May and August amounted to less than 6 per cent of any weekly income totals for the newspaper. As would be expected, when the movement declined in Puerto Rico, so did its contributions (both literary and monetary) to Cuba, and the Cuba–Puerto Rico link in the network – though not entirely dead – never recovered its previous level of activity.

Likewise, anarchist money flows from the Panama Canal Zone to Cuba were never a large part of the Cuban press' income, except for the above-noted 1911 contributions to *Vía Libre*. Still, although they accounted for a small percentage of ¡Tierra!'s contributions, we should not let those small amounts blind us to the importance they must have played for Panama-based workers and agitators who relied on ¡Tierra! for international information, propaganda and even their own canal-based news. One of the newspaper's longest financial contributors was Serafín G. González. While almost nothing is known about him, we can glean from issues of ¡Tierra! during the period 1906 to 1912 that his donations from Panama stretched from June 1906 to October 1912. Judging from the large amounts he sent (anywhere from US$2.24 to US$5.70), he was obviously collecting money from anarchist sympathizers. González was based in Colón for at least part of his stint on the canal and, given the trend of individual contributors donating an average of US$0.25 to US$0.50, would have pooled the resources of about ten or twelve people each time he sent money. At times, these contributions represented an important percentage of an individual issue of ¡Tierra! For instance, over the years his contribution amounted to almost 10 per cent of an issue's income. In July 1911 (at the height of anarchist activity in Panama and Aquilino López's growing role with the Havana-based *Vía Libre*), González's contribution to ¡Tierra! was equivalent to 12 per cent. Considering that most anarchists were finding their money redirected to *Vía Libre* at this time, González becomes a key figure in helping to maintain the tenuous relations between ¡Tierra! and the Canal Zone. This relationship appears to have ended in late 1912, when he provided nearly all of the paper's special collection designed to raise extra money outside of subscriptions for relieving the paper of its continuous deficit (¡Tierra!, 16 June 1906, 4; ¡Tierra!, 27 July 1907, 4; ¡Tierra!, 8 July 1911, 4; and ¡Tierra!, 19 October 1912, 4).

As reported in issues of ¡Tierra! between November 1912 and July 1913, money began to flow in even larger amounts from Panama to Havana beginning in November 1912 and running throughout 1913. Collected in the new Gatún Workers Centre, all but US$5 of the US$25 collected was to purchase copies of ¡Tierra! to help to alleviate its deficit or to purchase copies of other anarchist newspapers. More than thirty men signed their names to the collection list, setting the stage for a year of important financial flows from the Canal Zone to Havana. The bulk of the money came from anarchist centres in Gatún and Pedro Miguel, coordinated by M.A. Atiza and D. Macarro Sánchez in the former and Braulio Hurtado in the latter (¡Tierra!, 23 November 1912, 4; ¡Tierra!, 18 January 1913, 4; ¡Tierra!, 30 May 1913, 4; ¡Tierra!, 4 July 1913, 4). These contributions to Havana were increasingly paired with smaller contributions to Spanish-language anarchist newspapers developing in the United States with large US-based Cuban and Spanish readerships, including the New York– and then Los Angeles–based *Fuerza Consciente*, which received small amounts of funds from Culebra, Gatún and Colón from March 1913 to January 1914 (*Fuerza Consciente*, 15 March 1913, 4; *Fuerza Consciente*, 9 August 1913, 4; *Fuerza Consciente*, 15 October 1913, 4; *Fuerza Consciente*, 15 January 1914, 4). Like their contributions to ¡Tierra!, these donations and subscriptions represented only small amounts of a single issue's income, but the money from the Canal Zone was nevertheless a sign of dozens of men's continued dedication to the international anarchist cause, such that they continued to send scarce income abroad. Donations rose in 1913 and increasingly went to non-Cuban publications, suggesting that anarchism – far from being a withering movement in early 1912, as some have suggested – continued to thrive and gain new followers as construction on the canal drew towards a conclusion. For our purposes, it suggests as well that the international linkages between Panama and Cuba may have played a role in helping to sustain the movement in both countries, and thus contributed to financing the network.

When international contributors sent money to ¡Tierra!, those funds mostly went to purchase subscriptions or weekly issues of the paper. However, on occasion, money was directed to other activities, such as purchasing books and pamphlets from the newspaper's collection or funding specific anarchist causes for which the paper's editors opened receiving accounts. Interestingly, rarely did Puerto Rican anarchists send money for causes like helping the families of deported anarchists or financing legal expenses accrued by anarchists facing trial. In fact, of the few instances when Puerto Rican anarchists made specific donations to these causes, most were dedicated to financing an important cross-Cuba propaganda tour during 1907 (¡Tierra!, 8 July 1905, 4, and 12 June 1907, 4). Panama-based anarchists, on the other hand, sent more money to support anarchist causes in Cuba. For instance, ¡Tierra! on 8 July 1905 states that Luis Prats (the first anarchist in Panama to make a Cuban connection) sent money to support workers held in the Santa Clara, Cuba, jail and to support the planned propaganda tour. Issues of ¡Tierra! between April and November 1912 show that, under the influence of the Cuban-based anarchist Aquilino López, who arrived in mid-1911, Panamanian money went to help Cuban causes, including paying the legal fees of jailed workers and providing money to these workers' families. Also, money went to support the Havana-based family of anarchist schoolteacher Blanca de Moncaleano, whose husband had left Cuba to work at a school in Mexico. The couple would eventually reunite in the anarchist community of Los Angeles, California (¡Tierra!, 13 April 1912, 4; ¡Tierra!, 11 May 1912, 4; and ¡Tierra!, 23 November 1912, 4).

During these years, it appears that anarchists in Panama and Puerto Rico divided their contributions differently due to issues surrounding migration and familiarity. Puerto Rico's anarchists seem to have been largely island-bound, with only a few people like Angel Dieppa and Luisa Capetillo leaving the island to travel the network. Thus, most Puerto Rican anarchists would not have had a specific familiarity with Cuba or encountered Cuban-based anarchists and their families face to face. Panama's anarchists, though, came almost exclusively from Spain and Cuba, whose movements frequently interacted with one another via the exchange of newspapers and other publications, as well as the constant arrival of new anarchists from Spain in Cuba. Thus, the anarchists in Panama had a deeper knowledge of Cuban anarchism, and many would have spent time in Cuba. The arrival of Aquilino López from Havana in 1911 only strengthened this link between Cuba and the Canal Zone.

Consequently, ¡Tierra! can be seen not only as the key source in understanding the anarchist movement from 1900 to 1915 in Cuba but also as the key source in tracing the linkages of the broader regional anarchist movement. This newspaper, which generally published on a weekly basis, became not only the main voice of the movement on the island nor the main voice promoting the Cuban anarchist viewpoint abroad, but it also became the primary mouthpiece for smaller anarchist groups and movements in the Caribbean region.

As Juan de la Maleza from Mayagüez, Puerto Rico, noted in the 2 February 1907 issue of ¡Tierra!, he would continue to write about and support anarchist efforts for ¡Tierra! because "it is necessary that wherever ¡Tierra! goes it be known as a thunderous spokesman that intimidates the enthroned coward who collaborates with uniformed marksmen or police, united also with people of different uniforms but of the same caliber and perhaps worse, all working exclusively to molest, beat and strangle the poor working children of the people" (¡Tierra!, 2 February 1907, 4).

Migrating Freedom Thinkers: The Face and Framers of the Network

One of the constants we can identify in early twentieth-century anarchism is the transitory nature of the involvement of so many of the movement's members. Many of them were simply workers travelling from locale to locale to find work, taking their anarchist sympathies and energies with them. Several, though, were prominent writers and organizers who moved for political or economic reasons but then became insightful providers of information about the conditions and status of the movement abroad. In Puerto Rico, the female anarchist Luisa Capetillo travelled the areas, and Julio Ramos in his introduction to Amor y anarquía notes that we should see her as a "worker intellectual" who also democratized writing (Ramos 1992, 33). Ramos's point is that Capetillo rose from the same emerging working class for whom she spoke and wrote. Whether she rolled cigars or was a reader in the cigar factories, Capetillo knew her audiences intimately. When she picked up the pen to write on issues of labour, freedom or, in particular, women, she spoke from the experience of the masses. In effect, she democratized writing whether she was writing one of her many books or writing for the pages of ¡Tierra! for regional distribution from her home of the moment: Arecibo, San Juan, New York, Tampa or Havana.

Capetillo was only one of dozens of working-class anarchist writers in the circum-Caribbean who found themselves moving around their locales or the larger network. Their correspondence is key to illustrating how the anarchist network shared ideas, resources and people from place to place. On the international circuit, we should not forget the Spaniard Braulio Hurtado. His correspondence with ¡Tierra! after his arrival in Panama represents one of the few extant anarchist perspectives of political and economic issues not only in the Canal Zone but, just as importantly, in the new country of Panama proper. Likewise, Aquilino López spent a short period of time working, writing and propagandizing both in Cuba and Panama. His correspondence, fundraising and agitation – like that of Capetillo – helped to cement linkages within the regional network.

These figures are crucial because they not only help us trace their movements and interactions but also in a larger sense these key writers, editors and organizers were some of the vital links that formed the network's web throughout the region. They became the authoritative voices for the movements or newspapers that they helped to coordinate wherever they relocated. In view of this, it is appropriate to think of these people as transnational freedom thinkers who, like their counterparts in Cuba such as Antonio Penichet and Adrián del Valle, framed the struggle for their local and international audiences. They were the most visible links in the anarchist network. These individuals functioned as cultural brokers by moving to different countries and locales in those countries. As such, they helped to develop and coordinate the regional movement by organizing local anarchist groups, informing anarchists throughout the region about local events and interpreting those events through an anarchist lens grounded upon their experiences as active anarchist agitators elsewhere.

Of vital importance, these correspondent-activists framed the movement for a larger international audience. In other words, they represented, promoted and portrayed how the international anarchist movement developed around the region in distinct situations. Their audience was other Spanish-speaking anarchists not only in the regional hub of Havana but also throughout the region, the United States and Spain where ¡Tierra! was also distributed. In addition, these individuals and small groups provided a visible example for the lower-level, now almost lost to history, small-scale financial contributors who bought their writings and helped to underwrite their efforts, travels and occasional bail money.

Conclusion

Because of the strong linkages with Spanish anarchist movements and the tendency of the network's primary locations to be in Cuba, Puerto Rico and

Panama – areas controlled or heavily influenced by the United States – one should not be surprised that issues and critiques within the network were similar. These similarities reflected the interconnectedness of anarchists who sometimes travelled between the different points of the network. It also reflected how these lands were increasingly incorporated into US geopolitical and economic spheres of influence. Yet, while issues and critiques were similarly articulated, they revolved around and emanated from specific local and national conditions that shaped each locale in the network differently. It is important to consider anarchism as more than just a part of a country's labour movement. Rather, as noted earlier, anarchists constructed social movements that sought not only to improve working and living conditions for the labouring masses but also to critique and challenge the hegemonic elite in economic and political control. These social movements waged culture wars around issues of nationality, politics, health and education to different degrees. By challenging the elite on these key issues, anarchists tried to forge concepts of anarchist freedom in lands that were themselves newly freed from either Spanish or Colombian control. Yet these lands had quickly succumbed to neocolonial control by the United States while elites in Cuba, Puerto Rico and Panama tied their fortunes to the United States.

Consequently, each movement responded to the reality of its individual locale. Cuban anarchists built on an island-centred movement dating to the 1870s. The country's size, geographical proximity to the United States and important three-year struggle for independence before US intervention in 1898 meant that Cuban anarchists had to respond to issues that were of less importance than those in Puerto Rico or Panama. The size of Cuba's anarchist movement, complete with its numerous newspapers, periodic schools and alternative health system, had obvious benefits that could not be replicated throughout the network. Likewise, while Cuban anarchists could be found in many sectors of the economy, from printers and restaurant workers to cigar rollers, anarchists in Puerto Rico primarily came from the tobacco economy, and those in Panama appear to have been in the construction trades.

Still, despite the obvious differences and despite the fact that each part of the network was forced to engage in a culture war that reflected these differences, the linkages among the three are striking, and within these linkages we see important commonalities emerge. In short, while it is important to understand how each "national" or local movement encountered its situation and waged site-specific culture wars to promote anarchist concepts of freedom and progress, these men and women were first and foremost internationalists who sought to spread a common message of anarchist freedom throughout the Spanish-speaking lands in which they worked and through which they travelled. As such, they found common expression criticizing not only their political leaders but also the United States. While less so in Panama, anarchists in other parts of the network had to not only challenge US political or military influence but they also had to counter the spread of unions that had links to the US-based, anti-anarchist American Federation of Labor.

In dealing with their similar, though unique, social and political realities and in navigating the world of US imperial influence, anarchists in the Caribbean forged a transnational communication and financial network that witnessed more than just the sharing of money and ideas. Communicating and channelling money through Havana, as well as actually travelling between spots in the network, facilitated an internationalist consciousness. While internationalism was always a key ideological component of anarchism, this network put that ideology into practice. Not every anarchist could write correspondence or travel. Those who did, though, became the key freedom thinkers that framed as well as gave voice and a face to the internationalist dimensions of anarchism in the Caribbean basin in the first decade and a half of the twentieth century.

References

Bookchin, M. 1995. *Social Anarchism or Lifestyle Anarchism: An Unbridgeable Chasm*. San Francisco: AK.

Fuerza Consciente (Los Angeles), 1913–14.

Marshall, P. 1986. *Demanding the Impossible: A History of Anarchism*. London: Freedom Press.

Navas, L. 1979. *El movimiento obrero en Panamá (1880–1914)*. San José, Costa Rica: Editorial Universitaria Centroamericana.

Ramos, Julio, ed. 1992. *Amor y anarquía: Los escritos de Luisa Capetillo*. Río Piedras, Puerto Rico: Ediciones Huracáin.

Shaffer, Kirwin. 2005. *Anarchism and Countercultural Politics in Early Twentieth Century Cuba*. Gainesville: University Press of Florida.

———. 2013. *Black Flag Boricuas: Anarchism, Antiauthoritarianism, and the Left in Puerto Rico, 1897–1921*. Urbana: University of Illinois Press.

3.

ERIC WILLIAMS AND THE LABOUR MOVEMENT IN TRINIDAD AND TOBAGO

JEROME TEELUCKSINGH

ERIC WILLIAMS'S INTELLECTUAL AND INTERNATIONAL association with labour before his entry into politics in Trinidad and Tobago contributed to his revered status among the working class there. Williams gained valuable work experience with a major trade union body – the International Confederation of Free Trade Unions (ICFTU). During several months in Europe in 1955, his official portfolio was adviser to the ICFTU. His responsibilities included consulting with the International Labour Organization (ILO). Williams was also appointed secretary to the workers on the ICFTU's conference subcommittee which dealt with possible measures within countries and industries to stabilize employment and earnings of plantation workers (Williams to Wilfred, 23 October 1955; Williams 1969, 140). While working for the ICFTU, Williams kept in constant contact with friends and future founding members of the People's National Movement (PNM) in Trinidad and Tobago.

The ICFTU was impressed with Williams's work and invited him to present a report to the ICFTU executive board in 1955. Williams was informed that, depending on the quality of the report, it would be presented to the ILO Conference in Geneva in October 1955 (Williams to Misie, 6 November 1955). The first monograph completed for the trade union dealt with the topic of plantation economies. Williams was familiar with the topic and subsequently noted, "My work here has been based for the most part on the assessment of the various plantation workers' resolutions in the light of ILO provisions and developments in the plantation countries" (Williams to Andrew, 14 November 1955). Williams travelled to Geneva in November 1955 and held discussions with ILO officials regarding his assignment from the ICFTU, which dealt with international labour standards as applied to plantation workers. Not surprisingly, Williams received a favourable and encouraging response: "The ILO officials were enthusiastic over the undertaking. It will almost certainly lead to my attendance at other plantation conferences, if they can be fitted into my programme and schedule" (Williams to Donald, 25 November 1955). The two pamphlets Williams completed for the ICFTU were entitled *International Standards for Plantation Workers* and *The I.C.F.T.U. and the Plantation Worker* (Williams to Donaldson and Rogers, 28 November 1955; Williams 1969, 141).

The intellectual and research abilities Williams displayed resulted in the onerous responsibilities of speaking at both the ICFTU and ILO conferences; he also worked as general adviser to the workers (Williams to Mrs Tisha and Rolle, 1 December 1955). He did not complain about his workload and at the ILO conference, Williams was the featured speaker for the ICFTU. Interestingly, his speech was well received by all those in attendance except the Trinidad and Tobago delegation (Williams to Sam, 1 December 1955). This negative feedback did not deter Williams, and he optimistically stated, "There is much work ahead, with my ICFTU commitments and other ideas proposed here. The holiday committee sessions are indispensable" (Williams to David, Walter and Andrew, 4 December 1955).

At these international conferences Williams was admired and respected by trade unionists, labour leaders and policymakers alike. Also, while conducting research for the ICFTU in London, Williams expanded his network of friends in the international labour movement. These included Tom Mboya, C.L.R. James, George Padmore, Arthur Lewis and Aimé Césaire (Williams 1969, 142–43). As a result of these contacts, he could easily have found permanent employment with either the ICFTU or ILO or as a labour adviser in one of several countries. But his contributions to this sphere of labour would end abruptly as a result of the decision of this brilliant speaker and labour analyst to become involved in the party politics of Trinidad and Tobago. This decision initiated a long saga between the local labour movement, conscious of and anxious to exercise its independence and resistant to controls by government, and a government led by a man with impeccable trade union credentials, but whose commitment to the interests of workers was often subject to question.

News of the respect and admiration that Williams had received abroad quickly filtered into Trinidad and Tobago. Thus, upon his return in 1956,

Williams was in high demand among the working class. Not surprisingly, he was valued both as a speaker and adviser for various workers and trade unions. These commitments forced Williams to delay the completion of his report for the ICFTU. In a letter to J.H. Oldenbrook, general secretary of the ICFTU, Williams referred to the many requests for help he had received, such as that from Oli Mohammed of the colony's sugar union:

> He has enlisted my aid in talks to sugar workers in connection with his union's efforts both to retain its members and get new ones in the face of increase in union dues. I have spoken to workers in their thousands at St. Madeleine, where Walcott also spoke, and at Chaguanas, and as soon as I can find the time I have arranged to go to speak at Picton on trade unionism to people who are principally field workers. . . . Over and above this, I have had several meetings with fishermen in Cedros who want to form a union, with seamen in the overseas trade who are not catered for by Alexander's union, and with the steelbandsmen who have an association of sorts which so far has done nothing, while I have arranged to meet as soon as possible some workers on coconut estates who are considering the desirability of organising themselves. In all cases I have been asked to be the President of the Union concerned, but I have declined and I am limiting my assistance to technical advice. (Williams to J.H. Oldenbroek, 1 February 1956)

In September 1956, Williams witnessed a new era in which the concept of the old world was dominated by oil and sugar profits. This, he believed, was in opposition to the new world of self-government, with the focus now being the small producer (Williams, September 1956). By the 1950s, the Oilfield Workers' Trade Union (OWTU) was the strongest and best-organized union in Trinidad and Tobago. Undoubtedly, the oil industry had become the mainspring of the island's economy, and thus the leadership role played by the OWTU was crucial for the direction and future of the trade union movement. However, Williams had relatively little contact with this union.

Rumblings within Labour

In 1958, having spent more than two decades in North America and Europe, C.L.R. James decided to return to Trinidad. In 1959 Williams welcomed James as editor of the *Nation*, the newspaper of the PNM. However, their cordial relations soon soured because the two men had differing political visions, as a newspaper article later recalled: "His partnership with his former student and friend Williams came to an end as a result of the break-up of the West Indies Federation and, more particularly, as a result of Williams's rejection of a non-aligned position, in favour of the USA and its retention of the Chaguaramas Naval Base" (*Trinidad Guardian*, 2 June 1989). James's Communist activities were also a cause of concern to PNM party leaders, who believed James was spreading Communist ideas among its members and allowing Communists to enter the party (*Trinidad Chronicle*, 1 February 1959). In 1961 James addressed regular meetings organized by George Weekes and Walter Annumunthodo and other OWTU personnel who were members of the PNM (Ramdin 1982, 245). However, John Rojas, president general of the OWTU, disagreed with James's political philosophy and his incursion into the trade union movement. Rojas's failure to be more accommodating to the new ideas James propagated within the movement contributed to the ending of his presidency of the union in 1961. In a speech to the Senate in August 1962 Rojas claimed that Marxists were operating in some of the trade unions in the island and described the OWTU meetings addressed by James in Fyzabad, Pointe-a-Pierre and San Fernando as "communist cells". He also referred to the existence of "study cells" within the OWTU, which were attracting the radical and more educated elements in the union (Ramdin 1982, 245). Finally, he made reference to a conversation with James in July 1962, at the twenty-fifth anniversary celebrations of the OWTU, in which he claimed James had spoken of a revolution in Trinidad within eighteen months (Ramdin 1982, 243–44).

James soon broke ranks with the PNM and subsequently openly criticized his former friend's tactics. He believed there was "no sense of direction" in the PNM because Williams had "depoliticized and miseducated" every aspect of the country (interview with C.L.R. James by Henry Partap, *Express*, 7 April 1981; Buhle 1987, 18). It seemed almost that James was destined to form a political party with a strong focus on the working class: "It became necessary for him politically to challenge Williams, but it was too late. He had been known earlier as a writer and not as a political figure" (Cripps 1997, 105). Williams knew that the break with James could signal a further rift with the labour movement. At the fifth PNM convention on 30 September 1960, he had paid tribute to James's services as editor of the *Nation* (*Vanguard*, 17 September 1965), but a few years later, in October 1966 at a PNM meeting in San Fernando, Williams assured his listeners that he would crush any Marxist movement in Trinidad. One newspaper reported the prime minister's statements: "He said the Marxist group had started their activities in the sugar belt, using the workers there as 'pawns'. He hinted that that was one of the reasons his Government had to institute the Industrial Stabilisation Act" (ISA; *Evening News*, 5 October 1966). James possessed the qualifications necessary to become a powerful figure in the colony's labour movement. First, his international ties with labour organizations in the United States and Europe made him knowledgeable of their operations, tactics and strategies. This included his friendship with George Padmore, another prominent Trinidadian in the international black working-class movement. This gave him advantages as he persevered in his efforts to unite the workers of Trinidad and Tobago. Second, James's intellect could help both to define the course of the colony's labour movement and counter the ideas of the perceived enemy of labour – the scholarly Eric Williams. James had emerged from the heart of the PNM and those in the labour movement saw his knowledge of the ruling party's strengths and weaknesses as an important advantage in the ongoing struggle between the Government and the labour movement.

In August 1965, James and Stephen Maharaj formed the Workers and Farmers Party (WFP), which was formally launched in October 1965. James was also the founder and editor of the WFP paper *We the People*. Commenting favourably on the new party in an article in the OWTU paper, the *Vanguard*, George Bowrin made the bold statement that the PNM had "lost its magic", the Democratic Labour Party (DLP) was "demoralized" and the Butler Party was "a name only". Bowrin advised, "The WFP must offer a programme which promises real change if it is to receive substantial support from the people" (*Vanguard*, 20 August 1965). On 27 August 1965, the *Vanguard* published an appeal from the WFP stating the objectives of their political endeavour: "the Workers and Farmers Party believes that local businessmen, prospective industrialists, local workers and farmers have the capacity to build a modern economy based on our natural and quite exceptionally qualified human resources. Such an economy is an indispensable foundation for the life and development of the country and its relations abroad" (*Vanguard*, 27 August 1965). James held a similar view and sought to emphasize that the members of the WFP believed the country had reached a critical crossroads: "It recognizes the backward character of the economy, it recognizes the advanced character of the population – it knows that one of these has to go. Either the population has to be reduced to where it was in 1937, or the economy has to be made into an advanced and a modern economy" (*We the People*, 19 November 1965). The WFP, with its headquarters at 22 Ariapita Avenue, Woodbrook (Port of Spain), had emerged from the bowels of the OWTU. This new political party envisioned a government that was controlled by the working class, "by establishing a sound and scientifically based farming community, and by making labour aware that not only its rights but its contributions to all aspects of social progress are the constant concern of a Workers and Farmers Government" (*Vanguard*, 27 August 1965). The party chairman and officers included S.C. Maharaj (chairman), George Bowrin (first vice-chairman), A.S.A. Khan (second vice-chairman), C.L.R. James (general secretary), Dr S.H. Goopeesingh (assistant general secretary), C. Phill (treasurer), Dr J.M. Dube (public relations officer) and Basdeo Panday (youth organizer; *We the People*, 19 November 1965). However, the grandiose plans of the WFP failed to attract voters at the polls. The party received only 3 per cent of the popular vote and lost all their candidates' deposits. In Tunapuna, James, the defeated candidate, received only 2.8 per cent of the vote (Worcester 1996, 171). Despite its idealistic ambitions and claims of being representative of labour, the WFP never developed the comprehensive and necessary "organic links" with Trinidad's working class (Look Lai 1992, 199). The government also sought to discourage this attempt at working-class unity and political reform. In an article entitled "Human Rights Amidst Human Wrongs", Basdeo Panday, a member of the WFP, warned: "If you are employed 'with Government' you had better not let it be known that you are a member of WFP. Worse still if you are unemployed and looking for work. . . . So much for your right to join political parties of your choice" (*Vanguard*, 10 August 1965). A similar scenario unfolded in the formation of the United Labour Front (ULF) on 18 February 1975, the difference being that the ULF was able to secure ten of the thirty-six contested seats and become the official opposition in Parliament. The ULF functioned under a triumvirate leadership comprising George Weekes of the OWTU, Raffique Shah of the Islandwide Cane Farmers Union and Basdeo Panday of the All Trinidad Sugar and General Workers Trade Union. On 18 March 1975, the ULF attempted a religious march from San Fernando to Port of Spain. On that fateful day, thirty-seven persons were arrested, including union leaders Raffique Shah, Basdeo Panday, George Weekes and Joe Young. One month later, on 22 April, Weekes, Shah and Panday were found not guilty of the charge of leading a public march without police permission (*Trinidad Express*, 23 April 1975). Such animosity from the Williams regime was a concerted attempt to abort the efforts at unity among three of the country's major unions, which backed the ULF. Williams's fears that the political strength of the ULF would challenge the PNM were soon dismissed. In August 1977, Basdeo Panday was ousted from the ULF. Labour's short-lived experimental coalition had failed (Siewah and Arjoonsingh 1998, 28).

During the period of 1960 to 1964, there were 230 trade disputes in Trinidad and Tobago involving 74,574 workers with a loss of 803,899 work days (Cudjoe 1993, 373; Williams 1969, 311). The discontent of workers was clearly evident. Another wave of discontent began on 21 April 1969, when more than 650 workers took strike action against the Public Transportation Service Corporation. Several union members were fined as a result of their involvement in this bus strike, including Joe Young (president), Krishna Gowandan, Carlton Rosemin and Sylvester Mondesir of the Transport and Industrial Workers Union, Stephen Maharaj (leader of the WFP) and George Weekes (OWTU); Peter Farquhar, leader of the Liberal Party, and Earl Lewis, member of the editorial board of *Moko*, were also fined (*Trinidad Express*, 27 June 1969). The president of the Trinidad and Tobago Labour Congress, Senator Clive Spencer, warned that the labour movement would not allow a lockout of workers by the Public Transportation Service Corporation (*Trinidad Guardian*, 23 May 1969). The striking bus workers sought to confront and embarrass the prime minister on the ongoing crisis. The *Trinidad Guardian* reported on the union's tactics: "A demonstrator outside the magistrates' building had an anti–Dr Eric Williams poster. The 'bus-workers' union announced in Woodford Square that it would picket all public appearances by the Prime Minister starting from this afternoon with his 'Meet the Farmers' tour in La Pastora, Santa Cruz" (*Trinidad Guardian*, 14 May 1969).

The public responses to the protests included sympathy for Williams. For instance, during the bus strike, George Wiltshire (of Tobago) penned a letter to the editor of the *Express*, stating that the strike was really a struggle for political power by the trade unionists. Wiltshire appealed for the government's intervention: "It is high time that government do something positive to bring this act of illegality to an end, and restore sanity and balance in the society" (*Trinidad Express*, 15 May 1969). In a similar fashion, during a later strike at Texaco Trinidad Incorporated, another letter to the editor of the *Express* saw the workers' grouses as really being Weekes seeking political power: "The so-called powerful trade unionist that he once was in [sic] no more, and the primary reason for this is because he is straying from trade union matters and concentrating too much on Eric Williams" (*Express*, 25 April 1975). Certain sections of the public had lost sympathy for the constant strike action by unions.

For instance, in a letter to the *Trinidad Guardian*, A. Thomas (of Claxton Bay) expressed his dissatisfaction with the state of affairs: "I hope and pray that one day I will hear a trade union leader requesting workers to give an honest day's work instead of demanding a 120 per cent pay rise, cost-of-living boons, travelling allowance, more sick leave and a two-day work week" (*Trinidad Guardian*, 2 August 1974).

The OWTU was particularly severe on the Williams regime. James, a member of the WFP and renowned pan-Africanist, gave the OWTU a political renaissance which Butler had earlier ignited. In 1965, James believed the OWTU was an organization equipped for the political deliverance of the country: "The OWTU is fighting the battle of democracy, of parliamentary democracy in Trinidad and Tobago. . . . If the OWTU goes down not only Union rights go down. The liberties of every citizen of Trinidad and Tobago will not only be in peril, they will be tottering on the edge of extinction" (*Vanguard*, 17 September 1965). At a conference organized by the editorial team of the *Vanguard* at Palm's Club, San Fernando, James advised that the OWTU newspaper should be published weekly and undertake the responsibility of educating the public on such themes as West Indian history, creative arts and sociological analysis. James further advised on the role of the union's publication: "The *Vanguard* must see itself as filling a breach no one else in sight can fill. It is a union paper and it has to inform and educate labour and the public on all union matters. . . . Labour has to win over large sections of the population, particularly in an under-developed country, i.e. where organized labour is small" (*Vanguard*, 15 October 1965). It was evident that James attempted to consolidate the forces of labour to ensure it was a formidable opponent of the PNM. The OWTU did not hide its feelings of hostility towards the actions and policies of Eric Williams. The union often quoted from Williams's earlier statements to demonstrate the prime minister's apparent two-faced nature on matters relating to labour. Williams's views were usually confined to a column entitled "The Doctor Said". For instance, at the height of the debate on the ISA, the OWTU quoted from Williams' work *The Case for Party Politics in Trinidad and Tobago*, in which Williams then seemed sympathetic to labour: "We repudiate unambiguously, the indefensible efforts of the Ministers to intimidate the trade unions, split the workers' ranks, and set themselves up as little demigods recognizing only those they consider amenable. That road leads straight to totalitarianism" (*Vanguard*, 15 April 1966). Likewise, after repeated demands for wage increases, on 3 September 1965, the *Vanguard* quoted

Williams's comments made five years before in the PNM newspaper the *Nation* of 29 July 1960: "The increase of wages in the oil industry is not lost to the country. Not at all. The workers will spend the money in the country" (*Vanguard*, 3 September 1966).

The masterpiece *Capitalism and Slavery*, which made Williams famous in academia, was also cited by some trade unionists in Trinidad and Tobago as a means of criticizing Williams's attempts to undermine the labour movement. In an article in the *Vanguard*, Bernard Primus criticized Williams in this way: "It is almost natural that the Government and the Chamber of Commerce should have labour and trade unions as the whipping boy for all the economic ills of the country. This is the same old story told so well in Dr. Williams' *Capitalism and Slavery*" (*Vanguard*, 28 May 1965). The prime minister's other scholarly works were also cited in the *Vanguard*, as in the quotation from *The History of the People of Trinidad and Tobago* in which Williams had identified the trade unionist Butler as one of the three main persons contributing to the movement for self-government (*Vanguard*, 19 June 1965). In a similar fashion, E.R. Ramsahai, vice-president of the Federation Chemical Branch, OWTU, wrote about the 1937 riots based on an excerpt from *History of the People of Trinidad and Tobago* (*Vanguard*, 4 February 1966).

The double standards exhibited by Williams with regard to organized labour were exposed by the unions relentlessly, especially during the passage of the ISA in 1965. For instance, in May 1965, the *Vanguard* published Williams's statement of 13 March 1963 that "each party would pledge itself to the promotion, maintenance, and, above all, enforcement of proper civilized industrial relations based on collective bargaining". The view of the OWTU was that this was evidence that the government should not pass laws to ban strikes or interfere in the relations between employer and employees (*Vanguard*, 14 May 1965). Vas Stanford, president general of the Union of Commercial and Industrial Workers, believed there would be an "explosion" if the ISA continued to exist in the country (Ramdin 1982, 206). The "oppressive" legislation resulted in a temporary unity among unions. A joint action committee, comprising the National Union of Foods, Hotels, Beverages and Allied Workers, National Union of Government Employees, the Transport and Industrial Workers Union and the OWTU, embarked on a campaign to repeal the ISA.

For his part, Williams, in his work *Inward Hunger*, confessed to keeping the two major unions – oil and sugar – apart with the passage of the ISA:

> The subversive elements in the society, with James in the forefront, were at work; the background was an open attempt to link the trade unions in oil and sugar. I therefore presented a Bill to provide for the compulsory recognition by employers of trade unions and organizations representative of a majority of workers, for the establishment of an expeditious system for the settlement of trade disputes, for the regulation of prices of commodities, for the constitution of a court to regulate matters relating to the foregoing and incidental thereto. (Williams 1969, 311)

The statistics on work stoppages demonstrated that unions blatantly ignored the ISA. During 1970 there were fifty-five incidents of work stoppages, while in January 1971 there were fifteen cases of workers refusing to work. The growing disenchantment prompted the government to draft the Industrial Relations Act in 1971. However, this failed to reduce labour's antagonism. Eventually the Industrial Relations Act, 1972 (act no. 23), was passed and replaced the Industrial Stabilisation Act of 1965. The 1972 act defined the terms *union*, *worker*, *strike*, and *trade union*. The act allowed for the establishment of the Registration, Recognition and Certification Board. More importantly, the legislation protected workers' rights and offered freedom to the worker to join any union without fear of victimization from an employer.

During the Black Power era of the late 1960s and early 1970s, the OWTU felt the brunt of the Government's oppression. Eric Williams, as the minister of National Security, under the Emergency Powers Act of 1970, seized the union's books and victimized its officers. In April 1970, George Weekes was detained and other union members arrested, including Carl Douglas (assistant secretary, Palo Seco Branch), Winston Lennard (education officer), Nuevo Diaz (labour relations officer), Chan Maharaj (member of the Port of Spain branch). During this month, petrol bombs were thrown at the *Vanguard*'s printery, and an attempt was made to destroy the Paramount Building, headquarters of the OWTU. On 14 and 15 May 1970, the police seized the OWTU's books and records and invaded the union's headquarters and printery. The "days of terror" faced by the OWTU did not end in 1970. In August 1971, at the general council meeting of the OWTU, Weekes and two members were arrested on fraud charges. On 27 September at the court hearing, in a dramatic turn of events, Weekes cut his clenched fist and chest with a razor and shouted, "In the name of the Black Indian and African masses and in protest against the corrupt Williams regime I shed my blood" (*Vanguard*, 1 February 1980).

The divided and uncertain nature of the opposition served to also ensure Williams won the elections in the same year. For instance, after the issue of the ISA, the DLP suspended two of its members for supporting the government on the seemingly oppressive labour legislation (*Nation*, 29 November 1968). Between 1960 and 1980, the unions were fighting among themselves. For instance, in December 1957, two rival unions united to form the Trinidad and Tobago National Trades Union Congress (TTNTUC). John Rojas was president of the newly established union, which had forty thousand members. The first sign of trouble began shortly after George Weekes succeeded Rojas as president in 1963. Friction and internal problems developed in 1964 when three unions – Amalgamated Workers' Union, All Trinidad Sugar Estates and Factory Workers Trade Union, and Federated Workers Trade Union (FWTU) withdrew from the TTNTUC to form the National Federation of Labour with W. Sutton as president. A similar situation arose one year later with the withdrawal of the Postal Workers Union and the Seamen and Waterfront Workers Trade Union (SWWTU) from the TTNTUC. Thus, by 1965, the unions belonging to the TTNTUC were the Communication and Transport Workers Trade Union, Government and Transport Workers Trade Union, OWTU and the National Union of Government Employees. Throughout the 1960s and 1970s, there were indicators of serious schisms within the trade union movement. On 25 June 1972, for example, Robert Denny (president general of the Brotherhood of Construction and Industrial Workers' Union), criticized "fly by night" union leaders for preaching a doctrine of hate (*Trinidad Guardian*, 26 June 1972). Another incident of interunion hostility was in July 1975 with an election controversy in the Communication and Transport Workers Trade Union, which resulted in the expulsion of four members (*Trinidad Guardian*, 1 July 1975). Attempts to increase the membership of unions were also a source of controversy and contention. In November 1963, it was reported that 635 monthly paid members of the Civil Service Association "defected" to the SWWTU (Ramdin 1982, 247). A similar scenario unfolded in late 1974, as the Amalgamated Workers' Union accused the Contractors and General Workers Trade Union of "poaching" its membership (*Express*, 4 September 1974). In November 1975, the National Union of Government and Federated Workers, based on complaints by oil workers in Fyzabad, was reported to have been wooing oil workers to join their Port of Spain–based union (*Trinidad Guardian*, 1 January 1974).

Union leaders aspiring to the prized office of prime minister of the country were unable to penetrate the strongholds of the PNM. By 1975, it was evident that the WFP, DLP and ULF were no match for the machinery of the PNM with its various committees, conventions and party groups. It was not merely the racial cleavage between sugar and oil workers, representative of central and south Trinidad, which strengthened the PNM. Undoubtedly, the PNM enjoyed solid support among the unions in north Trinidad, and this ensured continuous electoral victories for Williams. But, it was the issue of race that largely explains the support of certain trade unions and working-class organizations for the PNM. Undoubtedly, the working class in the north, certain areas in south Trinidad, and also Tobago supported Williams. Unions with a large percentage of Afro-Trinidadians such as the Communication and Transport Workers Trade Union, the OWTU and SWWTU provided solid electoral support for Williams. The SWWTU, in 1974, was the fifth-largest labour organization, with a membership of 8,000 workers belonging to seven industries (of whom 2,021 were employed on the Port of Spain dock; *Express*, 30 November 1974). Thus, members of unions that were critical of and protested against PNM policies nevertheless gave Williams strong electoral support (interview with Alexander Phillips, 28 August 2001). Likewise, the National Union of Government and Federated Workers, which had a membership of 50,000 workers during the 1970s, comprised mostly urban Afro-Trinidadians who were staunch supporters of the PNM (interview with Selwyn John, 27 April 2001).

The WFP and later the ULF failed to defeat the PNM as a result of one prevailing factor – race. A political party composed of major unions lost to the PNM simply because race exerted a greater influence on the lives of a considerable segment of the working-class movement than issues relating to class. Unfortunately, the mass membership of some of the unions displayed a dual identity. Indeed, members supported their unions in anti-government demonstrations and marches. But their political allegiance was distinct from their occupational actions. For example, Indians in the sugar union would have been in union meetings supporting the efforts of Basdeo Panday or Raffique Shah to improve their working and living conditions. However, on Election Day, these workers would vote for the DLP, which was Hindu-oriented with an East Indian leader. Likewise, George Weekes would have appeared confident of victory in south Trinidad because of the massive crowds at meetings and his position in the OWTU, but Afro-Trinidadians belonging to the OWTU pledged allegiance to the PNM rather than the ULF. The Afrocentric character of the PNM and the Indian/Hindu-based DLP were social indicators of a postcolonial plural society which was still racially polarized. The mutual distrust and fears exhibited by both races since immigration had not disappeared. The quest for political power only served to perpetuate these inhibitions.

It would be simplistic to believe that race was the sole determining factor in Williams's success. There were other political parties headed by Afro-Trinidadians such as Tapia, led by Lloyd Best, and the Democratic Action Congress, led by Arthur Robinson. Both parties failed miserably to attract a significant percentage of the Afro-Trinidadian working class. In addition to his charisma and unrivalled intellectual ability, Williams possessed other vital assets, particularly his ability to deal effectively with the unions and to portray the PNM as sympathetic to the concerns of the working class. Undoubtedly, this enabled him to enjoy uninterrupted electoral success during the years 1956 to 1980.

Williams Strikes Back

During this period, the incidence of anti-government demonstrations coupled with the fines and arrests of union members projected an image of Williams as anti–working class and against trade unionism. Despite this, the prime minister still enjoyed considerable popularity among the unions and working-class organizations. The reasons for this were that Williams was able to manoeuvre domestic policies skilfully, while his public lectures at the "University of Woodford Square" helped him to appear sympathetic to the working class.

The formation of the PNM enabled Williams, as its political leader, to utilize the knowledge and experience gained during his earlier work with the ICFTU and ILO. There were representatives of labour on the general council (the governing body of the PNM) and its central executive. Among the persons holding positions of responsibility were Sam Worrell (labour relations secretary), Ulric Lee of the Industrial and Commercial Workers and Oli Mohammed of the sugar workers. Also included were workers from the communication, oil, seamen and waterfront sectors (Williams, 14 June 1956).

In a public lecture on 14 June 1956 at the "University of Woodford Square", Williams highlighted his political party's economic programme, which involved the improvement of the fishing industry, expansion of secondary industries, encouraging the development of foreign and local capital, assistance to small farmers, and provision of extra jobs for an expanding population (14 June 1956). He also revealed certain aspects of the PNM's Labour Programme which would have been attractive to workers in Trinidad:

It calls for the introduction into Trinidad and Tobago of the international standards worked out over the years by the International Labour Organisation.... The PNM policy is to bring the trade union leaders into the Central Executive, but to restrict the role of non-trade union members in union affairs to a purely advisory capacity.... The PNM through its trade union representatives, is associated with the ICFTU, the international trade union organization of the democratic countries, and through it with the British TUC and the powerful AFL-CIO merger in the U.S.A. (14 June 1956)

On 20 November 1959, the PNM chose Sir Solomon Hochoy to be the next governor of Trinidad and Tobago. This decision won valuable support from the labour movement and the working class. Hochoy had previously served as a civil servant and also as a popular commissioner of Labour. It was a strategic and well-planned move which would set the stage for the transition to independence.

In another of his lectures at Woodford Square, on 19 July 1965, Williams championed the cause of political unionism, stating: "The trade union element in any society is the bulwark of democracy.... The place for the trade unionist, his rightful place, is [sic] an elected member in the Lower House" (*Vanguard*, 21 January 1966). Almost a decade later, this view was reiterated by Weekes at a lecture at the University of the West Indies, Trinidad, when he argued that it was necessary for trade unions to be involved in politics as a result of "the breakdown of democracy".

The executive committee of the All Trinidad Sugar Estates and Factory Workers Trade Union invited Williams to address the sugar workers. In his speech at Couva Recreation Ground on 25 September 1955, Williams dealt with the problems facing the sugar industry – external markets, poor conditions of labour and "reconciling the economic interests of the investor with the social needs of the community". He envisioned the mechanization of the sugar industry and its subsequent challenges:

Production per worker amounted to 5 tons in 1939 and 9 1/2 tons last year. Thus higher and higher productivity coincide with the employment of fewer workers. That, Ladies and Gentlemen, is the fact which you and your union must courageously face – that the raising of your standard of living depends, paradoxically enough, on the reduction of the labour Force.... The sugar industry must mechanize or perish. Mechanization will reduce costs. But it will also reduce jobs. The raising of the standard of living and the rate of wages of sugar workers depends on the preservation of the sugar industry, the retention of present markets and the securing of new ones and the reduction of the number of workers employed by the industry. (25 September 1955)

It was evident that Williams simplified basic principles of economics for these workers, many of whom had only a primary school education. A decade later in 1965, he was invited to address the conference of the Cane Farmers Association at San Fernando (*Vanguard*, 12 November 1965).

Williams also sought to have the support of labour by including a union representative in his government. In 1965, Nathaniel Critchlow, president of the National Union of Government and Federated Workers, was appointed a PNM senator. However, Critchlow's appointment was revoked after he opposed the government's decision to pay daily-paid workers on a 60–40 cash-bond basis for their outstanding back pay. Critchlow was replaced by Carl Tull, who served in 1957 as the assistant general secretary of the Communication Workers Union (*Trinidad Guardian*, 3 August 1974).

At the eleventh PNM convention in September 1968, Williams announced his administration's plans to buy British Petroleum. This was the result of the cabinet's concern over the proposed retrenchment of 1,650 workers over a five-year period (*Nation*, 27 September 1968). The decision in 1968 to establish a national petroleum company was a major advance in the government's oil policy. This was not an initiative by Williams but of Weekes, president general of the OWTU, who had been campaigning for a national oil company (*Nation*, 4 October 1968). Even though Williams seemed to have succumbed to Weekes's earlier suggestion of establishing a national oil company, in April 1975 Williams said he would ignore the call of the OWTU for nationalization of Texaco Trinidad Incorporated (*Express*, 12 April 1975). However, he also announced the government's decision to acquire all of the Texaco gas stations in Trinidad and Tobago and Texaco's distribution of all domestic gas – a decision that certainly pleased the trade unions. Williams was fortunate that during his regime new oil deposits were discovered and there was an accompanying relatively high price for oil. In September 1969, John O'Halloran, minister of Petroleum and Mines, announced that Pan American Oil had again struck oil off the east coast of Trinidad (*Nation*, 19 September 1969). Interestingly, James firmly believed that the political success of Williams in the 1970s was mainly due to high oil prices:

> Let me tell you the prosperity in oil now experienced by this country had nothing to do with any policy of the Williams regime. It was a result of the decision by OPEC countries. And when they asked him to join, he refused. . . . In 1970, the whole country moved against him and in 1974, he was all ready to go because the country was bankrupt. The oil saved him. It saved everybody. (Interview with C.L.R. James in Buhle 1987, 18)

On the question of government policy towards sugar, as with oil, Williams was not inclined to take advice from union leaders. On 13 April 1975 at a meeting at Harris Promenade, San Fernando, Williams revealed that the cabinet had rejected the idea of paying TT$50 million for non-governmental shares of Caroni Limited, a step which had been urged by the union. He stated that he did not believe that Caroni Limited was worth TT$50 million (*Trinidad Guardian*, 14 April 1975). Basdeo Panday, then leader of the All Trinidad Sugar Estates and Factory Workers Trade Union, had previously been critical of Williams's statement that the government was planning to import sugar for its local market (*Express*, 12 April 1975).

At a PNM convention in September 1968, Williams highlighted achievements of his government. Among the items which would have appealed to the working class were the reorganization of the Agricultural Development Bank in 1968, the establishment of the Public Utilities Commission in 1966, the introduction of the social insurance scheme in early 1969 and plans to hold tripartite discussions involving the workers (*Nation*, 15 August 1969). Another move that won support among labour occurred in December 1968 when Williams designated 1969 as "Agriculture Year" in his budget speech. The prime minister promised that every effort would be made to focus attention on agricultural development (*Nation*, 6 December 1968).

In an ongoing effort to revamp the image of his party, on 3 August 1969 Williams launched celebrations in the country to observe the fiftieth year of the ILO's existence. He announced that in recognition of the special occasion two scholarships would be given – one each from the country's trade union and business sector (*Nation*, 15 August 1969). This attempt to create an impression of a labour-friendly administration received a minor setback in November 1969 when Lennox Hunte, senior lecturer at the Cipriani College of Labour and Co-operative Studies (Trinidad), revealed that the government had ratified only 10 of the 128 ILO conventions (*Trinidad Guardian*, 7 November 1969). It was ironic that Williams had once been associated with the ILO, yet as prime minister he did not see the necessity of ratifying many of its conventions.

The year 1970, during which the OWTU faced victimization for its outspokenness, also marked government's decision to seriously address the controversies surrounding the Industrial Stabilisation Act. On 28 August 1970, Errol Mahabir, writing in the *Nation*, sought to inform the unions and public of the outcome of discussions between the prime minister and the Trinidad and Tobago Labour Congress regarding the act. Mahabir stated that it had been decided that there would be a streamlining of the procedures governing the recognition of unions, a relaxation of the provision relating to strikes and lockouts, an enhancement of the status of the Labour Congress in matters such as inter-union disputes and registration of unions and the continued existence of the Industrial Court (*Nation*, 28 August 1970).

Amid the disturbances of the seventies, the formation of two unions between 1974 and 1975 was noteworthy. In 1974, Michael Als formed the Bank Workers Trade Union, which claimed to be the first to organize among workers in the banking sector in the country (*Express*, 12 April 1974). In 1975, the National Union of Domestic Employees was formed to organize domestic servants, babysitters, barmen, messengers, yard boys, chauffeurs and seamstresses. There seemed to be hope for increasing democracy in the labour movement.

In an address entitled "Government's Role in the Management of Public Enterprises", Williams shared his vision of agriculture in Trinidad and Tobago in 1976: "It is precisely because you have a big industrial revolution going on now in Trinidad, that one can anticipate an agricultural development. The essence of that agricultural development must be to take people away from the land, which is not difficult" (19 May 1976). Williams also gave the female labour force special attention, and this ensured the PNM received some support from this section of the working class. In April 1976 in an address to the Federation of Women's Institutes, Williams stressed the importance of women: "It is essentially a woman society. A family is dominated by the female element because that is the only element of certainty; that's the only element that you can be sure is there" (4 April 1976). It was increasingly apparent that Williams did not perceive women merely as commodities whose productivity was to be maximized. In another of his speeches, to the Business and Professional Women of Trinidad and Tobago, Williams emphasized the changes that had occurred in the lives of women: "The first is the women removed by technological advances on the one hand from the drudgery that's associated with housekeeping. And on the other. . . the relief from the drudgery and chore of persistent childbearing, especially when the child might not have been anticipated or planned or prepared for" (26 July 1976). Williams championed gender equality in the occupational sphere. It was an interesting development in that the colonial society, which was extremely patriarchal, was being radically changed by a visionary who was acquainted with the gender divisions of labour. In an address at the formal opening of the Harmon High School (Seventh-Day Adventist) in Tobago, Williams listed the vast options for young girls who were given equal job opportunities: "Not women in agriculture though they make better farmers than men. Horticulture. Perhaps factory processing. Textiles. Garments. An extension of the curriculum in respect of home economics and sewing. Electronics. The proficiency of women, young girls with these intricate computer parts which we have found out in Trinidad. There'd be room for the girls as well as for the boys" (30 May 1976). The government consistently emphasized its initiatives to improve relations with labour. For instance, on 23 April 1976 Williams, in the feature address of the Second Biennial Conference of the SWWTU, mentioned the cooperation between the two spheres: "I would make it explicit that in this tremendous economic transformation, restructuring one of the essential features partly in order to ensure the decision making remains in local hands, partly in order to deal with the inherent difficulties in Mr. Manswell's claim about the old attitude of investment – private capital would be majority shareholding by the Government or by agencies, working with the Government including the labour movement in all fields." The government's challenge of management was frankly tackled by Williams in a speech to the monthly meeting of the south branch of the Trinidad and Tobago Chamber of Industry and Commerce:

> Every day the government faces the question of, you are taking over something or other, I think right now it's cement, possibly also the remaining shares of Caroni – apart from the fundamental issues raised by that how is the government going to divest itself, if it is going to divest itself of any part of its shareholding and on what terms. Apart from that you have the question of Boards of Management . . . Would the change of ownership merely be a question of the big car that used to be held by the expatriate manager being transferred now to some local. Big car remains. Nationality and colour of manager change. Is that enough? (N.d.)

The PNM sought to bridge the divisions between the party itself, business and labour as it hosted tripartite conferences in 1964, 1966, 1967 and 1968. On 8 July 1968, the government held such a conference, but it was interpreted by

Basdeo Panday, a member of a major sugar union, as an attempt by the government to stage a "grand deception": "This is the trap that Dr. Eric Williams has laid for labour. He gets labour's representatives to sit down with him, and lay down proposals for solving the economic problems. At first, labour is under the impression that it is there merely in an advisory capacity – to give him ideas of how to run the country. But subtly labour's role is being shifted from one of advice to that of commitment" (*Vanguard*, 27 July 1968). In December 1969, the economic adviser to the prime minister, William Demas, suggested the government and private sector should offer technical and financial assistance to the country's labour movement. The PNM administration had taken the initiative, as it had recently held a tripartite conference on labour legislation which involved labour, business and the government (*Trinidad Guardian*, 23 December 1969).

In conclusion, during his time as prime minister, Williams was unable to prevent the unions from becoming politically involved or avert their frequent strikes. However, he sought, through overt and obvious tactics, to frustrate their political ambitions. The portrayal of the PNM as being labour friendly also served to ensure electoral support from union members. The early association with the ICFTU and ILO, his oratorical abilities and his intellectual superiority, which was highlighted by the international acclaim for his published doctoral thesis, ensured that Williams not only won votes but the hearts and minds of a significant segment of the working class in Trinidad and Tobago.

References

Primary Sources

All cited correspondence is from the Eric Williams Memorial Collection, University of the West Indies, Trinidad. The following addresses by Williams are held in the collection:

"Address to a Mass Meeting of Sugar Workers at the Couva Recreation Ground". 25 September 1955.
"The P.N.M. Restates Its Fundamental Principles". Address, 14 June 1956.
"Two Worlds in Conflict". Address, September 1956.

"The State of the Nation". Address to the Second Annual Convention of the PNM, 28 September 1957.
Address to the Federation of Women's Institutes, 4 April 1976.
Address to the Second Biennial Conference. SWWTU, 23 April 1976.
"Government's Role in the Management of Public Enterprises". Address at a Seminar on Effective Management, 19 May 1976.
Address to the Harmon High School. Scarborough, Tobago, 30 May 1976.
"Her Name Is Woman". Address to the Business and Professional Women of Trinidad and Tobago, 26 July 1976.
Address to the monthly meeting of the Southern Branch of the Trinidad and Tobago Chamber of Industry and Commerce, n.d.

BOOKS AND ARTICLES

Buhle, Paul, ed. 1987. *C.L.R. James: His Life and Work*. London: Allison and Busby.
Cripps, Louise. 1997. *C.L.R. James: Memories and Commentaries*. London: Cornwall Books.
Cudjoe, Selwyn, ed. 1993. *Eric Williams Speaks: Essays on Colonialism and Independence*. Welleseley, MA: Calaloux.
Look Lai, Walton. 1992. "C.L.R. James and Trinidad Nationalism". In *C.L.R. James' Caribbean*, edited by Paget Henry and Paul Buhle, 174–209. Durham, NC: Duke University Press.
Ramdin, Ronald. 1982. *From Chattel Slave to Wage Earner: A History of Trade Unionism in Trinidad and Tobago*. London: Martin Brian and O'Keeffe.
Siewah, Samaroo, and Satie Arjoonsingh, eds. 1998. *Basdeo Panday: The Making of a Prime Minister*. Tunapuna, Trinidad and Tobago: Chakra.
Williams, Eric. 1969. *Inward Hunger: The Education of a Prime Minister*. London: Andre Deutsch.
Worcester, Kent. 1996. *C.L.R. James: A Political Biography*. New York: SUNY Press.

PART 2

LITERATURE AND PERFORMANCE

4.

DOMINICA AS SPIRITUAL LANDSCAPE
Representations of Nature in Jean Rhys's *Wide Sargasso Sea* and Marie-Elena John's *Unburnable*

ENA HARRIS

> It was there [in Morgan's Rest] that I began to feel I loved the land and to know that I would never forget it. . . . It was alive, I was sure of it. Behind the bright colours, the softness, the hills like clouds and the clouds like fantastic hills. There was something austere, sad, lost, [about] all those things. I wanted to identify myself with it, to lose myself in it. But it turned its head away, indifferent, and that broke my heart.
> Jean Rhys, *Smile Please*, 66

THESE WORDS COME FROM Jean Rhys's unfinished autobiography, *Smile Please*. The land she speaks of is Dominica, the place of her birth and childhood. According to Rhys, the first "clear connected memory" she has is grounded in nature – it is an image of her head crowned by a wreath of frangipani flowers on her sixth birthday. It is a good memory that conjures sweetness, loveliness, a sense of innocence and security. And yet the last sentence from the just quoted passage reveals that Rhys ultimately felt as though the Dominican landscape rejected her, shut her out – that she remained an outsider in that space.

Paradoxically, although Rhys's forming identity is inextricably tied to the land, she is physically severed from it when she and her family leave for England. *Wide Sargasso Sea*, in some ways, represents Rhys's return to Dominica and to her childhood. Through the narrative of Antoinette (and her husband Rochester), Rhys is able to articulate the power and potency of the Dominican landscape and to illustrate how Europeans, white Creoles and blacks responded to and interacted with their natural surroundings. In particular, Rhys writes of the desire/need of both Antoinette and Rochester to "claim" nature, to discover Dominica's "secrets".

This chapter explores the ways in which both of these characters relate to outdoor spaces and the clime of Dominica within a constructed nineteenth-century literary context. It also examines how the Dominican landscape is woven into Marie-Elena John's novel *Unburnable*, paying close attention to how her protagonist, Lillian, is influenced by her interactions "Up There" on Monte Diablotin (the highest mountain peak in Dominica) and is drawn into a myth to which she is inextricably bound. The argument is made that both authors, through the narratives of their characters, personify Dominica and that the place "speaks" even in its silence. It keeps its secrets from strangers – from those not native who are unable to accept its difference – while offering echoes of the past to those with links to the natural space. Antoinette is never quite able to establish such a relationship and is eventually deprived of any opportunity to build a different kind of association with the land, while Lillian is drawn in by painful memories and is recognized as belonging to a specific spiritual and mythical history that is connected to the physical environment.

DOMINICA IN JEAN RHYS'S *Wide Sargasso Sea*

"I love it more than anywhere in the world. As if it were a person. More than a person": this is how Antoinette, the white Creole protagonist of *Wide Sargasso Sea* first tries to explain her attachment to Dominica to her new husband, Rochester, just arrived from England. But even as she expresses her affection for place – pointing out particular birds and flowers, showing him her favourite bathing pools, feeding him fresh water from a large green leaf – on some level, whether she is aware of it or not, Antoinette wishes to "claim" the natural surroundings as "hers": "The sky was dark blue through the dark green mango leaves, and I thought, 'This is *my* place and this is where I wish to stay.' Then I thought, 'What a beautiful tree, but it is too high up here for mangoes and it may never bear fruit,' and I thought of lying alone in my bed with the soft silk cotton mattress and fine sheets, listening" (Rhys [1966] 2001, 108; emphasis added). Antoinette identifies with the mango tree, there but apart and destined to remain barren. This observation serves as a strong foreshadowing of

Antoinette's fate. However, it is perhaps more important to notice the striking similarity between Antoinette's thoughts of her surroundings and those expressed by Rhys in her autobiography:

> The earth was like a magnet which pulled me and sometimes I came near it, this identification or annihilation that I longed for. Once, regardless of the ants, I lay down and kissed the earth and thought, "Mine, mine". I wanted to defend it from strangers. Why was I sure that in the end they would be defeated? They can't cut down the silent mountains or scoop up the eternal sea but they can do a lot. The trees and flowers they destroy will grow again and they will all be forgotten. (Rhys 1979, 66–67)

Both the character of Antoinette and young Rhys express a desire to "possess" ("my", "mine"); they also recognize the potency and persistence of the natural. Even as Rhys resents having been sent away as a child and just as Antoinette is also severed from Dominica by Rochester, both of them know that the landscape is resilient and cannot be destroyed.

There is one more relevant point to draw from this passage. The "they" to whom Rhys refers can be interpreted in a few ways, but in the nineteenth-century context of *Wide Sargasso Sea*, "they" most likely refers to Europeans and white Creoles. It is important to note the particular historical circumstances of Dominica as it relates to its colonizers and the role its physical presence played in the development of a certain air of mystery, adventure and intrigue that has been attached to the island. Patrick L. Baker provides a useful framework in his book, *Centering the Periphery: Chaos, Order, and the Ethnohistory of Dominica*:

> In the early seventeenth century, neither England nor France was anxious to colonize the severely mountainous, heavily-forested island of Dominica, which had little obvious agricultural potential . . . early settlement in Dominica was part of the strategies of the European countries to funnel resources toward themselves. But the competition . . . centred on the other island territories; the major effect on Dominica was to people it with refugee Amerindian people and provide an image of a somewhat mysterious, inhospitable place beyond the reaches of civilization. (Baker 1994, 43)

This impression of Dominica weaves itself into Rhys's text. As Rochester arrives at the docks and prepares to head toward the village of Massacre, a porter declares, "This a very wild place – not civilized. Why you come here?" Rochester soon agrees, adding the adjective of "menacing" to his description of the surroundings. He personifies Dominica and views "her" as excessively beautiful: "everything is too much, too much blue . . . the flowers are too red, the mountains too high, the hills too near" (Rhys [1966] 2001, 70). Initially, like Antoinette, Rochester articulates a need to possess not the beauty itself but what he senses behind it, some treasure he feels entitled to: "It was a wonderful place – wild, untouched, above all untouched, with an alien, disturbing secret loveliness. And it kept its secret. I'd find myself thinking, 'What I see is nothing – I want what it hides – that is not nothing'" (87). Although Antoinette shares this desire to understand fully and "have" this secret aspect of this Caribbean space, while growing up she observes that the black Dominican (and indigenous) population seems better able to connect to and interact with the land. Baker provides some perspective on why these links might have been stronger among the historically oppressed peoples of Dominica: "Land had a very different value for [ex-slaves] than it had for their former masters: they thought of it as an expression of freedom and identity rather than as an economic resource to exploit to exhaustion" (Baker 1994, 109). Again it is the concept of *possession* that prevents both Antoinette and Rochester from learning and sharing in all of the secrets. However, as Judith Moore suggests, "Antoinette learned not only to look without touching but without coveting or expecting, a stance that strikes . . . Rochester as simple-minded at best, at worst insane" (Moore 1987).

Rochester allows his lack of absolute control or knowledge as well as his feeling of "outsiderness" to feed his antagonism and fear of Dominica and its peoples. For him, nature becomes the enemy that surrounds him, particularly at night. He admits his angst to his wife: "the feeling of something unknown and hostile was very strong here. . . . I feel that this place is my enemy and on your side" (Rhys [1966] 2001, 129–30). Rochester's main fear is of difference, a difference that he also associates (negatively) with the black people he encounters in a place he refers to as his rival.

If the Dominican landscape is indeed a person, or perhaps the spirit of a person or peoples, let us briefly examine the nature of that being or beings. According to the name given to the island by its indigenous inhabitants – Wai'tikubuli, "tall is her body" – the presence is female and has been a witness to the atrocities inflicted by Europeans not only upon her "body" but also the bodies and minds of enslaved peoples. Antoinette knows this and understands that she is of the colonizers, the oppressors; consequently, she does not believe nature can be "on her side" as Rochester suggests. She tries to explain that the land does not favour her and that it can never be possessed by either of them: "It is not for you and not for me. It has nothing to do with either of us. That is why you are afraid of it because it is something else" (Rhys [1966] 2001, 130). I would add that it is not only because nature is "something else" that elicits fear but also that nature is undeniable. Rochester does eventually come to realize this as he declares before fleeing the island: "the dark forest always wins" (167).

Ultimately, a defeated Rochester, unable to puncture Dominica's "hidden place", makes the decision to sever Antoinette from one of her few comforts (aside from servant Christophine), the relationship with place that offered her some degree of joy and solace, by bringing her back to England with him. For Rochester, the Dominican landscape and Antoinette both represent an inferior yet overwhelming and dangerous kind of difference: "I hated the mountains and the hills, the rivers and the rain. I hated the sunsets of whatever colour, I hated its beauty and its magic and the secret I would never know. I hated its indifference and the cruelty which was part of its loveliness. Above all, I hated her. For she belonged to the magic and the loveliness" (Rhys [1966] 2001, 172). Yet, even as Rochester facilitates Antoinette's supposed descent into "madness", he is left empty and envious, knowing that at least part of the secret remains with her; the dark forest has indeed won.

Dominica in Marie-Elena John's *Unburnable*

> [Dominica was] an island so inaccessible and impenetrable that Columbus had bypassed it, describing it to Isabella and Ferdinand back in Spain, it is said, by throwing a crumpled sheet of paper at their feet.
> John, *Unburnable*, 3

Even before page 1 of Marie-Elena John's novel *Unburnable*, there appears a map of Dominica; the island is a central subject that is woven into both the "then" and the "now" of what Jane Bryce refers to as "a love story, a romantic thriller, and a historical romance" (Bryce 2006). John seems not only concerned with telling the story of her protagonist, Lillian Baptiste, and two earlier generations of women; she also illustrates the influence of Dominica as a site of remembrance and resistance, replete with historical resonance. John's novel takes on the challenge of telling the story of three generations of women. Her protagonist, Lillian, grows up hearing myths and rumours about her mother and grandmother that cause her psychological trauma. The accusation is that her grandmother, Matilda, who lived in a secluded mountainous area referred to as "Up There" and "Noah", was a murderer who confessed to her crime. Having been sent away as a girl to be raised in the United States, Lillian gradually develops an intense need to return to the physical place where both women lived in order to put the pieces of her family history together and prove Matilda's innocence. John moves her readers back and forth in time to tell each woman's fragmented story. Her audience joins Lillian in her quest for understanding and clarity.

In the "now" sections of the novel which take place primarily in the United States, John breaks apart stereotypes and exposes a general ignorance that exists about Dominica. At the same time, she acknowledges the presence and influence of the island's immigrants. In the "then" chapters of the book, stories of young Lillian, her mother (Lily), Matilda and other relations are gradually told.

In his seminal piece "The Antilles: Fragments of Epic Memory", Derek Walcott states, "What is hidden cannot be loved. The traveller cannot love, since love is stasis and travel is motion. If he returns to what he loved in a landscape and stays there, he is no longer a traveller but in stasis and concentration, the lover of that particular part of earth, a native" (Walcott 1999, 77). I argue that Lillian becomes a native of Dominica at the novel's end when she chooses to merge with the myths surrounding the women of her family. I believe that the Dominican landscape, to some degree, influences and helps to shape her fate.

Let us first examine Lillian's feelings when she sets foot upon Dominican soil for the first time in twenty years: "The initial immobilizing lurch of terror she felt as she stopped at the door of the small aircraft had retreated . . . she felt like something had fallen away, her physical being was now synchronized with her physical surroundings" (John 2006, 208). Teddy, her lover, who agrees to join her on the trip, has an initial response as a visitor that provides a stark contrast; it somewhat mirrors Rochester's impressions of Dominica. Teddy is uncomfortable in the dark and feels intimidated and overpowered by what he perceives as a looming Morne Diablotin. In an attempt to mask his uneasiness, he asks the housekeeper at their rented cottage, "What wickedness did this mountain do . . . to get named after the devil?" (ibid.). He is then schooled by this woman who explains that the mountain's name is actually that of a nocturnal seabird that used to nest on its high cliff: "it was said . . . that they were now extinct, and some white people from overseas had come looking for signs of them and had gone away not finding any". But they were around, she told Teddy, not many, but "they flew along the coast near the cliffs at night" (John 2006, 209). Again, Dominica's secrets are hidden from visitors, from all non-natives – well, almost all. The housekeeper does choose to share the secret with Teddy.

As Lillian and Teddy head "Up There", taking on Matilda's mountain, Teddy is unprepared for the hike and stops in his tracks when he sees what lies ahead: "They were in the middle of a genuine virgin rain forest, with all the shadowy mystique that came with the dark and the damp, with leaves the size of a child's body, pointed tips dripping beads of water, with its wide-open understory allowing them to ascend the mountain freely, unencumbered" (p. 244). As the two seem to be getting closer to the apex of the mountain, Teddy observes, "The rainforest was morphing into cloud forest" (p. 245). This brings us back to Rhys's own observation, "hills like clouds and clouds like fantastic hills". Initially, Lillian seems to do what Rhys had wanted so much to experience – to "lose herself" in the land. Lillian is able to hear the call of voices; in a manner of speaking, the Dominican landscape communicates with her and pulls her back into an important memory that had been repressed for a long time. Unlike with Rhys and Antoinette, Dominica's nature does not "turn its head away, indifferent" (Rhys [1966] 2001, 66). Yet even as Lillian comes closer to a deeper understanding of self, she teeters between life and death, dangerously balancing herself along the cliff's edge. She does the same, even when within the relative safety of her rented cottage; she is constantly leaning too far over the railing of its balcony.

CONCLUSION

Like Antoinette, Lillian is a character whose past haunts her and leads others to believe that she is perhaps destined for madness. Instead of continuing to work toward clearing her family name of the accusations made against her grandmother, Lillian chooses to submerge herself into the false myth that she first heard as a taunting song when she was a girl. She both counters and confirms the myth by deciding to jump off of the mountain as her Maroon ancestors had done to avoid capture. In so doing, Lillian feeds the story, yet she chooses the form she will take as she merges with myth. She creates the lyrics for a new song:

> a *soucouyant*: a woman who takes off her skin at night and flies around in search of victims . . . and it made sense to go back to where the Maroons had jumped; she would fly through the air for her country people – and at the bottom there were enough trees and branches to tear off her skin, so that when they found her she would be exactly what they wanted her to be: their nightmare come true: *a soucouyant*. It would be perfect for her song. (John 2006, 292)

Both Antoinette and Lillian descend into unlikely spaces of freedom via unusual means. They take control of their lives by ending them, one through fire and one through the mountain air. Returning to Walcott's words regarding a lover of the land as one who returns and remains rooted and committed to a place, it is clear that both of these characters become natives as they complete their journeys home and settle within Dominica's spiritual landscape.

References

Baker, Patrick. 1994. *Centering the Periphery: Chaos, Order, and the Ethnohistory of Dominica*. Kingston, ON: McGill-Queen's University Press.
Bryce, Jane. 2006. Review of *Unforgettable Fire*, by Jean Rhys. *Caribbean Review of Books*, August.
John, Marie-Elena. 2006. *Unburnable*. New York: Harper Collins.
Moore, Judith. 1987. "Sanity and Strength in Jean Rhys' West Indian Heroines". *Rocky Mountain Review of Language and Literature* 41 (1–2): 21–31.
Rhys, Jean. 1979. *Smile Please: An Unfinished Autobiography*. Berkeley: Creative Arts Book Company.
———. (1966) 2001. *Wide Sargasso Sea*. Penguin Classics New Edition: London.
Walcott, Derek. 1999. *What the Twilight Says: Essays*. New York: Farrar, Strauss and Giroux.

5.

INDEPENDENCE OR NATIONALISM?
A Fresh Look at Andreu Iglesias's *Los derrotados*

VICTOR C. SIMPSON

IN AN ANALYSIS OF *Los derrotados*, the first novel written by Puerto Rican author César Andreu Iglesias, María del R. Marín makes the following assertion:

> En la novela *Los derrotados*, César Andreu Iglesias nos ofrece, en forma artística, su mensaje de que el coloniaje será liquidado sólo cuando la clase obrera como tal se encare al problema. La conquista de la independencia nacional será el producto de la activación de las grandes masas, obra de todo el pueblo, no de minorías selectas, de gestiones diplomáticas ni violencias individuales.... La independencia dejará de ser un ideal abstracto cuando logre movilizar masivamente a la clase trabajadora. (Marín 1987, 32–33)
>
> [In *Los derrotados*, César Andreu Iglesias artistically presents his message that colonialism will end only when the working class confronts the problem. National independence will be won through the involvement of the masses; it will be the work of the people, not of select minorities, nor diplomatic manoeuvrings nor violent individual action.... Independence will cease to be an abstract ideal when the working class is mobilized in a significant way.]

Marín clearly believes that the essential message of the novel is one that reflects the thinking of the author, namely that the Puerto Rican nationalist movement is doomed to failure as long as an elitist, exclusionist ideology which does not integrate the working class into the struggle for independence continues to prevail. But this limited interpretation of the text is open to question. The conclusion seems to be based primarily on extratextual interpretation since it is difficult from the text to establish the primacy of this theme. Nilita Vientós Gastón is right when she questions the effectiveness of the author's effort to establish a link between the nationalist and workers' movements. As she puts it, "Los episodios sobre la huelga sobran y restan unidad a la obra" (Vientós Gastón 1962, 289; ["The episodes on the strike are superfluous and undermine the unity of the work"]).

Hence, whatever may have been the political conviction of the author, whatever may have been his intention in writing the novel, this chapter argues that the novel may be interpreted as not only heralding the death of the nationalist movement but also suggesting the futility of any serious movement for independence. While in the novel the nationalists are presented as failing and in other ways their shortcomings are highlighted, the text offers glimpses of another reality, one which may be seen as anticipating present-day reality in which there is very little interest in and no serious effort to obtain political independence. It is on the glimpses of this "new reality" that this chapter will concentrate.

Nation and Nationalism in Puerto Rico

The focus on the Puerto Rican nationalist movement in the novel invites a brief consideration of the concept of nation and nationalism. A good place to start seems to be Peter Alter's definition which sees nation as a social group "which, because of a variety of historically evolved relations of a linguistic, cultural, religious or political nature, has become conscious of its coherence, unity and particular interests. It demands the right to political self-determination, or has already achieved such through a nation state" (Alter 1989, 17). The definition offered by sociologist and historian Eugen Lemberg seems to reinforce this broad concept, except that the element of "political self-determination" is not included. For him nationalism represents a "system of ideas, values and norms, an image of the world and society" which makes a "large social group aware of where it belongs and invests this sense of belonging with a particular value.... It integrates the group and demarcates its environment" (8).

Common culture, language, history and geography (even when the latter does not parallel state boundaries) are usually considered to be important elements that integrate the nation. Additionally, Alter refers to "the nationalism of peoples which possess a state, and the nationalism of those who do not"

(Alter 1989, 8). There is also the distinction between the political nation and the cultural nation, the former rooted in the concept of sovereignty and the latter not needing to be "mediated by a national state or other political form" (14) but instead "based on the assertion of the moral and spiritual autonomy of each people" (Duany 2002, 5). These concepts have particular relevance to Puerto Rico, which, while it is not sovereign, sees itself as a nation and places great emphasis on the concept of cultural nationalism.

Puerto Rican Nationalism in Andreu's *Los derrotados*

Puerto Rico became a possession of the United States in 1898 and has been a colony (officially and unofficially) ever since. It is clear today that Puerto Ricans do not seek independence from the United States, and indeed there has never been a mass movement in that direction. However, the idea has always had some degree of support, and, especially between the 1930s and the 1950s, the local pro-independence, anti-American Nationalist Party (whence comes the repeated references to Nationalists in Andreu's novel and in this chapter) waged a violent campaign for national sovereignty, which brought swift and firm retaliation from the state. In any case, the issue of political status has remained a major point of discussion, even in the absence of significant or consistent effort to resolve it. Against this background the novel focuses on the attempt of a group of Nationalists to assassinate an American general in Puerto Rico and set fire to an American military installation. The main character in the novel is Marcos, who is an integral part of the assasination plot. It is his job to pull the trigger. When the attempt fails, Marcos finds himself in prison in the company of Paco Ramos, a union leader who engages him in a discussion in which he raises fundamental questions regarding the Nationalists' approach to the independence struggle in Puerto Rico.

Andreu was not an author who sought to, or even could, separate his political convictions from his literary endeavours. Indeed, in the era when he wrote, Puerto Rican authors, including and perhaps especially intellectuals with political convictions, typically used their literary skills to express support for and to advance their ideological agenda. On this basis, perhaps validly, this text is seen by many as reflecting the thinking of the author. Andreu had wide involvement in the politics of Puerto Rico for nearly fifty years. He was an active member of a number of political organizations and indeed a founder member of, and standard bearer for, some of these. He also found it necessary to change his political perspective, devoting as much energy to advancing his new convictions as he had done for the old. He was a socialist and also a nationalist in the sense that he supported the principle of Puerto Rican independence. Evidently, he saw an indissoluble link between the two. He did not join the Nationalist Party in spite of his commitment to independence because of what he considered to be its bourgeois orientation that did not allow for an integral role for the working class in the struggle for political independence. He tended to reject what he saw as the mystical, abstract, utopian concept of the fatherland espoused by this party, and he saw it as one destined to fail. These attitudes on the part of the Nationalists are roundly criticized in the novel.

When Marcos, the protagonist, and Sandoval, a Nationalist sympathizer, and indeed other Nationalists in the novel, suggest that the people are not ready to embrace what the Nationalists are fighting for, are they thinking only of an armed struggle? Or might his concern express an unintended prophecy about the status quo today? The idea projected is that Puerto Ricans generally are not very interested in the political issues of sovereignty and independence but rather in the problems they experience in everyday life which they do not directly associate with their political status. The struggle, as far as the people are concerned, is not one for independence, but for a better quality of life, economically and socially. And the historical record will show that no form of political nationalist effort (nationalist electoral politics, political struggle for independence, the politics of violence) has ever won the backing of even a sizeable minority of the population. Indeed, regarding the pre-1940 period, Henry Wells claims that the "political controversies were never very meaningful to the great mass of voters. Inasmuch as these ordinary citizens, the rural and urban poor, did not associate their poverty with the political *status quo* and did not regard themselves as victims of colonial exploitation, they could not get excited about the status issue" (Wells 1955, 27).

In understanding the picture of the Nationalist movement as painted by Andreu, Marcos's experience is incisive. He is driven by an ideal, but, on a practical level, he does not evince much confidence in the project he seeks to advance. There is a clear conflict, but the commitment to the ideal is such that, in spite of his doubts, he participates in an action that he believes will either fail or not have any significant effect. Throughout the novel, the author is at pains to portray the protagonist's ambivalence, his commitment to the cause, his conviction of the *rightness* of the path he is taking, and, at the same time, his repeated questioning of the *value* of what he is doing. In his view, the interest and commitment of the people are lacking. But, even so, he thinks that, maybe, the simple fact that he is doing something, that he is doing his part, is what matters most. This virtual acknowledgement of defeat, as well as the pragmatic reactions of other former and current Nationalist sympathizers as they are presented in the novel, points in the direction of the present political reality in Puerto Rico, a reality that is the result of a way of thinking that considers efforts to secure political nationhood as not only futile but even undesirable.

The attitude of Bienvenido, Marcos's older colleague, reinforces the author's negative portrayal of the Nationalists and the seeming inevitability of failure. The character's words are repeatedly simplistic, overly optimistic and platitudinous and betray much wishful thinking, somewhat removed from reality, including the reality perceived by Marcos, whose thinking the author effectively juxtaposes as he questions the basis for his comrade's optimism:

> ¿Te das cuenta de lo bien que andan las cosas?
>
> Marcos siguió con atención las palabras de Bienvenido y asentía con la cabeza. Pero dentro de sí, se decía: ¿Qué hay de bueno en las cosas actuales? . . . ¿De dónde sacará Bienvenido su optimismo?
>
> La conversación volvió al plano de la cuestión inmediata. Pero, en verdad, los planes de Bienvenido no eran muy concretos. Sólo repetía: lo importante es que haya algo grande. El algo que hacer no lo tenía claro.
>
> Marcos . . . sintió un poco de ira contra ese incorregible optimismo. Y echó un balde de agua fría sobre la exaltación patriótica de Bienvenido. (Andreu 1973, 26–27)
>
> ["Do you realize how well things are moving along?"
>
> Marcos followed Bienvenido's words attentively and nodded in agreement. But within himself he was saying: "What's so good about things as they are? . . . Where does Bienvenido get his optimism from?"
>
> The conversation returned to the question at hand. But, in reality, Bienvenido's plans were not very concrete. He just kept saying over and over again: "the important thing is that something significant happens". But he was not clear about what to do.
>
> Marcos felt a certain anger at such incorrigible optimism. In vain he tried to throw cold water on Bienvenido's patriotic exultation.]

Bienvenido's optimistic outlook and pronouncements are also contradicted by the attitude of Chevarri, the mastermind of the assassination plot. He sees himself as a patriot, but he is also assailed by doubts about Puerto Ricans' readiness for independence. Indeed, he questions whether they really "deserve" it. He is willing, on the one hand, to devote his energies to the struggle for independence, but, at the same time, there is an attitude of scorn towards a people that he believes is not deserving of his sacrifice. This line of thinking seems to give some justification to the widely held view that Puerto Rican Nationalists were in some respects conservative in their thinking and that their fight for independence, if successful, would have maintained the social status quo, leaving subaltern groups – women, blacks and others – in their traditional second-class position. And Chevarri's thinking may, in this context, be seen as prophetic regarding the effectiveness which Nationalist efforts may have: "Quiza su pueblo estaba ya perdido para la libertad" (Andreu 1973, 188; ["Perhaps this people is already lost as far as freedom is concerned"]). Of course, "libertad" is interpreted here strictly in terms of political independence. But, some critics and others who acknowledge the author's Marxist orientation would argue that Chevarri's frustration with "the people" is simply an indication of the bourgeois orientation of the Nationalist campaign, which has failed to integrate the masses into the nationalist project. And indeed, some of Paco's theorizings regarding "la patria" would seem to confirm this preoccupation. But whether Paco can be seen as representing a socialist future for Puerto Rico remains an open question. It seems clear enough that he is interested in contributing to the creation of a better life for his class of people; except for the idea that the job of nation building is a matter that includes the contribution of the proletariat, there seems to be no special orientation on his part towards a socialist future for the island.

Another major characteristic of the Nationalist movement as portrayed in *Los derrotados* is the sense of moral superiority that characterizes its adherents. There is a strong sense of idealism, dedication, commitment and self-sacrifice and a willingness to risk all for a cause that, in their eyes, transcends mundane preoccupations such as financial security, personal safety and family connections. Marcos wonders about the worth of sacrificing the life of his young, inexperienced comrade for a cause that seems futile, even though he himself has long been willing to sacrifice his own life. In fact, one major aspect of the author's portrayal of a number of the Nationalist characters is their evident preparedness to die for the cause. They are presented as people who believe in the need for personal sacrifice. The movement, as presented by Andreu, seems to be possessed of a martyr complex, a desire to become heroes. This attitude seems to fit with the idea of nationalism being "interwoven with religious predicates" in which "the nation is consecrated, it is ultimately a holy entity. Service, even death, for the sake of the nation's cohesion, self-assertion and glory are elevated by national rhetoric to the level of sacrifice and martyrdom" (Alter 1989, 10). In a confrontation with his wife, Marcos's belief in this regard is revealed through the author's effective use of the device of interior monologue, in which the depth of the protagonist's beliefs is reinforced by the juxtaposition of the contrasting perspectives of him and his wife. Marcos feels compelled not to express his thoughts because he believes that his wife would not understand: "¿Cómo explicar todo eso a Sandra? ¿Lo entendería acaso? ¡Imposible! Gente tan razonable, tan lógica, tan práctica, está incapacitada para entender la razón de lo irrazonable, la lógica de lo ilógico, lo práctico de lo impráctico" (Andreu 1973, 69; ["How can I explain that to Sandra? Would she understand? Impossible! People who are so rational, so logical and so practical are incapable of understanding the rationality of the irrational, the logic of the illogical, the practicality of the impractical."]). As he expresses it, he believes in ideals, in the principles of honour, dignity, nationalism. Without intending to be uncaring, he remains convinced that family considerations should not supersede his commitment to the concerns he considers to be loftier. Only a coward (and a cowardly nation such as Puerto Rico) would do less.

Marcos's perspective is that those who are unsympathetic to the Nationalist cause are cowards, in contrast to the brave, honourable Nationalists. This attitude reflects an acceptance of the theory of Puerto Rican docility popularized by the writer René Marqués, suggesting a weakness, ambivalence and lack of "manliness" – indeed a form of sickness – that Nationalists and their intellectual allies blame for the island's failure to pursue political independence. To Marcos, also, those who pursue mundane goals – however necessary – are sacrificing their dignity on the altar of materialism and temporary gratification. The oft-repeated contrast made between American materialism and Puerto Rico's supposed spirituality is brought into focus on more than one occasion. The culture, influenced by what is considered American, is immoral and the economy oriented to consumerism. In response to the comment that progress is evident throughout Puerto Rico, one Nationalist operative responds, suggesting that what is really taking place is a process of moral decline (Andreu 1973, 82, 86). In all this, the author seems to spare no effort to underline the weaknesses in the Nationalists' arguments.

The conclusion that one may draw from Andreu's portrayal of the Nationalists is that they are idealistic, out of touch with reality and tend to place excessive emphasis on symbolic action. They evince an attitude towards the masses that borders on elitism, and they possess a sense of righteous superiority over others. They have no plan to win the support of the population and whereas one operative believes that the people are not ready for the struggle, another expresses confidence that they are in fact yearning for its success. Andreu paints a picture of a movement whose action and attitudes are clearly not the stuff of which revolutions are made, and it seems that the strong affective element in their philosophy undermines their understanding of some of the harsh "battlefield" realities associated with their struggle. Indeed, one may wonder whether their sense of moral superiority may be a subconscious effort to buttress a cause whose success they do not fully believe in. In any case, as they are presented by Andreu, the inevitability of failure seems patent. And that failure historically anticipates, and indeed is integral to, the present political reality in Puerto Rico.

Reference has often been made to the ending of the novel, which gives a picture of Marcos incarcerated, with little hope of release, looking up to the skies filled with stars. Some commentators take this as a sign of hope, presumably for the Nationalists' struggle, or perhaps for the struggle for independence, whatever form this might take. In relation to this ending, Arcadio Díaz Quiñones says that "as they confront the new personal and collective challenges, the author seems to say colonial subjects have reserves of knowledge and experience that might carry them through. . . . A sense of defeat, but also 'a bias for hope' . . . could be the dialectical center that endows the novel with a certain ambiguity" (Díaz Quiñones 2002, 2). Certainly, in the fifties and even in the nineties, some intellectuals of Andreu Iglesias's era were still confident that independence would come sooner or later. Some may argue that it seems less likely to happen now than it did when the novel was written, not only because Puerto Rico still serves US purposes in economically and militarily strategic ways, but also, as several plebiscites since 1967 have shown, because Puerto Ricans are not interested in political independence, even if "the processes that allowed a relative improvement in the quality of life for most island residents during the past decades are at their limits" (Negrón-Muntaner and Grosfoguel 1997, 4). If there is one thing that points back to the futility of the Nationalist struggle in which Marcos is portrayed as a standard bearer, it is the reality today that Puerto Ricans overwhelmingly prefer some form of political relationship with the United States which they see as beneficial, rather than to "stand on their own" politically.

Marín argues that the failure of the Nationalist operation and the death of the young idealistic revolutionary Camuñas, as described in the novel, symbolize the end of the Nationalist dream and suggests that, on the contrary, the more realistic approach of the workers' movement is in the ascendancy. The reality, though, is that this failure, as well as the nature of the struggle itself and the attitude of the participants as presented by Andreu, can be seen even more broadly as indicative of the hopeless state of the whole movement of political nationalism, including the Marxist version. Indeed, the resistance of the workers as depicted briefly in this text is not necessarily reflective of a patriotic socialist struggle as much as a struggle for basic human rights which do not depend for their validity on the fulfilment of a nationalist agenda. Indeed, the text seems to confirm the fact that working-class leadership during this period of American control was concerned with winning for workers some of the rights and benefits that their mainland counterparts enjoyed. Paco Ramos, the workers' representative, does not evince any Marxist orientation and does not seem to see the workers' strike in terms of the class struggle that is so fundamental to Marxist thinking. And the tension and conflict that continually accost Marcos not only raise questions regarding the validity of the Nationalist struggle but may also point to the possibility or desirability of an alternative approach that does not see political independence – and less so through an armed struggle – as essential to the development of Puerto Rico.

Over against the Nationalist activity, the conflicts and doubts that beset some of its adherents and the unbridled optimism that characterizes others, one is able to observe glimpses of a reality that has now completely eclipsed both the Nationalist violent struggle for independence and the socialist non-violent pursuance of the same goal. There is no definitive expression of this perspective as an alternative to the radical nationalism of the main character. The reader is made aware of it by means of intermittent references by different characters with conflicting perspectives on the matter. One character, who is clearly representative of a certain kind of creature spawned by the individual economic opportunities created by the programme of industrialization and development, is evidently supportive of this alternative. The references by don Reimundo, Marcos's father-in-law, to Muñoz Marín are significant in this regard. And perhaps there is none more significant than when he says: "Hay líderes que en su juventud fueron nacionalistas. El mismo Muñoz Marín estuvo por la independencia. El lo ha dicho: ¡errores de juventud!" (Andreu 1973, 61; ["There are leaders who were nationalists in their youth. Muñoz Marín himself was in favour of independence. He said it himself: 'The mistakes of youth!'"]). Reimundo is a typical product of the colonial situation, one that at the historical juncture at which the novel was written was seen to be in the ascendancy and may more validly represent a counterfoil to Marcos than Paco does. A number of authors who were contemporaries of Andreu (René Marqués, Emilio Díaz Valcárcel, Pedro Juan Soto) portray this type of character to represent the trend, as they see it, towards the abandonment of traditional Puerto Rican values in exchange for foreign values that tend to include the undervaluing of what is Puerto Rican in favour of what is American. The reference to Muñoz also seems to reflect a reality already existing at the time the novel was written with respect to the course the island was taking on the issue of nationalism and independence, a course that would seem to have been confirmed by subsequent developments.

Muñoz was the governor who, after having been a forceful proponent of independence (to the extent that he was expelled from the Liberal Party because of his failure to relent on the issue) abandoned the idea of pursuing independence for Puerto Rico. Different interpretations have been given to this political about-face. Some see it as the result of political pressure from the United States – a concession that he was forced to make "para posibilitar el trato privilegiado que Puerto Rico requería para ser transformado en un 'showcase' norteamericano en la Guerra Fría" (Grosfoguel 1997, 71; ["in order to facilitate the special treatment that had to be granted to Puerto Rico in order to transform it into the American 'showcase' during the Cold War"]). Other more favourable explanations suggest that Muñoz had come to realize that the general population was not concerned about the status question but rather about the depressing economic and social conditions in which they lived. According to Henry Wells, Muñoz

> discovered that they were not disturbed by Puerto Rico's then colonial relationship with the United States. He learned moreover that they were not in favor of independence because they were afraid of the consequences that might ensue – political instability and civic disorder of the Central American variety – if Puerto Rico were to become a sovereign republic. He also learned first-hand the depths of their economic distress and the need they felt for governmental action to better their lot. (Wells 1955, 28)

Whatever may have been the influential factors, it seems evident that he came to the conclusion that at the time political independence was not in the best interests of the country. His view, presumably, was akin to that expressed in the novel by don Reimundo, who represents one of his supporters and admirers. After suggesting that Puerto Ricans would starve without the help of the United States, Reimundo angrily says to Marcos: "¿Es que no te acabas a convencer de que sin los Estados Unidos, Puerto Rico no valdría nada? Mira a esos otros países . . . Santo Domingo, por ejemplo. Allí meten preso a cualquiera por cualquier cosa. ¡No hay libertad!" (Andreu 1973, 60; ["Haven't you been convinced yet that without the United States, Puerto Rico would be worth nothing? Look at those other countries . . . Santo Domingo, for example. They put you in prison for any reason there. There is no freedom!"]). The exaggeration of political instability and economic deprivation implied in the reference to Santo Domingo has special significance in relation to Puerto Rico in that, while one senses a purely self-serving and materialistic motive in Reimundo's comments, there is a line of current thinking which, though somewhat more refined and cast in the context of a globalized world in which neoliberalism and economic neocolonialism are the norm, argues similarly against political nationalism.

As if to compensate for the abandonment of the ideal of political nationalism, Muñoz began to privilege the concept of cultural nationalism which was to become an essential plank in the construction of the new Puerto Rico. According to John Hutchinson, cultural nationalists see the essence of a nation as "its distinctive civilization, which is the product of its unique history, culture and geographical profile" (Hutchinson and Smith 1994, 122). Their aim is to highlight "their distinctive national civilization . . . celebrate cultural uniqueness and reject foreign practices, in order to identify the community to itself, embed this identity in everyday life and differentiate it against other communities" (124). According to Jorge Duany (2002, 123), "In 1955 the establishment of the Institute of Puerto Rican Culture consolidated the project of defining, promoting, and defending national identity. Scholars, writers, and artists were recruited to codify the values, symbols, rituals, and practices that would represent the Puerto Rican nation to itself and to the world." Perhaps, most significant in all this is Duany's observation that whereas cultural nationalism tends to be a "small-scale movement", in Puerto Rico, it "has acquired a massive following" (ibid.). This may be explained, perhaps, by the suggestion that, in the absence of political sovereignty, Puerto Ricans need something that would help them to be able to identify themselves as a nation. Muñoz also saw it as a political movement which would serve as well to pacify, maybe neutralize, Nationalist opponents, and perhaps it may be seen also as a way of "fronting up" to the United States and resisting the pressure towards cultural assimilation in the only way that was perhaps left to the island (without political, economic or military power of its own).

Such a rationale would seem to justify the view which John Hutchinson attributes to Hans Kohn and others that "cultural nationalism is a regressive force, a product of intellectuals from backward societies, who, when confronted by more scientifically advanced cultures, compensate for feelings of inferiority by retreating into history" (Hutchinson and Smith 1994, 127). It may be explained also by the fact that local political leaders (who traditionally tend to be the catalysts in struggles for political liberation) have been able to convince their followers that the benefits derived from association with the United States outweigh the concomitant disadvantages and also that they cannot be matched by those promised by a sovereign Puerto Rican state. As a result, it seems evident that in Puerto Rico cultural nationalism has replaced political nationalism as the means of expressing Puerto Ricans' uniqueness as a "nation". Most Puerto Ricans are clearly not interested in establishing a nation state, while maintaining that they are indeed a "nation". The obvious preference is for maintaining some form of political relationship with the United States, which automatically eliminates the independence option. It seems, therefore, that the reference to Muñoz Marín is a very significant hint that can be taken from the novel that the idea of political independence has no more force and that the future of Puerto Rico may now lie in what Muñoz represents, which is not nationalism in the traditional sense (indeed, not even oriented toward political sovereignty) but rather a "new colonialism" – an arrangement with the colonial power which would permit the free expression of the Puerto Rican "national culture". And if, as Duany suggests, "cultural nationalism may be a more useful ideology than political nationalism where a large portion of the population has become transnational" (2002, 284), then the concept seems particularly applicable to Puerto Rico.

Arlene Dávila laments the "second-class" status accorded to cultural nationalism, especially in a climate in which recent studies have been giving more prominent attention to cultural and related elements in the construction of the concept of nation, quite independent of the traditional political, and indeed geographical, requirements. She observes that "constant in the analysis of cultural nationalism is the recognition that the forging of a cultural identity from an ethnic past or from recent inventions is an effective basis for political mobilization among people seeking to establish themselves as national entities, irrespective of any objective state or territorial boundary" (Negrón-Muntaner and Grosfoguel 1997, 232). And, as she suggests, this is clearly applicable to Puerto Rico, "where cultural nationalism is elaborated by a variety of interests to emphasize the cultural aspects of Puerto Rico as a nation and a distinct community" (ibid.).

Another example which this novel provides and which serves to reinforce the suggestion being made is a conversation between Federico and Adalberto, two intellectuals whom Marcos meets in a bar. In the midst of their excessive drinking, they manage to maintain some degree of lucidity as they, from opposing perspectives, engage each other on the subject of the political winds of change that seemed to be blowing at the time. This conversation – at least one side of it – acknowledges the developing political realities. Both of these characters were, in the past, sympathetic to the cause of independence. Federico maintains this posture, or at least, as he puts it, he no longer believes in anything. He certainly does not embrace the political reality which accepts the colonial situation. The idea of some "arrangement" between Puerto Rico and the United States is ludicrous to him. In contrast, Adalberto believes that he has progressed with the times. As he says to Federico, "Aquellas ideas ingenuas tenían que crecer. Mis ideas han crecido, como ha crecido Puerto Rico. ¿Qué significa hoy el concepto de nación, por ejemplo? En el mundo actual, la nación no existe. Es un concepto obsoleto que se ha llevado el río de la historia" (Andreu 1973, 91; ["Those ingenuous ideas had to change. My ideas have grown, as Puerto Rico has grown. What is the meaning, today, of the concept of 'nation', for example? In today's world, the nation does not exist. It is an obsolete concept that has been washed away by the river of history"]). He is ready to embrace the change that is taking place. He is pragmatic, not committed to a worn-out ideal that seems impractical. Today, one finds that arguments such as this are not just the stuff of novels but of serious thinkers who believe that the ideal of political nationalism should not be seen as essential to the development of the Puerto Rican nation. Independence is seen as a sure way to pauperize the working class further in exchange for benefits for an elite minority. Adalberto's view in this regard may be summed up as follows: the best thing for us is some form of accommodation with the United States which will allow us real freedom, indeed more freedom than some so-called free nations enjoy, and at the same time, we maintain our Puerto Ricanness, or sense of being a nation with our language and other important elements of our culture. Another hint to be found in this novels is that, perhaps, not only the "old" Nationalist idea but indeed any idea of independence is dead or dying rapidly.

Towards the end of the novel, one finds another conversation, which is really not a conversation as much as it is a diatribe, launched by Federico this time, against what he and other characters in the novel see as the developing pro-American system and the concomitant decline in values. Though sympathetic to the Nationalist cause, Federico says that there are many reasons he does not support the action of Marcos and his associates. As he puts it, with a certain comical cynicism, "Esos atentados no resuelven nada. Imáginate que Carlos hubiera matado al general Kelly. ¡Pues viene el general Jelly a ocupar su puesto! ¿Y si matan a Jelly? ¡Pues, viene Helly! Nada, chico, que todo sigue igual" (Andreu 1973, 242; ["Those attacks solve nothing. Imagine Marcos had killed General Kelly. Then General Jelly would take his place and if they kill Jelly, then Helly would take his place. Everything continues the same"]). And he seems to conclude that failure is inevitable, as he continues: "No puede triunfar porque la época no le ayuda. Precisamente por eso, en su desesperación, recurre a esa clase de acciones, como quien pretende vencer un gigante con una pedrada" (Andreu 1973, 244–45; ["Marcos cannot succeed because the times do not help him. Precisely for that reason, in his desperation he has recourse to that kind of action, like a man trying to conquer a giant with a stone"]). These are the words of a Nationalist sympathizer, saying that nationalism in the extreme sense is dead. If the author presents such a person espousing this pessimistic perspective, might the reader not by extrapolation assume that most Puerto Ricans (who do not support the Nationalist cause) would not be thinking in terms of political sovereignty as an ideal to be pursued?

It is of interest to note also that even among the Nationalists, committed as they are to a violent struggle to attain independence, which is often synonymously referred to as nationhood, there is some sense that Puerto Rico is already a nation. They do seem to have a broader sense of what "nationalism" means. Don Antonio, a tried and tested Nationalist, proffers the following opinion: "Yo creo que existe un pensamiento puertorriqueño. Existe, porque existe la nación puertorriqueña" (Andreu 1973, 171; ["I believe there exists a Puerto Rican way of thinking. It exists because there exists a Puerto Rican nation"]).

And he continues, affirming that both the Nationalist leader Pedro Albizu Campos, committed to political independence by whatever means necessary, *and* the current national leader (at the time of the writing of the novel) who has no commitment to independence, have contributed to the development of Puerto Rican thought, which, as suggested earlier, cannot be separated from the idea of a Puerto Rican nation.

This conversation continues with one character saying that nothing that "denaturalizes" Puerto Ricans would last, only that which affirms and enhances what is Puerto Rican, and in her view those things are "Puerto Rican Values". This can be read as an affirmation of the importance of culture apart from the need for political independence. What is of special interest here is that, at all levels of a society where political sovereignty and independence (and more so a violent struggle to achieve them) have no appeal, an essential aspect of the focus, the alternative focus, is on Puerto Rican values and the need to maintain and affirm them. This is cultural nationalism and, clearly, it is integral to the thinking of the Nationalists, though not to the exclusion of political nationalism. There is in this a concept of being a nation, of being an autonomous people, an awareness of self that is totally unrelated to the idea of political status, even though the latter idea is a source of continued debate. This reality tends to underscore the validity of the contention that the new orientation which was taking root at the time of the writing of *Los derrotados*, and of which the reader is given glimpses in the novel, is now firmly entrenched in the psyche of Puerto Ricans and which makes it possible to see the novel from a contemporary perspective as heralding not only the death of the Nationalist project but also of any project whose goal is political independence.

Conclusion

Given the thinking outlined above, perhaps one can argue that the Nationalists (at least the thinkers among them) were not so different from the Muñoz Maríns and Puerto Ricans over the past fifty years who have been content with the more affective elements of nationhood. Maybe, buried within some aspects of Nationalist thinking are the same seeds that eventually germinate into the reality one sees today in Puerto Rico. And even though, obviously, Nationalists are not content to limit their claim of nationhood to this level, there is clearly a level at which the thinking of these two broadly opposing groups coincides.

While it may not be valid to argue that the novel somehow unequivocally supports the attitude of most Puerto Ricans today regarding national sovereignty, it does seem, if only in an indirect way, to anticipate that reality. Puerto Ricans today are strongly nationalistic, they believe that they have a certain degree of independence, yet they are seen by many as a colonized people. All this seems to suggest that, when all is said and done, the question of political status is not paramount. To my mind, this is a subtle message that one can glean from Andreu's novel.

Note

1. All translations are by the author.

References

Alter, Peter. 1989. *Nationalism*. Translated by Stuart McKinnon-Evans. London: Edward Arnold.

Andreu Iglesias, César. 1973. *Los derrotados*. Río Piedras, Puerto Rico: Ediciones Puerto.

Díaz Quiñones, Arcadio. 2002. *The Vanquished: A Novel*. Translated by Sidney Mintz. Chapel Hill: University of North Carolina Press.

Duany, Jorge. 2002. *The Puerto Rican Nation on the Move: Identities on the Island and in the United States*. Chapel Hill: University of North Carolina Press.

Grosfoguel, Ramón. 1997. "La recolonización neo-colonial". *El Nuevo Día*, 20 November, 71–72.

Hutchinson, John, and Anthony D. Smith, eds. 1994. *Nationalism*. Oxford: Oxford University Press.

Marín, María del R. 1987. "Militancia nacionalista y lucha obrera en *Los derrotados* de César Andreu Iglesias". *Prisma* 2 (2): 21–35.

Negrón-Muntaner, Frances, and Ramón Grosfoguel. 1997. *Puerto Rican Jam: Essays on Culture and Politics*. Minneapolis: University of Minnesota Press.

Vientós Gastón, Nilita. 1962. *Indice Cultural (Tomo 1) 1948–55 y 56*. Río Piedras, Puerto Rico: Ediciones de la UPR.

Wells, Henry. 1955. "Ideology and Leadership in Puerto Rican Politics". *American Political Science Review* 49 (1): 22–39.

6.

PERFORMATIVE BONDAGE
Caryl Phillips's *Dancing in the Dark*

AGNEL BARRON

IN THE NOVEL *Dancing in the Dark* (2005), Caryl Phillips portrays the lives of Bert Williams and George Walker, two African American performers who, in the early twentieth century, became the most successful performers of their race. Replete with verbal and structural irony, the novel focuses on their private lives and shows the very high price they paid for their "success". Told in three "acts", *Dancing in the Dark*, like many of Phillips's novels, is dialogic and polyphonic. Through a technique of free indirect discourse, the voices of all the major characters, and occasionally that of a minor character, are heard seemingly in a constant discourse with each other. Through their discourse the story is told and interwoven in it are excerpts from the performances of the characters as well as reviews and critiques of these performances that help to set the historical framework of the story.

Phillips's major theme in this novel is the marginalization of the black performer in nineteenth- and twentieth-century America. Of the two performers, Phillips's primary focus is on Bert Williams, whose narrative dominates the story. Through his portrayal of Bert's life, Phillips examines the role of the African American performer/artist. He uses the term *performative bondage* to refer to the way in which Williams and Walker, and the entertainers who succeeded them, are held captive by stereotypes and white expectation. He shows that historically, African American performers have been artistically constrained by being expected to "perform blackness" for the majority group. Phillips, however, looks at the extent to which these performers were complicit in their artistic enslavement and degradation by failing to challenge what bell hooks describes as "colonial imperialist paradigms of black identity which represent blackness one-dimensionally in ways that reinforce and sustain white supremacy" (quoted in Hall 2004, 111). Phillips captures this situation in his delineation of Bert's life and the way in which Bert's identity is severely undermined by his lack of professional freedom – a situation that ultimately destroys him.

Phillip's retelling of Bert's story from a socio-historical perspective locates him firmly within contemporary literary discourse as a writer who believes that literature cannot be divorced from history. By taking a historical event and presenting it in a fictional way, Phillips shows, in the words of M.H. Abrahms (1999, 183), "a reciprocal concern with the historicity of texts and the textuality of history". History is a text to be interpreted, and the text is a product of the historical conditions of an era. He shows the intertextuality of history and literature by including historical records in his fictive narrative of the lives of these real performers. He seems to be implying that, as Ian Maclean suggests, "there is no escape from the historical situatedness of understanding, because it is the ontological ground of our being-in-the-world" (1986, 126). In doing so, he subscribes to the subjectivist, historicist account of meaning which posits that "meaning is an historical event determined by the context in which it occurred and possibly also by the historical situation of its interpreter" (123). Hence, he often textualizes historical subjects from the perspective of contemporary society to highlight often ignored subtexts which inform the subject. This is what he does with Bert Williams in *Dancing in the Dark*. He reinterprets his life from the vantage point of a black artist in the twenty-first century to determine its meaning and relevance, and to highlight the way in which his minority status in American society affected his career.

For theorists such as Michel Foucault, discourse or any mechanism that allows meaning and value to be conveyed is a form of representation. I maintain that the "performance" of Bert is thus a discourse. By re-creating a discourse that examines Bert's performance, Phillips engages in a metadiscourse that seeks to interpret and contextualize Bert's life from the perspective of the present. Hence the text is an interrogation or critical analysis of the role of the black entertainer in American society. Specifically, Phillips demonstrates the tendency of the dominant discourse to reduce the black artist to a one-dimensional role determined solely by race and shows that, by accepting this crude essentialism and not seeking to resist it, some black entertainers have been complicit in its promulgation.

Bert is a Bahamian immigrant who journeys with his parents to the United States. Here we see a recurrent theme in Phillips's work, namely, the fate of the migrant who makes the journey from the fringes of empire to the centre, a concern that Benedicte Ledent terms Phillips's "post-migratory ethos" (Ledent 2002, 82). Bert's parents first go to Florida but fail to make a living there. His father then decides to go to California where the family settles and "begin[s] to learn how to become coloreds and niggers, foreigners and the most despised of home grown sons" (Phillips 2005, 25). Bert's father hopes that Bert, a good student, will opt to go to university, but Bert chooses to join a medicine show and pursue a career as a performer.

We are given some insight into Bert's childhood in his "wooing narrative" to Lottie, whom he subsequently marries. We are told that the "clowning and performing" which were a part of his life from school days is used to mask the vulnerability he feels at not fitting in and being teased by the other children. He continues to hide behind this mask of "buffoonery and desperate clowning" after he leaves school to become a performer (Phillips 2005, 25). He takes a brief hiatus from this life and attempts to pursue a normal occupation as a bellboy but fails when he realizes that this is yet another "performance" in which he is not afforded the luxury of speech and there is no laughter or applause to reward his performance. Society's complicity in his degradation is established, for his career choices are very limited and they all seem to involve his self-abasement. Bert returns to the medicine show and, after a series of misadventures, goes to San Francisco, where he meets George Walker on a street corner. They team up and perform together as "plantation darkies", "coons" and primitive "natives" of Africa (29). The derision meted out to them by white audiences takes a toll on them mentally and this, along with the fact that they barely manage to eke out a living, propels them eastward across the United States in search of greener pastures. They change roles along the way. George plays the "straight man" while Bert plays the shuffling, clumsy, dim-witted Negro, and they find that the audiences respond more favourably. Against the objections of his partner, Bert decides to wear black face make-up, reneging on an earlier decision they had taken never to do this. They tour the vaudeville circuit in New York, and their act is so successful that they make their way to Broadway, where their play *In Dahomey* becomes the first all-black play shown on Broadway. However, in spite of this success, Bert begins to fall apart, and it is clear to his wife that he has lost his way.

At the age of thirty, a world-weary and despondent Bert is heralded as a success as he achieves the height of fame, but his professional success is ultimately a form of personal failure, for he has achieved it by conforming to and perpetuating the demeaning stereotypes which the white audience holds of the black man. In the initial stages of his career, Bert attempts to rationalize this objectification by claiming that his subjectivity is not determined by his objectification but by his sense of who he is. As time goes by, he realizes that this is not so, for the undignified objectification which he suffers begins to undermine his very sense of self and identity.

In an extract from an interview, the real-life personage upon whom Phillips bases the character of George notes that white performers caricatured blacks by donning blackface and presenting a stereotype of blacks and "the one fatal result of this to the colored performers was that they imitated the white performers in their make-up as 'darkies'" (Phillips 2005, 119). Hence the absurdity of a black performer imitating a white performer "imitating a black man". George realizes that this mimicry was the undoing of the black performer, who, in appropriating this stereotype, is essentially appropriating and perpetuating his objectification.

George begs Bert to leave this character behind, insisting that he does not belong in the twentieth century, but when they try to stage a "different" play it fails, according to the critics, because it contains too little of this character. Bert's performance without blackface is met with public outcry and critical condemnation, and he feels compelled to return to wearing the mask. This scenario begs the question: Was presenting this character and then trying to take him away unsuccessful because he had been presented in the first place? This is perhaps the question that torments Bert, in that an affirmative answer implicates him in the condemnation of the "coloured performer". While he may not have been responsible for the professionally limiting situation in which he operated, he contributes to it and reinforces it. He is thus complicit in his own oppression and that of his people. He does not challenge the discourse but simply enters into it as "supplicant" (Phillips 2005, 15).

This lack of artistic autonomy erodes Williams's personality, his friendships, his marriage and his working relationship with his partner to the point where he becomes alienated from everyone. The root of his unhappiness stems from his dissatisfaction with the role he plays and his lack of fulfilment as a performer. He feels as though he has failed his family, and he is not at peace in his newly bought home for although he has achieved material success, he has lost his self-respect.

As their career continues, George worries that Bert's "unfortunate blackface performance and his disturbingly accommodating personality are becoming confused in his partner's mind" (Phillips 2005, 110). This occurs after their return to America from a tour of Britain when their promoter suggests that they play Columbus Circle, a less prestigious venue than Broadway. George is incensed at this and wants Bert to express his anger and stand up to the promoter, but Bert remains silent. They do not perform in Columbus Circle but instead go to court to break their contract.

In addition to the erosion of his personal identity, Bert realizes that he has done little to uplift his race. The implications of Bert's actions on the future of the black performer are probed when, after his company's tour of Britain, on the return voyage home, Bert asks himself a series of questions which sums up his predicament and personal torment: "Is the colored performer to be forever condemned to pleasing a white audience with farce? . . . Is the colored performer to be nothing more than an exuberant childish fool . . . who must be neither unique nor individual? . . . Can the colored man be himself in twentieth-century America?" (Phillips 2005, 100). Bert's responsibility to his race as a black performer comes into greater focus as his career winds down. His realization that he has not been an agent of social change but has accepted and partaken of the dominant ideology of a racist society – and in so doing has been complicit in the oppression of his race – weighs heavily on him.

There is a sense in which Bert constantly looks at himself through the eyes of others. His need to explain his choice to wear blackface and the apologetic way in which he speaks to Lottie of this shows that he is keenly aware of how others look at and judge his performance. Moreover, his deep sense of shame at performing in front of his father and black audiences indicates that he uses them to judge himself and, in so doing, externalizes his own internal turmoil. W.E.B. DuBois, the African American philosopher who examined the "lingering effects of slavery and the impact of continuing racism on the psyches and self-conceptions of African-Americans" (Hall 2004, 38), notes that blacks possess a "double-consciousness, this sense of always looking at one's self through the eyes of others, of measuring one's soul by the tape of a world that looks on in amused contempt and pity" (quoted in Hall 2004, 38). We see this "double-consciousness" reflected in Bert's view of himself and of his performance. It is also evident in the views of a group of affluent "coloured gentlemen" who visit Bert and "admonish" him for reinforcing the views that whites have of blacks, noting that "we exist in *their* imagination as you portray us and you reinforce their low judgment of us as dull and pitiable" (Phillips 2005, 178–79). They are concerned with the effects of his performance on the public perception of blacks, for they view him as undermining their attempts to escape the legacy of slavery by articulating an authentic subjectivity and creating an authentic identity which is inextricably bound up with the way in which blacks are perceived by the white majority. Bert responds defensively to their criticisms by asking the question, "Am I responsible for how the Negro is viewed in America?" (179), thus bringing the role and responsibility of the entertainer into question.

This scene interrogates the way in which cultural representation contributes to society's views of individuals, and, in a society as defined by race as American society, it questions the way in which black cultural representation contributes to white society's views of blacks. Moreover, while Bert's stereotypical performance reflects negatively on all blacks, his role is decidedly gendered to caricature black men. Hence, the novel scrutinizes the role of the black male entertainer. Although Bert's critics never openly respond to the question, their answer is clearly in the affirmative. They imply that even if he is not solely responsible for perpetuating society's myths and stereotypes of the black man, he is contributing to the problem. When he asks them whether he should abandon the stage, they reassure him that this is not what they want but that they want him to "perform in theaters that neither bar nor Jim Crow Negroes, and . . . in the guise of somebody whose persona and demeanor is closer to that of the new, twentieth century Negro, as opposed to a low type who is a deliberate travesty of our race" (Phillips 2005, 188). In this way, he can help "drag [his] troubled profession toward dignity" (180). They see it as part of his responsibility to shape the identity of the black man and are urging Bert to become involved in what Homi Bhaba refers to as "performative agency" (cited in Hall 2004, 115). However, Bert maintains that he is trying to humanize this character and give him some dignity. There is a sense in which Bert seems to identify with this character and is almost reluctant to discard him. Here we see the effect of the racist discourse on Bert's behaviour and selfhood. Bert internalizes the discourse of race and the position of the black man in that discourse as inferior and powerless to change his position, and this becomes "naturalized" (Hall 2004, 96).

The social construction of identity is explored. Bert fails to see that although identity is socially determined, individuals can enter into that social discourse and can help shape their identity. He fails to see that although power is circumscribed by "historically specific terms and limits", it can be appropriated: hence, he does not act as an agent in "aesthetic creation" (Hall 2004, 93, 5). His performance does not slyly interrogate the assumptions behind the stereotype; he simply perpetuates them (Hall 2004, 115). In this way, his choice to perform in a stereotypical manner can be viewed as socially irresponsible. This decision also suggests that Bert defines success by white standards. He does not consider himself successful playing to black audiences in black theatres. Only when he has made it to Broadway, the mainstream of American theatrical society, does he consider himself successful. However, the price he pays for this success is great.

Bert loses his self-respect, his health and, ultimately, his life in the pursuit of his trade. His life is presented as tragic. He is a man of intelligence and personal dignity. However, he never seeks the opportunity to practice his craft in a manner that would humanize him and his race. Instead, he allows himself to become trapped in a career of portraying the black man in a one-dimensional, degrading and personally humiliating way which conforms to the stereotype of the hapless black, a character who ironically exists only as a figment of the white imagination.

In the end, both men are destroyed by their careers. George becomes "tired of pleasing white folks" and notes that "a man can kill himself trying to please white folks" (Phillips 2005, 133). This appears to be the case, as he collapses during a performance soon after he makes this statement. He is diagnosed with syphilis and he dies a few months later. Bert also collapses on stage years later as a result of physical and mental exhaustion and dies shortly after. Before this incident, as he is in the waning days of his career, Bert looks back on his life and weeps when he realizes that he has "foolishly spilled his life".

Although today African American entertainment has moved from the periphery of American culture and now occupies the mainstream, the legacy of the historical racism faced by performers like Williams and Walker still affects the black entertainer. In an essay entitled "The Burden of Race", in his book *The New World Order*, Phillips comments upon this fact, noting that although African American entertainment has moved from the periphery of American culture and now occupies the mainstream, some contemporary black American artists deal with the ongoing legacy of historical racism by "embracing an 'aesthetic' defined by race". He argues that this "retreat to black essentialism" limits the humanity of those who subscribe to it (2002, 12–14). As opposed to promoting artistic freedom, such a position stifles it; as opposed to becoming progressive agents of change, the artist becomes a reactionary. Thus, the concern is that some contemporary African American performers, like their predecessors, are wittingly or unwittingly limiting their artistic and creative freedom.

References

Abrahms, M.H. 1999. *A Glossary of Literary Terms*. New York: Harcourt Brace.
Hall, Donald E. 2004. *Subjectivity*. New York: Routledge.
Ledent, Benedicte. 2002. *Caryl Phillips*. New York: Manchester University Press.
Maclean, Ian. 1986. "Reading and Interpretation". In *Modern Literary Theory*, edited by Ann Jefferson and David Robey, 122–44. Totowa, NJ: Barnes and Noble.
Phillips, Caryl. 2002. *A New World Order*. New York: Vintage.
———. 2005. *Dancing in the Dark*. New York: Vintage.

7.

FREEDOM OF THE SPIRIT AND AFRICAN CULTURAL RETENTIONS
The Case of East Port of Spain, Trinidad and Tobago

SANDRA GIFT and
OBA KENYATTA OMOWALE KITEME

THIS CHAPTER SITUATES EAST PORT OF SPAIN against a socio-cultural backdrop that offers an appreciation of the spiritual and sociolinguistic roots of artistic expressions in what is generally viewed as an economically depressed and crime-ridden urban area of Trinidad and Tobago. The authors view this urban environment through the lens of its cultural heritage as represented in the artistic achievements of some of its people. The community's cultural heritage has been significantly shaped by its history, and, in order to understand this history, the authors have drawn extensively on the work of Bridgette Brereton, Caribbean historian, and Maureen Warner-Lewis, Caribbean sociolinguist, among others. This essay has also been informed by discussions with Caribbean publisher Gerard Besson. The historical background described in the chapter serves as a basis for understanding the degree of African cultural retentions evident in the performing arts created within the community of east Port of Spain today.

The performing arts in east Port of Spain, Trinidad and Tobago, have been significantly influenced by African cultural retentions. Around 1870, groups of Africans and their descendants constituted the most significant group of settlers in north-east Port of Spain. East Port of Spain has been described as being at first "a haven for the emancipated African slaves, like the Ibos, Radas and Mandingos to practice their ancestral rituals. Then out of their chants and lamentations to the rhythms of tribal drumming came bongo, tamboo-bamboo, dame lorraine, kaiso, j'ouvert . . . and steelband" (Carr 1989, 6). According to

Newsday, 25 March 2007, east Port of Spain is referred to by other names such as East Dry River, Urban Slum, de Ghetto and Behind the Bridge.

In 1818, the majority of enslaved blacks in Trinidad were born in Africa. This was unlike the situation in the longer-established colonies. There were "13,980 natives of Africa and 11,629 Creoles. . . . Just over 60 per cent of the Creoles were Trinidad-born, while the rest had come from the other British colonies, or from the French and Spanish Caribbean" (Brereton [1981] 1989, 55). Enslaved Africans were brought to Trinidad from a very wide geographical area. The single largest group (39.4 per cent) was brought from the Bight of Biafra. There was significant intermarrying between enslaved Africans from different regions, resulting in the diminution of the individual identities of their distinct African ethnicities.

Hollis Liverpool (2001), Trinidad and Tobago calypsonian and author, comments that, diversity of languages and differences in their customs notwithstanding, enslaved Africans came from "a relatively small part of Africa that represented one cultural area with a high degree of similarity and unity" (Liverpool 2001, 16). Despite the tendency at the time to place a higher value on European values and customs over non-European, Africans retained their own customs and values. Later, freed Africans and groups that came to Trinidad through intra–West Indian migration also brought with them cultural influences that helped to shape the cultural landscape of east Port of Spain.

Like Europeans and Asians, enslaved Africans brought with them a memory bank – their cultural heritage that contributed to the shaping of their world view in the New World. There could be no pure form of any African cultural retention or tradition. Enslaved Africans and their descendants inevitably forged new societies in the New World, constituted in part from a variety of African backgrounds and in part from their experience of enslavement in the Americas. Thus was fashioned the African continuum, one shaped by the new environment, transformed and reflecting African cultural retentions evident in "African folklore, textiles, sculpture, architecture, music, language and religion" (Liverpool 2001, 20).

During the 1870s and early 1880s, vagrancy and lawlessness, caused by unemployment and overcrowding, were problems in Port of Spain. East Port of Spain and the city environs of East Dry River and Sea Lots today continue to be plagued with high levels of poverty and crime, fuelled by continued immigration to the area from other Caribbean islands, the gun and drug trades and general underdevelopment as a result of the failure of national development policies.

According to the 1996 report *The Determination and Measurement of Poverty in Trinidad and Tobago: Indications from the 1992 Survey of Living Conditions*, published by the Ministry of Social Development, 54 per cent of the country's poor households were located in East Dry River and Sea Lots, long known for their depressed conditions and overcrowding, while 12.7 per cent resided in the San Juan/Laventille area, part of east Port of Spain. The poor were identified as "those individuals falling under a poverty line fixed at TT$623 per capita" (Ministry of Social Development 1996, x).

Lasana Kwesi, writer, poet and chair of the San Juan/Laventille Regional Network, in an article titled "Place Set Apart", observes that East Dry River is targeted by politicians for votes, but politicians subsequently abandon the people to dire neglect and social isolation. According to an article in *Newsday*, they are "left to their own devices with the hardships of poverty, unemployment, unemployable non-skilled beings, illiterates and semi-illiterates, dependency-laced government labour programmes, female-headed households, absentee fathers, delinquent and crime-prone youths, drugs, rampant indiscipline, a gun cultured generation with teenage pregnancies and unwanted babies looming large in the background" (Ministry of Community Development 2007).

EAST PORT OF SPAIN: YORUBA VILLAGE, A RETROSPECTIVE

During the sixteenth to eighteenth centuries, the number of Yoruba people caught up in the transatlantic trade in enslaved Africans was small, mainly war captives and law offenders. However, in the late eighteenth century, England opened a slave market at Lagos, a Yoruba town, to rival France's slave forts at Porto Novo (Ajase) and Whydah, in neighbouring Dahomey. There was consequently a significant increase in enslaved Yoruba involved in the transatlantic trade in enslaved Africans in the early part of the nineteenth century. The British were the principal traders in Yoruba people. The trade having been outlawed in 1807, under British law Yoruba arriving in British colonial ports after that date were free. The freed Yoruba were put ashore at several places, including the British West Indian islands. They were used as a ready-made source of labour by the West Indian plantocracy after emancipation in 1838. The recruitment of West Africans as indentured labour to work in the West Indies began in 1841 and ended around 1867. During this time nine thousand Africans arrived in Trinidad. Between 1807 and 1841, freed Africans had previously landed on the island of Trinidad. They also worked in other Caribbean islands

(Grenada, Tobago, St Lucia, Montserrat and Guadeloupe). In Trinidad, the geographic areas in which many free Africans (including many Yoruba) settled included Dry River in the lower Belmont/east Port of Spain area. This area of Port of Spain was also called Yarriba Village or Yarriba Town (Warner-Lewis 1997, 43). These workers lived in conditions of semiservitude. When at the end of their three- or five-year contracts they were free of indenture, they "settled in language enclaves" (7). Other Yoruba settlements or "blocks" were located in north, central and south-east Trinidad (Warner-Lewis 1994). Today a plaque conceived and executed by Stetchers Limited for the city council of Port of Spain as a public service announces "You Are Now Entering Yoruba Village" with a brief account of the history of Yoruba Village.

The Yoruba, like other African-born peoples, entered a society shaped by European colonialism and imperialism in which skin colour and its degrees of shades formed the basis for assigning individuals and groups to superior or inferior roles. In addition to the disadvantage of skin colour, Africans generally were looked down upon for their lack of "Eurocentric cultural values and mannerisms" (Warner-Lewis 1997, 37). However, Warner-Lewis notes the characteristics of the Yoruba people that drew attention to them and which speak to their cultural self-assurance: their internal social organization, their dedication to commerce, independent occupations, land acquisition and their capacity for integration into civil society. Their embrace of Catholicism also recommended them highly.

There was intense neighbourhood solidarity within and between Yoruba language "islands" in Trinidad (blocks of Yoruba people speaking Yoruba). Family and social occasions, work routines, and trips to large neighbouring towns provided opportunities for mother tongue usage. Secular and religious occasions also brought together Yoruba people. In addition to social functions, religious ceremonies to the Orisha or deities were led by those dedicated to the Orisha faith or trained as Orisha priests. Cultural forms which constituted secular entertainment included "story-telling, games such as *ayo*, and dances that featured singing and playing of percussive instruments like the drum and the beaded calabash" (Warner-Lewis 1997, 44). Warner-Lewis comments that Yoruba communities' network of social activity was not documented and had to be reconstructed from oral evidence. Warner-Lewis's research uncovered a competence in Yoruba discourse in Trinidad that was innate and that went beyond sacred topics and functions. She asserts that the retention, in the second half of the twentieth century, of languages such as Yoruba serves as a pointer in "assessing the relative cultural, if not numerical, strength of African communities in the previous century" (36).

The generation born in Africa imprinted its languages on the memory and mimetic capacity of survivors. Other groups perceived that the Yoruba diligently trained their children to use their mother tongue. However, the numbers of Yoruba language speakers and their competence in reproducing the language both gradually declined. Nonetheless, African languages continued to serve as a code for second- and third-generation speakers. Yoruba was used in contexts associated with work, religion, entertainment, and social relationships. Yoruba songs also served to boost one's ego; to express community togetherness, undeclared feelings of love, admiration, grief over broken homes; and to mourn the dead and the departed.

Religious ritual was another sphere of use of Yoruba language, facilitated by an increase in the worship of Yoruba Orisha deities among the Trinidad population. In considering the shrinking of Yoruba language functionality in Trinidad, Warner-Lewis found that the affective use of language has proven hardiest. She notes that the dilemma between cultural possession and cultural loss has been "the ambiguous destiny of succeeding generations of Africans" since the first arrival of enslaved Africans in the New World (Warner-Lewis 1997, 16, 19).

African religious practices were rejected as true worship by whites and coloureds steeped in European culture. Using legal provisions, these groups were as harsh as possible in their treatment of the faithful of African religions. They also disapproved of many lower-class black customs and festivals and did their best to suppress them. Formerly enslaved Creoles and their descendants made up the majority of black folk. Alongside them were immigrants from the eastern Caribbean, who themselves were formerly enslaved, their offspring, as well as Africans from many different West African tribes who had been freed and "surviving ex-soldiers" who earlier in the century settled in Trinidad. Even though the overwhelming majority of blacks were not born in Africa, the African element was the strongest in the Creole culture. Notwithstanding the fact of a decreasing proportion of natives of Africa in the Trinidad population, many elements of West African life, culture and religion survived in late nineteenth-century Trinidad. These cultural elements were denigrated by white and coloured leaders of Trinidad society who elevated European cultural patterns. Throughout the nineteenth century, legal restrictions were placed on African musical forms. A key West African instrument, the drum, provoked the most hostility. The values informing these responses were naturally those of the dominant culture in colonial Trinidad, which was British and Christian and encompassed the institutions of the law, church, school, the government and the English language. The people resisted the repressive laws against their music, and this resistance was reflected in the calypso art form in the 1880s. The prohibition of the use of the African drum gave rise to tambour-bamboo bands. After the early 1880s a proliferation of improvised instruments (tambour-bamboo, bottle and spoon) were integrated into calypsos and carnival music. Eventually European instruments became more *en vogue* as accompaniment for calypso.

Elements of the Yoruba Religion in Trinidad

It would appear that African cultural retentions in east Port of Spain, particularly in the sphere of religion, have had an impact on the nature of the artistic products created within the community. Nature worship, ancestor reverence, the worship of deities called Orishas which represent elements of nature and spirit, drumming and dancing are all central features of the Yoruba religion. In some celebrations, precise rhythms intended for particular Orishas are played by percussionists and drummers. An important concept in the Yoruba religion is that of the crossroads, represented by the Orisha Eleggua. Inherent in this concept is the idea of a meeting point of the possibilities, including magic, and the concern to negotiate a painful past and uncertain present in order to move forward. Followers of the Yoruba religion are described as "self-determinists" who are not inclined towards self-negation. It is possible, therefore, that African folk who were Yoruba faithful, whether overtly or covertly, recognized their own value – in spite of the overwhelming efforts of the colonial authorities to have them believe otherwise – and sought to create a culture that mirrored that from which they had been separated. In so doing, they actually created something new reflecting a worldview that was in fact a new entity – part African and part Creole – but which provided them with the means for a "magical freedom" in the midst of poverty and oppression.

Leaning on the Past to Create a Future

The Success Laventille Networking Committee, among other non-governmental organizations working in east Port of Spain – concerned about poverty and crime in the area and believing that the history of its people holds both an explanation and an answer to its development challenges – has set out on a campaign of public information and education. Through a community newsletter, *Ujaama News*, the committee promotes knowledge about the history of Yoruba Village (east Port of Spain) and the roots of the negative associations which now are seen as characteristic of the area. The newsletter serves as a vehicle for empowerment of the people of east Port of Spain by promoting self-knowledge, traditional African practices, cultural self-assurance and a view of themselves as heroic survivors rather than as victims. The committee tries to reduce crime by highlighting positive characteristics which traditionally defined the Yoruba people, such as self-help, seeking their own interest and honouring community leaders. The Success Laventille Networking Committee holds culture up as a metaphor for the liberation of this community of Afro-Trinidadians in modernity, and it has as one of its goals "transforming Laventille into a respected community" (*Ujaama News* 2003).

CALYPSO, ART, STEELBAND, AND RUDOLPH "VALENTINO" CHARLES, THE LAVENTILLE RHYTHM SECTION AND CARNIVAL

The calypso, believed to be the reinterpretation of a traditional African topical song, is considered to have attained its highest form of expression in Trinidad. Around 1900, many calypsonians criticized coloureds and whites who were part of upper- and middle-class society. Calypso was used as a means of retaliation for society's devaluing of calypso and black folk culture. In the immediate postemancipation period, calypsos tended to be inflammatory, closely linked as they were to the Canboulay parades, which were described as "African freedom celebrations" (Boyce Davies 1985, 69).

One of the earliest antecedents of the calypso, sung by Attila, protested the suppression of African culture and dealt with Africans' determination to hold Shango ceremonies even though they had been banned. Some of the earliest known calypsonians were excellent exponents of the Yoruba language and used it in their renditions. Executer, Beginner, Atilla, Roaring Lion and the Growling Tiger all sang Yoruba songs; these songs were sung entirely in the Yoruba language and were largely of a spiritual nature, honouring Yoruba deities Sango, Ogun, Oya and Osun, among others. Later, Rose, Nelson, Sparrow, Blakie, Squibby, Ella Andall, Singing Sandra, Andre Tanker, Sugar Aloes,

David Rudder and a host of other modern-day singers used the Yoruba language in their renditions.

David Rudder, for example, born in Belmont, east Port of Spain, from his earliest years was exposed to the Spiritual Baptist religion through his grandmother. He was raised in close proximity to a pan yard and a Shango yard, influences that coloured his music. At the heart of his songs is the chanting of the Shango Baptists. In "Shango Electric", one of his renditions from his CD titled *International Chantuelle*, Rudder, the griot, recounts an encounter between two Orishas, Shango and Elegba. Shango, god of thunder and lightning, is considered a central figure of the Orisha religion. His energy is symbolic of African resistance against an enslaving European culture. He is said to rule the colours red and white and to be the owner of music, dance and entertainment. Elegba, one of the most respected deities in the Yoruba tradition, has wide-ranging responsibilities. He is the protector of travellers and the god of roads, and of crossroads in particular. Shango laments young people's rejection of their heritage and their lack of a sense of direction, of who they are. Rudder sings:

> oh why do the children stray?
> They don't even look to their elders today
> Like headless chickens running around and around
> They don't even know where they're coming from

He asks Elegba:

> Legba, send me through their cable system
> I'll be coming in flaming red
> I've got to find a way to wake the children
> To make them stand up and raise their head, their head, their head oh

THE ART OF CHIEF ABIODUN (LEROY CLARKE)

At first viewing, Clarke's art seems dark and mysterious, lacking popular appeal. However, his work shares Rudder's purpose of projecting an artist/philosopher who has the intention to enlighten and guide a lost people. Rudder is no doubt more successful than Clarke in this quest, as his music has a wide appeal and his influence is therefore likely to be much greater than that of Clarke. Within the Orisha community of Trinidad and Tobago, however, Clarke is revered as artist and elder and has been bestowed with the title Chief Abiodun.

A strong African-influenced spiritual and philosophical ethos is evident in the art of LeRoy Clarke. J.D. Elder (2003a), the late Trinidad and Tobago anthropologist, viewed Clarke's art as a "liberation breakthrough" and identifies a nexus between Clarke's aesthetic and the aesthetic which informs African religions. For Elder, the ancestors' spirits arose in Clarke, reanimating their eternal presence in his work. He likened the artist to Elegba, shepherd and teacher, standing at the crossroads.

The mask of the female face is identified as one of the dominant features of Clarke's paintings. In African religion, the mask is a symbol of the ancestors and in rituals represents the presence of the living dead (Elder 2003a, 89). The ancestors symbolized in the masks provide assurance to those alive that they will serve as intermediaries with the Supreme God so that the living and their families might enjoy health, prosperity and longevity. Humanism is a basic principle in African religion, and this is reflected in Clarke's art in the tribute he pays to the female and in his seeking repentance for wrongdoing as, for example, the defamatory stereotypes of women in popular songs (ibid.). Clarke, the artist, is considered to have created an artistic hieroglyphic that is radical and uniquely his own, one that he uses to communicate his message about diasporic black folks' struggles, oppression and progress.

The source of Clarke's inspiration to commit himself to painting and writing for the rest of his life was his recognition that the spirit of Africans had become fragmented. Caroline C. Ravello (2003) describes all of Clarke's work as revolving around philosophical, phenomenological and psychological imagery of the redemption of Africans from the abyss of a society into which they had been flung without having a say. Clarke's *El Tucuche* series, therefore, named after Trinidad's second-highest mountain peak, stands as a metaphor for finding oneself. Ravello cites Trinidad and Tobago art critic Geoffrey Maclean, who comments that Clarke's journey in his art "is a continuation of the living spirit of Africa, transplanted to Caribbean soil". She also turns to Makemba Kunle for an appreciation of Clarke's work, who writes of the artist, "Marked from birth with gifts of vision and expression, nurtured 'Behind de Bridge' in the cradle of steel pan, Shango, bad john, chaneled through rites of manhood and warriorhood . . . [Clarke] went [on] to shape a world view" (23, 24).

Steelband and Rudolph "Valentino" Charles

The steelband as we know it is an offshoot of the tambour-bamboo bands. Elder (2003b) situates the steelpan, as musical instrument, as an instance of "seminal artistic breakthrough and liberation from the powerful thralldom of Eurocentrism, in the area of the arts and culture" (Elder 2003b, 88). Nettleford (1995) places on the Caribbean research agenda the need to understand, for example, why it is that it is from the unlettered yards of Port of Spain that the innovation in steel pan music emerged. Some of the earliest known steelbands, such as Mission to Moscow and Bar 22 founded in the 1929–30 period, were formed after state legislation was passed banning the playing of the drums, an important feature of the Yoruba culture that dominated the hills and plains of Laventille, Belmont, Gonzales and Morvant. Several Orisha yards dotted these areas at the time, when African spirituality governed the lives of African folk.

Rudolph "Valentino" Charles, the Moses of Laventille, long after his death remains an iconic figure in the pantheon of steelband heroes. From a respected family in the depressed community of Laventille, he gravitated to the panmen from Desperados, a Laventille steelband, at a time when there was fierce rivalry among steelbands. As he was able to read music, he went on to become captain of Desperados, a position so highly respected that it was unchallenged, in the words of *Newsday*, by even "the most 'ignorant' battle-scarred bad-john" (25 March 2007, 29). Under Charles's exemplary leadership, Desperados became one of the top steelbands in Trinidad and Tobago. In 1970, the band was declared winner of the national steelband competition, "Panorama", a victory that resulted in tours to Europe and the United States. The success of Desperados then and in following years attracted members and supporters from all over Trinidad to the band. Not paradoxically, David Rudder saw his career skyrocket with the release of his 1986 album and two songs which won popular appeal nationally and internationally, including "The Hammer", the story of the deceased Rudolph "Valentino" Charles.

Percussion Band: The Laventille Rhythm Section

The Laventille Rhythm Section is the vehicle for another cultural product created in east Port of Spain, percussion music influenced by African rhythms. Wayne Bowman (2007), Trinidad and Tobago music critic, in a review of the group's most recent CD, titled *Pure Rhythm*, describes the group members as skilled musicians who, in their performances throughout the world, have brought great pride to Trinidad and Tobago. It was the Laventille Rhythm Section that raised the spirits of the national football team, the Soca Warriors, on their journey to the 2006 World Cup in Germany. (At the World Cup, more than half of the Trinidad and Tobago cultural contingent came out of the heart of Yoruba Village.) Bowman describes one of the CD's selections, titled "Shango", as exhibiting "the raw rhythm of the beat that was developed by African slaves . . . in Trinidad as they tried to hold on to the ancient religion of their forefathers" (*Sunday Express*, 4 March 2007).

Carnival

West African traditions combined with new elements in Trinidad helped to shape and define the carnival tradition (Liverpool 2001, 13). Carnival in nineteenth-century Trinidad offered blacks an important means of expression, and this included "letting off steam". While in contemporary Trinidad carnival has become a space that celebrates the notion of oneness, even if temporarily, the "jamet carnival", as it was called during the time of the Canboulay Riots in 1881, represented a counterforce to respectable society's judgements and values. Carnival was the focus of the subculture shaped by urban blacks in the slums of Port of Spain. This subculture was based on the barrack yards, controlled generally by "the jamets, the singers, drummers, dancers, stickmen, prostitutes and badjohns" (Brereton [1981] 1989, 135). In the 1860s and 1870s, jamets dominated carnival, using it to settle old grievances, which resulted in conflict among bands. Carnival before emancipation belonged to upper-class Creole whites and had been an elegant social affair. This changed after 1838, as the formerly enslaved and other members of the folk group increasingly participated in carnival while the upper class abstained. Taken over almost entirely by the barrack yard jamets who organized themselves in bands, carnival became a time for challenge, with the stick-fighting arena being the supreme battleground and the place for the display of skills in song and dance.

Canboulay is a procession of masked folk with lighted torches, beginning at midnight and lasting into the next morning with drumming, singing, shouting and fighting between rival stickfighters. The tradition of Canboulay is accompanied by call and response, singing and percussion reflective of African cultural retentions. Although the bands resisted police attempts to suppress Canboulay in 1881, the efforts of the government to do so finally prevailed in

1884. Today, however, it is once again observed as an important element at the start of carnival. As in the 1870s when carnival presented the poor masses with an important escape valve, today carnival continues to play this role for similarly marginalized groups. Despite the purging of obscenity from carnival (which was strong before 1895) and the remaking of carnival in the image of the upper classes, there remain in carnival explicit sexual themes, transvestism and "smut" in calypso; the spirit of the "jamet carnival" survives, and protest and anarchy characterize the participation of some of the masses in search of an outlet.

Carnival portrayals, as reflected in masquerade, also reflect African cultural retentions in Trinidad. West African traditions of masquerading existed long before the transatlantic trade in enslaved Africans and could be observed in ceremonies and festivals (Liverpool 2001). Characters such as the Moko Jumbies, Bats, Dame Lorraines, Midnight Robbers, Blue Devils and Perrot Grenades (some of these representing dangerous spirits restrained by chains) continue to be typical of Trinidad carnival not only in east Port of Spain but throughout Trinidad and Tobago. These same characters – though with African names – can still be found in the Ogun, Osun, Oya, Gelede and Egungun festivals of Nigeria today, all in their original splendour.

CONCLUSION

Africans and their descendants in east Port of Spain used culture to convey a political vision, one of resistance to oppression and a refusal to negate the cultural continuities that they were able to create for themselves. To the extent that they were able to communicate this vision through their cultural products, African folk became their own liberation fighters and revolutionaries. Their artistic expressions, products of the creative imagination, provide important insights for understanding human society in this area of Port of Spain. Several of the artists who have emerged from east Port of Spain have done so with their feet firmly rooted in African cultural retentions. Writing in *Newsday* (25 March 2007), Lasana states that the people of east Port of Spain are eternally optimistic and deserve to have their views and aspirations respected, that they are a vast "human resource still waiting to be discovered". The history of Africans, Creoles and their descendants in the barrack yards of east Port of Spain no doubt holds many stories of pride, dignity and survival. As is made clear in the *Newsday* article by Lasana, in addition to the artists it has produced,

Behind the Bridge has given to Trinidad and Tobago other outstanding citizens among whom are Sir Hugh Wooding, a "formidable legal mind", Makandal Daaga "whose 'Black Power' mantra rattled the status quo until the doors of opportunity were opened to qualified locals", and Professor Courtney Bartholomew, "internationally renowned medical doctor in AIDS research".

Increasingly, culture is being viewed by international development agencies such as the United Nations Educational, Scientific and Cultural Organization (UNESCO) as a critical dimension of sustainable human development that ought to be recognized and incorporated into policies that target poverty alleviation. As noted on its website, UNESCO has been promoting the concept of cultural industries or creative industries, which in some countries embrace the visual and performing arts, manufacturing of musical instruments and cultural tourism. The term *cultural industries* refers to industries that merge the creation, production and commercialization of intangible and cultural contents in the form of either goods or services. These goods or services are usually protected by copyright. The development of sustainable cultural industries that build on what has already been created and sustained by the folk of east Port of Spain should be examined seriously as a means of addressing unemployment and alleviating poverty in the community, with the required financial investment on the part of the government and the private sector. This is particularly important in the context of globalization, with its attendant threats and opportunities.

The arts in east Port of Spain, and the performing arts in particular, represent one very rich and promising area of human endeavour for the pursuit of a development strategy centred on the concept of cultural industries – there are likely to be others. There has been rapid growth in trade in cultural goods over the past two decades, though that trade so far has involved a small number of countries. This reflects a rising demand for cultural goods and services. Astute national and regional development policies should seek to take advantage of the opportunities presented by this trend. Certainly east Port of Spain would have a great deal to contribute in the pursuit of such a development strategy. The arts must not be seen only for their entertainment value or as a means of controlling the population nor used merely for "showing off" when wanting to project a good image of the country abroad. Rather, the arts must be treated as an area of investment to attract hard currency to directly benefit the creators of the cultural products of the people. In the twenty-first century, this must become an essential step in the ongoing trajectory of freedom.

REFERENCES

Bowman, Wayne. 2007. "Laventille Rhythm Section Scores Another Hit". *Sunday Express* (Trinidad), 4 March.

Boyce Davies, C.E. 1985. "The Africa Theme in Trinidad Calypso". *Caribbean Quarterly* 31 (2): 67–86.

Brereton, Bridget. (1981) 1989. *A History of Modern Trinidad, 1783–1962*. Oxford: Heinemann Educational.

Carr, A. 1989. *A Rada Community in Trinidad*. Port of Spain: Paria.

Elder, J.D. 2003a. "Totem and Icon in Clarke's Art". In *LeRoy Clarke, of Flesh & Salt & Wind & Current: A Retrospective*, edited by C.C. Ravello, 99. Port of Spain: National Museum and Art Gallery of Trinidad and Tobago.

———. 2003b. "Towards a Caribbean Aesthetic". In *LeRoy Clarke, of Flesh & Salt & Wind & Current: A Retrospective*, edited by C.C. Ravello, 88–90. Port of Spain: National Museum and Art Gallery of Trinidad and Tobago.

Liverpool, L. Hollis. 201. *Rituals of Power and Rebellion: The Carnival Tradition in Trinidad and Tobago*. Chicago: Research Associates School Times Publications/Frontline Distribution International Inc.

Ministry of Social Development. 1996. *The Determination and Measurement of Poverty in Trinidad and Tobago: Indications from the 1992 Survey of Living Conditions*. Port of Spain: Author.

Ministry of Community Development, Culture and Gender Affairs. 2007. "Remembering the Maafa: Bicentennial of the Abolition of the Trade in Enslaved Africans, 1807". *Newsday*, Sunday supplement. 25 March.

Nettleford, Rex. 1995. *Inward Stretch, Outward Reach*. New York: Caribbean Diaspora Press.

Ravello, Caroline C. 2003. "Retrospectively Speaking: Clarke, Esteemed Umpire of Taste". In *LeRoy Clarke, of Flesh & Salt & Wind & Current: A Retrospective*, edited by C.C. Ravello, 21–24. Port of Spain: National Museum and Art Gallery of Trinidad and Tobago.

Warner-Lewis, Maureen. 1994. *Yoruba Songs of Trinidad*. London: Karmak House.

———. 1997. *Trinidad Yoruba: From Mother Tongue to Memory*. Kingston: The Press, University of the West Indies.

8.

MYTH AND RITUAL IN HOSAY, RAMLEELA AND CARNIVAL AS EXPRESSIONS OF A VIBRANT CARIBBEAN CULTURE

EDITH PÉREZ SISTO

THROUGHOUT THE WORLD, IN ALL times and under every circumstance, mythology has flourished. James Frazer's theory supports the idea that all myths are, or originally were, the forms of words which accompanied a magical or religious rite. Furthermore, "myths are not merely explanations of the rites; they are in many instances the actual words used in the performance of the rites" (1959, 386). Myth is the living reality, believed to have once happened in primeval times, continuing ever since to influence the world and human destinies (Pérez Sisto 1993, 16). According to Northrop Frye, ritual constructs a "calendar and endeavours to imitate the precise and sensitive accuracy of the movements of the heavenly bodies and the response of vegetation to them" (1957, 119–20). Furthermore, ritual re-creates the historical events and deeds of societies' heroes.

Historically, myth follows and is correlative to ritual. It is the "spoken part of ritual, the story which the ritual enacts" (Wellek and Warren 1949, 191). These critics are of the opinion that ritual is performed for a society by its priestly representatives in order to avert or procure; it is an agenda which is recurrently, permanently necessary, like harvests and human fertility, like initiation of the young into their society's culture and a proper provision for the future of the dead. But, in a wider sense, "myth comes to mean any anonymously composed story telling of origins and destinies: the explanations a society offers its young ones of why the world is and why we do as we do, its pedagogic images of the nature and destiny of man" (Wellek and Warren 1949,

191). In Trinidad, rituals and rites have undergone many changes due to the incorporation of new elements from various cultural sources, such as Black Religion (Shango), Shi'i Islam, Hinduism and Western mythology. On the island of Trinidad, the myths and rituals of those who came to make this place their home have prevailed and survived through time. What human beings have in common is revealed in myths. Myths are stories of our search through the ages for truth, for meaning, for significance. We all need to tell and to understand our story, the story of our ancestors. We all need for life to signify, to touch the eternal, to understand the mysterious, to find out who we are. Such understanding becomes relevant in a multiethnic society such as Trinidad and Tobago, where all year round Africans, Muslims, Indians, Chinese, Europeans, Syrians, Lebanese, Amerindians and people of mixed race display and re-create their cosmologies in elaborated multicolour and polyphonic festivals, leading to reinforcement of a sense of belonging.

The mythical re-creation of sacred stories is based on an archaic ontology that did not differentiate between the sacred and profane. Mythical re-presentation is anti-historical and archetypal (Eliade 2000, 156). Thus, during these festivals one can observe an insurrection against concrete, historical time, in other words, a desire for a periodical return to the mythical beginning and hatred of any attempt at autonomous history, that is, of history without an archetypal order (144–45). An archetype is "a figure, a daemon, man or process that repeats itself in the course of history wherever creative fantasy is fully manifested" (Jung 1959, 513). Any archetype is essentially a mythological figure, the formulated result of countless experiences we inherited from our ancestors.

THE HOSAY FESTIVAL: ADAPTATION AND READAPTATION OF SHI'I MUSLIM TRADITION IN TRINIDAD

During the first ten days of Muharram, Shi'i Muslims, regardless of where they reside, commonly observe Husayn's sacred commemoration. The tragic circumstances surrounding Husayn's redemptive suffering and vicarious death resonate throughout the Shi'i world, providing a central paradigm for a Shi'i theological emphasis on personal suffering as a method for the achievement of salvation (Korom 2003, 7). There is great merit associated with weeping for Husayn, and even just "remembering the event can absolve sin" (17). Canetti argues that "the suffering of Husayn and its commemoration become the essence of Shi'ism, which is a religion of lament more concentrated and more extreme than any to be found elsewhere. . . . No faith has ever laid greater emphasis on lament. It is the highest religious duty, and many times more meritorious than any other good work" (Korom 2003, 17). The celebration of Hosay began in Trinidad during the 1850s with the arrival of indentured servants from the Indian subcontinent, who made the voyage to work in the great sugar plantations of southern Trinidad. The first Hosay procession most likely was held around that time (Nunley and Bettelheim 1987, 126–27). The mythical and archetypal representation of the sacrifice of Husayn and Hasan re-create the archetypal image of the "victim"; this figure is full of social connotations, religious associations and psychological paradoxes. The secular and sacred aspects of the archetypal image of the "victim" appear in a multiplicity of forms such as injustices, wounds and sacrifices. The archetypal image of the victim is the personification of the way in which a group imagines itself to be suffering. This is the "sacred victim" with its accompanying associations of eternity and transcendence: "the sacred aspect of this archetypal figure remits to its depth as an interior psychic figure and its meaning" (Jung et al. 1991, 300).

This archetypal image "paralleled the experience of the East Indians [Indo-Trinidadians] in Trinidad, who say their brothers died on board the ships or on the plantations" (Nunley and Bettelheim 1987, 127). Hosay became a powerful festival, wherein the sacrifice of the martyred brothers was acted out and mirrored by the real sacrifice of the Indians who travelled to Trinidad. Here ritual and reality meet, and people are transformed. Thus, "mythology is the product of the collective unconscious . . . the unconscious wisdom which rises up from the depths of the human psyche in answer to these unconscious questions. The unconscious knowledge of the background of life and of man's dealing with it is laid down in ritual and myth; these are the answers of . . . the human soul and the human mind" (Neumann 1948, 13). Each year in the St James neighbourhood of Port of Spain, the festival is celebrated by the building of four *tadjah* and the Husayn and Hasan moons, each by a separate building crew. Each night prayers are said and ritual food is shared among the builders and invited guests. Aside from the drumming, the ritual activities are an "insider" phenomenon: "These activities socially bond the various groups together in ways unknown to outsiders. But the last three nights of the Hosay open up the observance to the general public because the central ritual performed on the eighth, ninth, and tenth of Muharram are processional rituals performed outside the yard" (Korom 2003, 176). The festival procession begins on the evening of the eighth of Muharram (called Flag Night) led by large hand-pulled carts decorated with flags crowned by the *panjtan* (standards), reminiscent of the *alams* (also called standards). The ninth of Muharram is dedicated to Husayn's older brother, Hasan (Small *Tadjah*, or tomb-like house). A smaller *tadjah* is placed on each yard's platform along with some of the flags. These are moved onto the streets to the accompaniment of drumming. At the end of the performance, participants break the fast by killing a goat in the halal style. The meat is used for making curry to be shared by everyone in the yard on the following evening. At sunrise the large *tadjah* are "crowned" by the men with large domes that complete the structures (*gummadge*). Upon completing this phase of the ritual, the space once occupied by the *tadjah* becomes profane (a dining room for the sacrificial meal). Meanwhile, the two moon yards prepare themselves to bring out their moons, which rest positioned to face Mecca. After the *baksh* (blessing) of their sacred objects, they chant "I say, Hosay" over and over again, until the consecration rite is complete after five revolutions of the *chowk* (meeting place). Each moon man wears a *chomatee* (leather suspender harness) attached to a *kamarband* (belt) around the waist, at the centre of which is a metal cup in which the bottom of the moon's vertical post is placed when he is dancing. The two moons meet and kiss, or touch, symbolizing the last meeting of the brothers. The moons also kiss each *tadjah* when they pass them. Some of the older female members of the Indo-Trinidadian community throw rice and cloves at the structures when the moons kiss the *tadjah*. Local tradition holds that the *tadjah* is dead from the end of this evening's performance (Korom 2003, 188).

According to John Nunley and Judith Bettelheim (1987, 127), "the *tadjah* stops parallel to each tomb and touches it in a symbolic kiss, releasing the spirits of Husayn and Hasan into unbounded space". This is an archetypal representation of the eternal motif of the brothers who meet and kiss for the first time. Frank Korom argues that "participants believe that the spirits of the two brothers enter into the large *tadjahs* on the midnight of Flag Night". This is said to make them come alive, and to prove their presence "a drop of blood is believed to appear under each of the *tadjahs*. They are also believed to shake violently as the spirits are entering" (Korom 2003, 177). The power of Hosay lies in the fact that it is a mythological saga re-created every year in which archetypal motifs are, according to Jung, "similar to cultural motifs represented everywhere and throughout history. Their main features are their power, depth, and autonomy" (Jung 1959, 511). Korom suggests:

Hosay in Trinidad seems very different from the Iranian and Indian forms at first glance.... The observance becomes marked by gaiety.... The Trinidadian form of the rite becomes "carnivalized".... In Trinidad the rituals are at the centre personal and subjective. From the subjective core, we move to the kinship unit or family circle within which ritualistic and customary activities occur in the esoteric, private realm of the "yard" compound. From here we move out to the tertiary ring of the small community of Shi'i worshippers on the island. (2003, 7)

The principal objects of the Indian festival are the *taziya* and the *Alams*. In Trinidad, however, the moon shape is probably derived from the Indian *alam*, judging from the crescent shape of a particular *alam* associated with the *nal sahid*, or sacred horseshoe, as well as the crescent moon of Islam itself. The two Indo-Trinidadian moons derive from a number of Indian festivals, objects and practices. They are built with bamboo armatures decorated with cloth, tinsel paper, and mirror. In the Husayn structure, red stands for the martyr's blood, and the green of the Hasan moon refers to the colour of the poisoned brother's skin. Three peacock feathers, a *panjtan* and a knife blade, symbolic of the battle of Karbala, surmount the Husayn moon. From the crescent portion of the Hasan construction protrude twenty-three knives, the two hands and the *culce*, the green shamrock-shaped objects at the top of the crescent. Each object has a sack suspended on the top of the heavily decorated side; the sacks are said to be filled with sacred material.

Answering the needs of Muslims and Hindus, the *alams* of India play a central role in the festival. The strong animistic side of Hinduism has relegated certain *alams* to the status of spiritual objects as, for example, the horseshoe-shaped crescent in Hyderabad, India.

The crescent shape, and the peacock feather decoration of this horseshoe *alam*, as well as the fact that incense is burned before it, all link it to the Indo-Trinidadian moon with respect to shape, materials and ritual use (Nunley and Bettelheim 1987, 132). Like Indo-Trinidadian moons, Indo-Trinidadian *alams* are often decorated with gold and silver embroidery, tassels and fringes, and the open hand, while some feature swords emblematic of the weapons carried by Ali.

The horseshoe shape of the Indo-Trinidadian moons suggests that these objects symbolize horses. Both are decorated with bridle-like cords suspended from the sides, and the *culce* surmounting the Hasan moon resembles the ears of the horse. The moon dance is reminiscent of the movements of a bucking horse; as the two moons meet in the procession, they prance in a circle like horses. One can imagine that the moons represent the brothers on horseback, mounting an attack with outstretched hands and bared knives. This is a symbolic play, marking the return of the dead for revenge. The moons have become a powerful symbol in Hosay in Trinidad, synthesizing many aspects of the Indo-Trinidadian tradition.

The festival "became a national statement in a land of many nationalities" (Nunley and Bettelheim 1987, 127) and thus makes the observance public by bringing the ritual items outside. This "not only allows for spectacle but also enables a large audience to experience the aesthetic beauty of the *tadjahs* while simultaneously creating new sets of meanings concerning the significance of the event" (Korom 2003, 176). The question of convergences, diffusion and independent development has always intrigued scholars of multifarious cultural traditions in the Americas. The *tadjah* is not found only in the Hosay festivals of the Caribbean; as a matter of fact, this motif worn as a headdress, carried in the hands, or built large enough to require a moveable platform, appears in festivals on both sides of the Atlantic.

The Ramleela Festival: Adaptation and Readaptation of Hindus in Trinidad

Ramleela narrates the story of Shri Rama. The events of the life of this lord incarnated, Shri Rama, are condensed in the most popular book of the Hindus, *Shri Ramcharitamanasa*, written by Tulsidasa. The way in which the story of *Rama* is communicated every year has pedagogical consequences because the more one is exposed to a philosophical, educational or religious premise, the more it will impregnate one's everyday existence. Thus, by performing every year this complex theological, ideological and philosophical belief or devotional poetry in an imaginative way, a unique experience is created for those involved not only as actors but also as audience.

The monumental epic Ramayana (story of Rama) is thought to relate to the two north Indian tribes of the late Vedic Age (*c.* twelfth to tenth centuries BC), the Kosala and the Videha, since in the epic these names are those of the kingdoms allied by the marriage of Rama, prince of Kosala, and to the daughter of Videha's illustrious king, Janaka. Of the many extant versions, the oldest is ascribed to the sage Valmiki, supposedly a contemporary of Rama. Research, however, indicates that the epic was written down in its present "Valmiki" form shortly before the beginning of the Christian era. It consists of twenty-four thousand verses (*sloka*) divided into five hundred songs.

The Ramleela story begins with an incarnation of the God Wisnu (Vishnu) in the newborn son of a Kosala king of Ayodya, Dasarata, whose kingdom lay near the slopes of the Himalaya. In the shape of Rama the firstborn of Dasarata and his wife Kausalya, Wisnu was to fight and conquer the king of demons, Rawana, who ruled Alengka (Langka). During preparations for Rama's coronation and attending festivities, the king's other wife, Kaikeyi, reminded him of a vow made to her long ago, in which Dasarata had promised to grant anything she might wish. Kaikeyi demands the banishment of Rama and the coronation of her own son Barata. The king is forced to keep his vow but dies soon afterwards. Rama honours his father's obligation and goes into exile, followed by Sita and his devoted brother Laksmana. They wander through the forest and settle at a place called Tjitrakuta. There they are found by Rama's crowned half-brother Barata, who implores Rama to return. Rama refuses but gives his half-brother his sandals to take back to Ayodya, legitimizing Barata's rule in Rama's name. Rama disappears. Rawana appears in the disguise of a begging Brahman. A white monkey, Hanuman, appears and leads Rama to the king of the monkeys, Sugriwa. After many adventures and clues obtained from the brother of the bird Djatayu (Sempai), Hanuman is captured by the demons, who set fire to his tail in an attempt to burn him. But Hanuman jumps from roof to roof and sets houses on fire. Rawana is alarmed and decides on war. The armies cross to Alengha, and violent battles ensue. In the end Rawana is slain by Rama with an arrow. Rama and Sita are reunited. Sita is subjected to an ordeal by fire which proves her stainless virtue, but her captivity continued to cast shadows upon her reputation. Rama banishes his devoted wife. She gives birth to twins, Lawa and Kusa. Years later, Rama performs the great horse sacrifice; Valmiki comes with his two apprentices. Rama recognizes the youths as his sons and, repentant, asks Sita to return. She refuses and appeals to the goddess of the earth to receive her and disappears into the cleft in the opening earth. Rama eventually regains heaven in his original shape of Wisnu.

The Ramleela narrative reiterates the virtue of moral and social order, which will bring happiness to the world. Evidently, dark and evil forces may threaten and disrupt social order, but divine intervention will ultimately restore order, peace and harmony among mankind. The Ramleela narrative provides the foundation for harmonious family life reflecting on better community life, which in turn will benefit the wider society. Among the aspects dwelled upon one can find brotherly love, portrayed in the sacrifice of Lakshaman, who spent the fourteen years in exile accompanying his brother Rama instead of enjoying the luxuries of palace life; fidelity and chastity, the example for which is Sita and her sacrifices in banishment, who, even when abducted, remained true and faithful; friendship, as portrayed in the Vali-Sugriva episodes; devotion, which is demonstrated through the actions of characters such as Bharat, Lakshaman, Nishaad, Keval, Sugriva and Hanuman; and, finally, self-control, exemplified when the evil destructive forces manifested in lust, anger, hate and egoism yield to Rawana (or Ravana), who at the very end is destroyed by Rama.

Tulsidasa managed to convey the eternal motifs of humanity by depicting its struggle against evil forces. The symbolism of Rawana's death reminds us of the basic truths of all scriptures: that human glory and greatness do not lie in wars, suppression, lust, injustice and arrogance but in justice, kindness to all, building up villages and cities, helping the downtrodden, and making life easy, peaceful and happy for all, thus raising the standard of living and increasing the wealth of the entire population.

In the Rama legend plays, scenography acquires a style aimed at manipulating the space and audience participation in a variety of ways. Rama legend plays are cycle plays, performed for ten days as one unit; each canto of the Ramayana is presented daily. The audience is on all sides of the open space, which symbolically represents Rawana's kingdom and Rama's kingdom. The action flows in all directions, reaching all the spaces occupied by the audience. There are bamboo branches creating a dividing line between performers and audience. Indo-Trinidadian Ramleela performance is an open-air event which takes place in every village.

According to the Maha Sabha National Ramleela Council:

> People learn the story of Rama and from this are able to develop the thought-provoking ideas and lessons of life that emanate from it. These patterns of life encourage people to inculcate sincere habits in their life styles. They are always in a better position to understand and appreciate our many forms of puja and rituals and see the reason for it. . . . We can never really evaluate the benefits that are derived from this period of fasting for both players and audience alike. The bounties of this are immeasurable. There is great community involvement at this time and people generally adhere to keeping their fast before entering the site which has become holy ground. Even the evil elements in our society either keep out or leave their evil tendencies behind. (1994, 7)

As stated by one of the members of the Pierre Road Ramleela Committee interviewed at their 2004 performance, "Our forefathers who came to Trinidad didn't know how to read, so some of them put on the re-enactment of the Ramleela as a means of transmitting and teaching aspects of our culture. Through Ramleela we try to deliver to the villagers the message. Our way of life can be seen through our deeds, our service to man and community" (the Samatan Dharma Maha Sabha of Trinidad and Tobago). According to a member:

> Ramleela started as a play, but gradually developed into something bigger. I have been involved in Ramleela since I was ten years old. It's the culture in which I was born. The Ramleela starts with prayers, it's a religious festival, we are to show respect to the Earth because it's a nature thing. We must pay obeisance to the Earth before we enter the holy ground, which each year is specially prepared.

The Indo-Trinidadian community involved in Ramleela lives and experiences the festival in all its dimensions. For a period of ten days the name of Rama lingers on in their thoughts and words and eventually penetrates their actions.

The fact that Ramleela takes place in an open arena provides for a certain interaction between performers and the audience. The Maha Sabha National Ramleela Council stated, "The Non-Hindus are able to understand and appreciate our way of life, thus creating a more harmonious society. By looking on at the play and listening to the songs that are sung, people generally develop a more picturesque meaning of these songs." (1994, 7).

Trinidad's Carnival: African Adaptation and Readaptation

From the beginning, Carnival has functioned as a ritual for regenerating or reshaping time. Carnival cannot be represented but must be lived; one has to adhere to its laws, which are beyond the ordinary limits or borders, a kind of backward existence in which restrictions which determine structure are suspended, that is, the hierarchical order of things is suspended. This reshaping of order is a basic human need because lineal time is a frightful aspect of nature. Thus, at least once a year, the ritual aims to allow people to take over and re-shape or reorganize time and nature.

From the ancient ruins of Egypt, we hear the echoes and remembrances of the annual ritual to *Wosir* – the oldest account of a festival which can be directly associated with the origins of carnival – "celebration which took place during the five days outside of time, that is, outside of the 360-day year. Wosir was a god of rebirth, a promise of universal resurrection. . . . Descriptions of the closely related ritual for Auset strongly suggest that the participants in this Osirian drama also wore disguises, that is, they were masqueraders" (Smart 1996, 30).

Smart refers to Budge's description of the play *Wosir* as follows:

> This act . . . represented the "coming forth" of Osiris from the temple after his death. . . . A solemn service was performed in the temple before the body was carried from it, and offerings were eaten sacramentally, and then the procession set out for the tomb. When it reached the door of the temple it was received by a mighty crowd of men and women who beat their breasts. Many of the men in the crowd were armed with sticks and staves, and some of them pressed forward the procession with the view of helping the god, whilst others strove to prevent them. Thus a sham fight took place, which, owing to the excitement of the combatants, often degenerated into a serious one. (Ibid.)

There is evidence that "the Osirian mystery plays are the source of the Greek theatre. Thus, the Latin carnival, a Christianization of pre-existing Roman religious rites, had its source in Africa too" (Smart 1996, 30). This theory is plausible since the Romans conquered Greece in 146 BC. As Gilmore suggests, "the Roman Empire stretched from northern Britain to Mesopotamia and included all the countries around the Mediterranean. The Romans became great admires of Greek culture and literature, and much of Roman art and Latin Literature was based on Greek models" (Gilmore 2003, 17). Furthermore, there is evidence that Greeks travelled to Egypt, thus providing fertile ground for mythological borrowing. Budge provides a full description of two festivals that were performed in Rome – perhaps ancient reminiscences of the Saturnalias? There were two important festivals for Auset in Rome referred to, one in November and the other in Spring. At the head of the great procession came men who were dressed to represent a soldier, a huntsman, a woman, and a gladiator. These were followed by men dressed as magistrates, philosophers, fowlers, and fishermen" (Smart 1996, 31). The myths of the African world have survived in the "collective unconscious" (Jung 1959) of those who were forced to come to the Caribbean. The re-creation of this ancient festival would be "activated" in Trinidad by archetypal primordial images which would be drawn from mythological sources. The term *myth* refers to a story that is important for the group and not necessarily untrue. Thus, mythology is all around us and is reflected in everything we do, particularly in the festivals. African religious ideas as they evolved not only in Trinidad but also in the Caribbean as a whole did not lead necessarily to an open and joyous celebration of life. In fact, these ideas helped to sustain people in the struggle for survival under the harsh and oppressive conditions of life in slave and plantation society. African religious practices and their varied cosmological views became part of a people's survival mechanism – perhaps the most important. The bliss of a better future was experienced in anticipation, as it were, in the ecstasy of the dance and other rituals involved in worship, but religious practices had to do with the anxiety to survive, without too much trauma, the crises of life (Bisnauth 1989, 100).

There is a massive and decisive African contribution to Trinidad's carnival, regarding its three major forms: masquerading, music and calypso. Although systematic attempts at "deculturation" during slavery eradicated African traits on most levels of organization, the artistic expressions, those sprouting from the *spirit*, could not be annihilated. Thus, African singing, dancing, drumming, chanting, storytelling, divining and rituals were kept alive in the collective unconscious; they manifest themselves in everything they do, particularly, in their carnival.

Ian Smart and Kimani Nehusi (2000, 117) define Trinidad's carnival as "the African Trinidadian's Carnival of emancipation, commemoration, reconstruction and creativity". The theory proposed by Smart explains how the slaves and their descendants could continue being human, having been exposed to such an aberrant brutality. Theoretical evidence supports the fact that Trinidad's carnival started with the "Cannes Brulees" in which the enslaved as well as the freed participated in masquerading activities during the carnival season. Wood states, "The French speaking slaves before Emancipation . . . celebrated Canboulay (Cannes Brulees), a torchlight procession to commemorate one of the few excitements of the plantation, a fire in the canefields" (in Smart 1996, 243). Also, "since public visitation of ancestors was not possible under the restrictive plantation system, the intensity with which the Africans entered into carnival tradition derived from a perception of carnival as the only legitimate public means of actualizing their tradition of ritual masking, albeit, on a not wholly ritual occasion" (Aiyejina and Gibbons 2000, 7). Hill gives a detailed description offered by a Dominican priest of the ritual which took place in Carenage, Trinidad, in 1883: "Following emancipation, which took place on 1 August 1883, they resolved annually to celebrate this day by a solemn festival for perpetual memory. The festival began at daybreak with a high mass, loud music, consecrated bread, a procession, etc. And it continued for three days during which, in the course of festivities, there were indescribable dances and orgies, remembrances of African life" (Hill 1997, 31). This ritualization helps the individual or community to manage the menace of the absurd. Abrahams argues, "Licentious play brings the group together and allows it to rehearse confusion and embarrassment in a context that is under control. On such occasions nonsense is a community focus in channelling creative energies in socially useful directions" (1983, 81). The Canboulay celebration was not just an annual celebration of freedom but also a ritualized expression of that newly acquired freedom. Canboulay was the dramatic enactment of scenes associated with the obscure and terrible time of slavery. In fact one can rightly affirm that the newly free ex-slaves were symbolically re-elaborating the return to the primordial. Canboulay was banned in 1884 as a result of riots. However, by that time carnival was legally and officially fixed to the two days preceding Ash Wednesday.

The African descendants who participated in those first carnivals evidenced the oppressing reality through playing mass, which in turn became a political weapon. Furthermore, popular and folk music are the mirror on which surface the essence of a people is reflected. Through it one can say what in other situations would not be possible or even acceptable. Through the penetrating rhythm of the steel pan, Calypsonians satirize their opponents and mock them – exorcising their frustrations through happiness. These instances of satire allow the victim to be victorious even momentarily.

But is this not the ultimate mandate of calypsonians? By commenting negatively or positively on all aspects of life, they awaken people's consciousness and raise issues which otherwise would not be discussed. Thus, in a mocking, joking atmosphere, relevant aspects of the society are brought to the surface and rationalized in a controlled environment. This is the political function of calypso. The calypso is an oracle of survival from bondage and slavery. Calypsonians are the heart of society, the custodians who fearlessly monitor injustices or lapses of human rights for their people. The celebration of the carnival and the interpretation of the calypso have overflowed the frontiers of the population; it has become an expression of the culture of Trinidad and Tobago.

The religious nature of carnival has given way to a different manifestation, which is ideologically based. However, the ritualistic nature of the festival has survived, masked under a different disguise. Nevertheless, the festival provides a unique opportunity for integration. The masks that the devils wear and their impulsive personality are the trademarks of these festivities. As Earl Lovelace (1979, 120) says:

> Every Carnival Monday morning . . . with only the memory burning in his blood, a memory that had endured the three hundred odd years to Calvary Hill felt, as he put on his dragon costume, a sense of entering a sacred mask that invested him with an ancestral authority to uphold before the people of this Hill, this tribe marooned so far from the homeland . . . the warriorhood that had not died in them.

The African sensibility of masquerade is a major focus of festival arts. Despite their different origins, Africans in the Americas understand and practise the masquerade, combining music, dance, costume, sculpture and drama in a single performance. Traditional African aesthetics also can be characterized as assemblage – "animal and human bones, raffia, beads, shells, horns, metal, and imported cloth might all appear on a single masquerader" (Nunley and Bettelheim 1987, 128).

FINAL REFLECTIONS

Mythology is the song of the imagination, inspired by the energies of the body. Thus, ritual and mythology put us back in touch with the essential typology of spiritual life. Ritualizing your mythology keeps you in line.

Ramleela means different things for different people. It depends on how one perceives the performance – whether as an opportunity for enjoyment, for learning, for sharing with family and friends, for gambling or just for partying. However, its potential as a means to transmit values and morals to the wider society is unquestionable. The Ramayana is a mirror of the highest ideals of Hindu culture and civilization. It is firmly rooted in the psyche of every Hindu and every individual that has read or listened to it. It answers the spiritual cravings of the common person and the ruler, and inspires them with faith, love, hope and peace. The story of Rama epitomizes a living Hindu culture unfolding the everyday contemporary difficulties of family life. It reflects merciful compassion and teaches that the essence of detachment is that at times people must endure pain to give pleasure to others. It characterizes human conflicts and dilemmas at the personal, family, community and national levels. It provides psychologically sound advice and solutions based on Hindu religious thought and practice. Every personality in the Ramayana has been a role model to Hindus in the past and will continue to be so for generations to come. The themes and motifs dealt with in the Ramayana are archetypal; thus, their appeal to different cultures and the main reason the story can be a relevant and pertinent way to teach, shape or *mould* society, particularly young children. These themes and motifs teach audience and performers to value and preserve their cultural heritage, and in the process they reinforce a sense of identity.

Because of its strong ethnic and religious tones, some people could feel bias towards this festival. However, the representation of the mythological saga in Ramleela aims at describing the ideal hero, the ideal husband, the ideal son, the ideal king, the ideal wife, which eventually would be re-presented by those touched by its archetypal motifs, eternal to humanity and endlessly represented in different scenarios under a different disguise.

In the re-creation of the mythological saga of Hosay, we find that the hero's first task is to experience consciously the antecedent stages of the cosmic cycle, to break back through the epochs of emanation. The second task is to return from the abyss to contemporary life to serve as a human transformer of demiurgic potential. Husayn had the power to transcend time itself. Thus, if the deeds of an actual historical figure, such as Husayn, proclaim him to have been a hero, "the builders of his legend will invent for him appropriate adventures in depth. These will be pictured as journeys into miraculous realms, and are to be interpreted as symbolic, on the one hand, of descents into the night-sea of the psyche, and on the other, of the realms or aspects of man's destiny that are made manifest in the respective lives" (Campbell 1949, 321). Imam Husayn's suffering and death are an archetypal and mythological motif; the reactualization of the event is the central Shi'i ritual observance of the year. Muharram is a metahistorical phenomenon because the observance related to it makes possible individual identification with, and direct experience of, Imam Husayn's suffering. During the observance, subjective apprehension is spatially and temporally bound to the historical battle of Karbala. The archetypal motif is made present through the pious actions of Shi'i Muslims around the world. The will to be a sacrificial victim has been considered a moral virtue by various religious systems. What suffering redeems is not merely the victim's affliction but rather the experience of its meaning: "Husayn's biography exhibits the variously rationalized theme of exile and return; a prominent feature in all legend, folk tale, and myth, 'when the hero is a great patriarch or prophet, the wonders are permitted to develop beyond all bounds'" (Campbell

1949, 323). Participation in the annual Muharram renewal is humankind's chief role and responsibility in this lifetime, according to Shi'i perspective. In patriarchal societies, "collective masculinity is a value-creating and educative force. From a psychological point of view, every ego and every consciousness is gripped and formed by it. In this way the masculine side helps the developing ego to live through the archetypal stages individually and to establish contact with the hero myth" (Neumann 1948, 433). This in turn permeates the groups' values.

According to Korom, the maintenance and survival of Hosay in Trinidad proves "the continuity and change with regard to theology and symbolism but also community process in religious performance. The festival is religious and ritualistic on the most esoteric level, but also cultural and national on more widely engulfing levels" (Korom 2003, 193). Its meaning and interpretation, as understood by performers, artisans and audience members, have multiple functions. On the one hand, for the small community of believers (two or three hundred) the religious and mystical dimension, familial activity, and Indo-Trinidadian identity are highlighted through the inside, esoteric activities that occur during the private forty days leading up to the processions. On the other, the general public interprets the three nights and one day of procession as a celebration; nevertheless, they cannot apprehend the complex theological and ritualistic activities involved in the festival. Thus, during these days the sacred and profane are intertwined. As Korom (2003) suggests, the festival is esoteric, sacred and ethnic on the inside, while exoteric, profane and national on the outside. Hosay observance has not only survived; through celebrating diversity, it has also creatively responded to the various needs of a nation state constituted by a polyethnic citizenry.

Carnival functions as a ritual for regenerating or reshaping time. Thus, during carnival one can observe an insurrection against concrete, historical time; there is a desire for a periodical return to the mythical beginning, to history without an archetypal order (Eliade 2000). In addition, the permutations of Chinese, Indian, African, European, Syrian-Lebanese, Amerindian and mixed-race participation in Trinidad's carnival show the festival's permeability. On looking back at the terrible restrictions placed on black people under slavery, one realizes how precious these two days of revelry are.

These festivals share common aspects such as the social organization of the yards in which events take place, thus providing ample evidence of cultural creolization. Their practices are connected to social issues surrounding ethnic identity formation and the undying importance of racial relations in a nation still in the process of defining itself and its national culture. The myths that link us to our social group, the tribal myths, affirm that we are part of the larger organism. Society itself is a part of a larger organism, which is the landscape, the world in which the tribe moves. The main theme in ritual is to link individuals to a morphological structure larger than that of their own physical body. Hosay, Ramleela and carnival are emblematic of Trinidad's polyethnic population. They manifest multiple discourses about national culture, race, and ethnic identity – at the core of which myth and ritual gravitate.

As festivals rooted in ritual and myth, Hosay, Ramleela and carnival are expressions of a vibrant Caribbean culture – constantly transforming, reshaping itself to readapt to environmental, historical and social circumstances. Myths are intimately bound to culture, time, and place, and unless the symbols, the metaphors, are kept alive by constant re-creation through the arts, the ritual, and the festival, the life just slips away from them.

References

Abrahams, Roger D. 1983. *The Man-of-Words in the West Indies: Performance and the Emergence of Creole Culture in the West Indies.* Baltimore: Johns Hopkins University Press, Johns Hopkins Studies in Atlantic History and Culture.

Aiyejina, Funso, and Rawle Gibbons. 2000. *Orisha Traditions in Trinidad.* Research and Working Papers Series. St Augustine, Trinidad: Faculty of Social Sciences, University of the West Indies.

Bisnauth, Dale. 1989. *History of Religions in the Caribbean.* Kingston: Kingston Publishers.

Campbell, Joseph. 1949. *The Hero with a Thousand Faces.* Princeton, NJ: Princeton University Press.

Eliade, Mircea. 2000. *Le mythe de l'eternel retour: Archétypes et répétitions.* Buenos Aires: Emecé Editores S.A.

Frazer, James. 1959. *The New Golden Bough.* New York: Phillips.

Frye, Northrop. 1957. *Anatomy of Criticism.* Princeton, NJ: Princeton University Press.

Gilmore, David D. 2003. *Monsters: Evil Beings, Mythical Beasts and All Manner of Imaginary Terrors.* Pittsburgh: University of Pennsylvania Press.

Hill, Errol. 1997. *The Trinidad Carnival: Mandate for a National Theatre: The Classical Study of Carnival.* London: New Beacon.

Jung, Carl. 1959. *The Archetypes and the Collective Unconscious.* Vol. 9, pt. 1 of *Collected Works.* Princeton, NJ: Bollingen

Jung, Carl, et al. 1991. *Mirrors of the Self.* Barcelona: Editorial Kairós, S.A.

Korom, Frank. 2003. *Hosay Trinidad: Muharram Performances in an Indo-Caribbean Diaspora.* Philadelphia: University of Pennsylvania Press.

Lovelace, Earl. 1979. *The Dragon Can't Dance.* London: Andre Deutsch.

Maha Sabha National Ramleela Council. 1994. *Ramleela 1994.*

Neumann, Erich. 1948. *The Origins and History of Consciousness.* Bollingen Series 42. Princeton, NJ: Princeton University Press.

Nunley, John, and Judith Bettelheim. 1987. *Caribbean Festival Arts.* Seattle: University of Washington Press.

Pérez Sisto, Edith. 1993. *Myth and Ritual in Lovelace's "The Dragon Can't Dance".* Caracas: Trabajo de Grado de la Maestría en Educación, Mención Enseñanza de la Literatura en Inglés, Universidad Pedagógica Experimental Libertador (mención publicación).

Smart, Ian. 1996. *Amazing Connections: Kemet to Hispanophone Africana Literature.* Washington, DC: Original World Press.

Smart, Ian, and Kimani Nehusi. 2000. *Ah Come Back Home: Perspectives on Trinidad and Tobago Carnival.* Washington, DC: Original World Press.

The Samatan Dharma Maha Sabha of Trinidad and Tobago. N.d. *Ramleela the Divine Sports of Ram.* Siparia, Trinidad and Tobago: Soms.

Wellek, Rene, and Austin Warren. 1949. *Theory of Literature.* Orlando: Harcourt Brace Jovanovich.

PART 3
EDUCATION AND LANGUAGE

9.

MUSEUM EDUCATION AS A MEANS TO PROMOTE EQUAL OPPORTUNITIES

HILDE NEUS VAN DER PUTTEN

[T]he treasures of the world are made by people like me through the exercise of skills and imagination. I do not have these skills and my imagination spins different dreams. Nevertheless that potential is also in me.
Kwame Anthony Appiah, *Cosmopolitanism*

A MUSEUM IS NOT A MUSEUM when it has no visitors. It is just a dusty stronghold storing antiquities, rarities and *objects d'art*. A museum has the obligation to open its doors to the public and disclose its collection, treasures of the world made through the exercise of skills and imagination by people like us. Traditionally, most museum visitors in Suriname (and probably in most of the Caribbean countries) were tourists or people who had gone to live in the metropole and now and then return for vacation. This raised the problem of how to attract visitors from among the local population. Since, often, museums are not especially equipped for young people, educational officers had to find ways to translate the collection of objects to be of interest to the public of Suriname and distinctively to children. This they tried to achieve through several plans of action.

It is important for schoolchildren to visit museums because experiencing one's cultural heritage is a multifaceted means of looking at history and of understanding how the past relates to the present. Thus, visiting museums can be a major contribution to the education of young people. In reality, we observe that many schools from poorer regions and rural areas (or countries as such) do not participate in museum programmes as frequently as schools from rich countries or from better-situated schools in close proximity of the museum.

This chapter focuses on the history of the Suriname Museum Foundation and the problems this institution has faced over time. It will argue the importance of museum education for children and relate some of the solutions by which we can achieve a better attendance and more impact of museum education on schoolchildren. Thus museum education may function as a way of promoting equal learning opportunities for children. More significantly for Caribbean people as descendants of enslaved people, attaining a knowledge and understanding of their heritage is an integral part of the process.

Museum Tradition in Suriname

During colonial times, many artefacts were collected in Suriname and transported to the mother country, that is, the Netherlands. In Europe, collections of rarities, antiques and ethnographies grew into museums. The famous Scottish-Dutch soldier and author John Gabriel Stedman wrote *Narrative of a Five Year Expedition against the Revolted Negroes of Suriname* (1796). He collected artefacts from Amerindian and maroon people and shipped them to Holland in the eighteenth century. They are currently kept in the Royal Institute of the Tropics (KIT) in Amsterdam. Another well-known Dutch example with Suriname collections is Teylers Museum in Haarlem, founded in 1798 (Van Wengen 1992). This was not just for collecting purposes but was also of educational value: the more people knew about production, farming and native life in the colonies, the better they could prepare for their travels and endeavours in the tropics.

Since 1864 the Suriname Society for the Preservation of Knowledge handed over their zoological collection to the state of Suriname, and the Colonial Museum became a fact in 1875. The importance to education was soon acknowledged since the government placed the institution under the supervision of the inspector of Education. Nevertheless, the institute deteriorated and the remains were turned into the School Museum, which was finally closed down in 1925. By 1930, most of the artefacts had been sold at public auctions. A number of educational institutions sent letters of protest to the minister of Colonies in The Hague, but to no avail.

In 1947 the Suriname Museum Foundation was established. The reason for its founding was a growing national awareness that had arisen during the Second World War. By that time, it was customary for foreign visitors to collect valuable cultural items and transport them out of the country. This was the case with Creole head ties, an entomological collection and a number of Amerindian and Maroon artefacts. A law against this was passed in 1952, but observation of it leaves much to be desired. As a result of an exhibition on Suriname in 1953 organized by the Ministry of Education, the foundation managed to acquire a building to present its own displays and store artefacts and the colonial library. In 1965 Parliament decided to allot the fortress (Fort Zeelandia) to the Museum Foundation. This building was opened as the Suriname Museum in 1972 (Van Putten and Ferrier 1999). At the beginning, the museum existed merely to exhibit artefacts; it did not consciously aim to educate its visitors.

THE SURINAME MUSEUM'S DEPARTMENT OF EDUCATION

Education is a recent field in museology. Following worldwide developments since 1970, the Suriname museum slowly picked up the pace in museum education skills. Notwithstanding the enormous difficulties the museum in Suriname had to face in the past, some of the temporary exhibitions were accompanied by an educational programme. Examples of this included *Weddings in Suriname* (October 1987–May 1988: 4,021 visitors); *Let Them Talk* on Creole clothing and head ties (July 1988–July 1989: 4,920 visitors); *Javanese in Suriname* (August 1990–August 1991: 3,164 visitors); *Wonebori* on the Amerindians (September 1992–May 1994: adult visitors 3,158, children 3,328). However, the museum did not have its own educational officer until the last exhibition was mounted; previously people with the necessary expertise were seconded to the museum from the Ministry of Education's Department of Culture. The *Wonebori* exhibition was also the first to institute a separate count of visitors who were adults or children. To design and implement these exhibitions, most of the time staff from other departments of the Ministry of Education were involved. In 1981, a successful teach-in was organized at Fort Zeelandia. As a result, school visits no longer took place only at the end of the school year, when the teaching programme had finished. However, for a number of years, a climate of political unrest discouraged schools from visiting the fort.

Only since 1999 has the Suriname Museum had an active Department of Education. The first year was a start-up year, with only one employee. However, in 2000 the department began an active programme designed by three teachers, who pooled ideas. Two of the three teachers were pensioners who volunteered, while one younger teacher decided to work at the museum without pay. Currently, two people are employed with the Department of Education. The main task of the Department of Education is to build a bridge between the museum and the public. A museum should not be object oriented but visitor oriented. It should not be defined just by what it holds but also by what it does (CLMG 2006, 2). Through research, the Department of Education may advise the museum management of the educational value of objects or propose a subject for display. Additionally, it also develops texts to accompany the exhibitions and educational programmes for visiting schools. It is their task to inform the public of the history of Suriname and Fort Zeelandia through permanent exhibitions and temporary displays on interesting topics in culture and arts.

From object-oriented presentations with guided tours to explain and connect the objects, museum education has evolved into concept-oriented presentations. Museums should provoke curiosity; a story is told to the public and the object underscores the story (Van Wengen 1992; Ganzeboom and Haanstra 1989; Sectie Geschiedenis Hogeschool Interstudie 1988). The curator, educational officer and designer work together in building an exhibition that holds a mirror to society and is optimal in terms of content, object, information and explanation, aesthetics, evocation, colouring, lighting and pacing. The Department of Education of the Suriname Museum executes a number of the tasks (similar to those outlined by Hooper-Greenhill [1991]) in building an exhibition and is linked to several education-related organizations in realizing the goals.

Audience

Fort Zeelandia is visited mainly by tourists. Every Sunday a number of volunteers present the public with two guided tours through the fort. Normally this is done in the Dutch language. However, English is provided on request. The fort is situated near major hotels and entertainment venues; this strategic location is hard to miss. Tourists write their experiences in a guest book: their comments are mostly very positive. This does not imply, however, that the staff of the museum is not looking for ways to extend the number of displays and the depth of information in order to provide a better service to the public (Bettenhausen 2006).

The reason that members of the public in Suriname are less frequent visitors to the fort is because traditionally they are not educated to appreciate the role of the museum. In the past, exhibits in museums worldwide were often designed by curators who were primarily scholars, rather than educators. This resulted in a common perception of museums as remote and forbidding places for those without the prior knowledge to understand the exhibits. Furthermore, people are not very well informed about their own history. A certain amount of engagement is required to be aware of the preservation and education of one's history and heritage. The only way the museum can reach the local target group is through education. It is very important to develop a certain attitude towards culture and preserving one's heritage from childhood (Donawa 1993). The Department of Education focuses its attention, therefore, mainly on schools. By designing a plan and evaluating this strategy, the museum can reach its goal of attracting as many schoolchildren from as many age groups and levels as possible. In Suriname, visiting museums is not a school curriculum–related activity. The Ministry of Education and Community Development has no strategy to incorporate the teaching of cultural heritage appreciation in schools. This means schools are not obliged to visit any cultural heritage–related site, even once a year. The lack of incentives originating from the Ministry of Education does not exempt school directors and teachers from being creative and visiting the museum, even though there are no special facilities. Some schools within walking distance of the museum have all the opportunities but still do not go on field trips.

From experience the museum has learned that schools are more likely to arrange visits to the museum in the period from January until the end of August. The second half of the year does not yield a large crop of visiting schools because of the long summer break and other activities.

In 1988 an exhibition entitled *Suriname in Archaeology* was mounted in the annex of the Suriname Museum. This programme was developed by the archaeology department of the Ministry of Education and Community Development and housed at the museum annex. The educational programme was especially designed for secondary school students in the fourteen-to-sixteen age group. For a period of nine months, almost three thousand students visited the programme (Archeologische Dienst 1988). This number could have been higher if the Department of Education had developed a programme targeted at different levels. For instance, presently the exhibition *The Heritage of Slavery* has a programme designed for primary as well as secondary school students. The main organizer of *Suriname in Archaeology* in 1988, Benjamin Mitrasingh, writes a regular page on culture in one of the local newspapers. In 2005 he stated that the Suriname Museum has remained a "temple of the muses". In view of his comments that children in Suriname are not able to acknowledge their own background and remain estranged from their own cultural heritage, the museum does everything in its power to work on these educational goals. Notwithstanding the statistics, Mitrasingh thinks the museum has not grown into a centre of education (Mitrasingh 2005).

In a survey conducted in 2001 by Mitrasingh and Badal, the conclusions are, to say the least, contradictory. The report says that since 1982 there is no real museum in Suriname, rather exhibitions housed in museum buildings: "Visiting a temporary exhibition within such a building or complex, cannot be considered a museum visit." However, in the conclusions, the report states that 70 per cent of the interviewed respondents have visited a museum in Suriname (Mitrasingh and Badal 2002). This survey was conducted nationally among 3,836 mostly young respondents. Apparently Mitrasingh is not well informed, because since 2000 the number of schoolchildren coming to the museum annually has risen from 750 to more than 5,000. Almost every year a programme especially created for these children is implemented.

Politics

The Suriname Museum is a foundation. This means there is no formal government influence on its policies. Unfortunately this also means that the government does not provide sufficient financial support for the upkeep of the buildings or the hiring of personnel. Plans have been drawn up to change this, as described in an unpublished government report entitled "Integraal cultuurbeleid" (Directoraat Cultuur, Ministerie van Onderwijs en Volksontwikkeling 2007). However, since the budget earmarked for culture is extremely small, improvement is not to be expected in the near future. The limited budget affects the entire operational structure in a negative way. The Suriname Museum depends on selling entrance tickets, donations and financing support from the Dutch government. As a consequence, museum policy is still dictated, rather than merely influenced, by budgetary considerations.

At the opening of an art exhibition in 1990, the minister of education (later president of the Republic of Suriname) Ronald Venetiaan declared, "The museum not only has the task of collecting paintings, statues and other works of art. It also has to make these accessible to the public. Additionally, it has the task of conserving and keeping collections that are historically as well as culturally of obvious importance to Suriname, and this task will undoubtedly be a tough one" (1990). Unfortunately, over time this task has not become any easier. Dedicated personnel who had the knowledge and the heart to take care of the collection have moved on or passed away. At present, the biggest contribution the government could make would be to employ knowledgeable people and make them available to help develop the museum.

Museums are traditionally a Western concept. In *Census, Map and Museum*, Benedict Anderson points out that the immediate genealogy of museums can be traced to the imaginings of the colonial state. Together with censuses and maps, the museum shaped the way in which the colonial state imagined its dominion (Anderson 1991, 163). This means that museums are political. Anderson states that, up until the early nineteenth century, the colonial rulers had very little interest in the antique monuments and cultural heritage of the people. Nevertheless, as we have seen, it was Dutch colonial rule that led to the first museum in Suriname. Anderson points out that post-independence states inherited a form of "political museumizing" (183). In spite of this heritage, the museum is often one of the few remaining neutral public spaces where people can discuss, learn about and reflect on life (CLMG 2006, 2). This is very important for governments to understand: an appreciation of the role of museums in promoting cultural understanding and responsible citizenship should lead to much greater financial support for these institutions. A recent description of museum goals makes it clear: "Since museums are all about collecting artifacts and stories about cultures, discussing them with the public and generating debate, learning enjoyment and understanding from them, they represent exactly the processes and skills people need to explore the similarities and differences of identity in modern society, and nurture the roots of citizenship and cohesion" (4).

Networks outside the Museum

The Department of Education tries as much as possible to connect with the national curriculum developed by the Ministry of Education and Community

Development. On a semiregular basis, it consults with the curriculum development department. This has resulted in the inclusion of several museum science topics and displays, the discussion of museum visits and collections, as well as the applications of archaeology being incorporated in school textbooks (Ministerie van Onderwijs en Volksontwikkeling 2004). Historical figures like Quassi or Ernst Jan Matzeliger get attention in both the textbooks and the museum displays. The history department of the Teachers' Training College also participates from time to time in discussions on education. During holidays special groups, such as orphanages or vacation schools, can visit. The museum also tries to reach special groups like elderly people by providing them with entrance tickets at reduced rates. At an international level, the museum keeps good contact with several museums, especially in the Netherlands. These museums contribute by supporting several departments in expanding their activities. A number of students from Dutch universities and the Reinwardt Academy, the largest school in museum sciences in western Europe, have fulfilled their internship at the Suriname Museum. They have brought with them fresh ideas on displaying and creating educational materials. Because of lack of finances, members of the museum staff do not have many opportunities to attend conferences or training sessions; however, the existing international links, although small and limited, contribute to the advancement of education in the Suriname Museum.

Marketing

In general, the fort is well known to the public. Tourists find descriptions of the museum venue and exhibitions in travel books on Suriname and tourist guides. Many tour operators include a visit to the museum in their city tour. Anderson points out that monumental archaeology linked to tourism allows the state to appear as the guardians of a generalized but also local tradition. This is illustrated by the fact that the reconstructed monuments often have smartly laid out lawns around them and explanatory tablets with dating (Anderson 1991, 181). Fort Zeelandia is a good example of an old monumental building with historic features like dates and plaques on the buildings. Because of such features, it is not surprising that many museums in the Caribbean are housed in historical monuments. The building in itself is an advertisement for the museum.

When a new exhibition is opened, a number of journalists from national newspapers, radio and television are invited to attend. This means free publicity in the local media. In addition, it is necessary to keep the public informed and interested. So invitations are sent out to schools when teachers' conferences are organized. Every other week the biggest local newspaper publishes "Museumstof", a one-page article on an object or an activity connected to the Suriname Museum. People can react to these articles, so the museum gets feedback from the public.

The goal of marketing is to attract as many visitors to the museum as possible. Because of the increase in the number of tourists coming to Suriname, the museum is also receiving an increased number of visitors. Among these are tourists travelling on cruise ships. It is clear to the local tour operators that the museum is representative enough to give short-term visitors a good impression of Suriname. Anderson uses the term *logoization* to explain how monuments, besides flora and fauna, are depicted on postcards and in schoolroom textbooks (Anderson 1991, 182). Nowadays, a lot of objects are decorated with monumental representations. They include buttons, postcards, drinking mugs, T-shirts, calendars and even telephone cards. The museum shop sells a number of these articles as souvenirs as well as for purposes of advertising.

Local guests, however, need more encouragement. To some extent, the school population is covered by our educational programme. Meanwhile, adults might be stimulated to visit the museum through television programmes and radio talks or by the enthusiastic reports of their own children. When school pupils see an exhibition and tell stories at home, this might encourage their parents to visit as well.

EVALUATION

Before starting an exhibition, it is necessary to do some audience research to be able to evaluate the likely impact of the exhibition not just on regular visitors but especially on visiting youth. As an example, an exhibition entitled *Nursing* was developed in the Netherlands as a result of research and a book on the experiences of Surinamese nurses who left to work in Holland in the 1950s and 1960s. This display was offered to the Suriname Museum Foundation. The Department of Education considered it insufficiently targeted to attract a school public, so a programme was developed to teach the children the history of nursing in Suriname before 1950, visualized with texts, objects and old photographs. This introduction to the exhibit was housed on the ground floor. The second floor had the exhibition from Holland. On the top floor of the building, a display was mounted on the local hospitals, the medical services in the interior parts of the country and on information about the nurses training institutions in Suriname. This made an exhibition from abroad interesting for our main target group.

As is common in Caribbean countries, small children (age group 4–8) were not in the habit of making field trips to the Suriname Museum (Bilodeau 2005, 28). But in trying to provide museum education to as many age groups as possible, we should also look into the needs of small children. In the case of *Nursing*, a special activity was designed for this group. A large number (781) of small children were invited to dress up as doctors and nurses for their visit to the exhibition and were given a story-related picture for colouring.

The age group between ten and fourteen years (primary grades 4–6) is the one that visits the museum most regularly, because the teacher can easily include a fieldtrip in the curriculum. With secondary schools it is much more difficult to plan visits, because these surpass the regular school scheme and several teachers have to be involved. These may be some of the logistical problems mentioned in the survey conducted by the Commonwealth Association of Museums that account for the small number of secondary school children who visit the museum (Bilodeau 2005, 28). Displays on subjects specifically taught in school programmes are most likely to be visited by schools: for example, national history, slavery, emancipation. Some topics can be interesting to a large range of age groups, but the means by which each group is approached may vary. In 2003 and 2006, when no special school programme was offered, the number of visitors fell significantly. In 2003 this was due to the fact that the educational officer was abroad for studies. In 2006 it was not possible to effectuate a school programme for external reasons. Nevertheless, it can be concluded that, because of the visiting habits resulting from previous programmes, the number of children has risen from 750 visiting in 2000 to 1,249 in 2003 and 2,594 in 2006.

In 2005 the Commonwealth Association of Museums conducted a survey on children in museums in the Caribbean (Bilodeau 2005). The resulting report gives a review of basics in museum education to help identify the ideal situation. It also gives an assessment of the current situation in museum education. From this survey it can be concluded that the Suriname Museum comes sixth out of twenty-one institutions assessed for their educational programme and number of visiting children. Considering the fact that a structured yearly programme has only been developed in recent years, this is a good result and shows that the scope of people reached by the Suriname Museum is widening.

Modes of Education

Schools and museums have evolved throughout their history in interconnected ways. Since the period of the Enlightenment in Europe, the need for improvement in living conditions and in opportunities for education has been acknowledged increasingly. With growing government interest in and responsibility for education came a growing recognition that museums could provide a means of popular education. Nowadays there is a growing sense within postcolonial states of the importance of museums in providing active learning opportunities and promoting nation building (Cummins 2004). Learning is a trajectory in which knowledge is created by the processing of experiences. This is a most important concept in education. As a result, we can all conclude that textbooks are not sufficient to transfer knowledge about history to the pupils in schools. There are different styles of learning: abstract conceptualization, concrete experience, active experimenting and reflective observation. This is theorized by David A. Kolb (1984, 15), who promotes the theory of experiential learning: "with the recognition that learning and development are lifelong processes, there comes a corresponding responsibility for social institutions and organizations to conduct their affairs in such a way that adults have experiences that facilitate their personal learning and development". And of course, this is not just the case for adults but also for children and teens. Learning is most satisfactory when understanding is physically and perceptually supported by material experiences (Russell 1994). Children do not need just to learn the facts; they also need to learn to think. They have to be the centre of the activity.

The Department of Education of the Suriname Museum Foundation has developed a paved route to be followed accompanying every major exhibition. First, with every new display, the department gathers information on the topic of the exhibition and identifies the target group for visiting. Once the educational materials have been developed, teachers are invited to the museum for training. They are informed about the programme and provided with educational materials. In 2000 the Department of Education developed a folder with loose leaves, so material might be added with each new exhibition. Normally, when teachers are invited to the museum for the workshop, two days are spent on primary schools and one on the middle and higher levels. The latter group includes teachers in social sciences, humanities and Dutch language. The language teachers are invited because many times the programme can be enriched by adding literature to the subject: oral history, storytelling, novels or poetry. The number of participating teachers at these gatherings is growing. This shows a certain thirst for information and new ideas in addition to the regular school curriculum. At the first teachers' conference in 2000, 125 participated. This number has grown to almost 200 in 2007. Since this concept has been evaluated and proven successful, the Department of Education at the museum plans to continue to organize teacher training conferences.

Depending on the nature of the exhibition and the age group, the museum's Department of Education supplies several types of support: direct teaching services include guided tours, provision of special guides or use of booklets or pamphlets with information and questions. Museum visitors are encouraged to use their skills of observation, reason and imagination to explain what they see, and they are encouraged to contextualize their answers (Salter 1998).

In an educational programme, several modes of learning can be incorporated to give meaning or imagery to a person in relation to the display:

- presenting background information from different sources in different audio-visual ways (texts, sound, movies)
- presenting oral history, fiction in stories or poetry to enhance the personal experience
- inviting the visitor to brainstorm, fantasize or reflect
- stimulating the visitor to internally evaluate the information and be encouraged to do more research
- enabling the visitor to associative interconnections
- stimulating all the senses, creating an atmosphere and feeling, and being aesthetic in colour and texture (Bilodeau 2005, 28)

In choosing the subject of the exhibition, the Department of Education depends on the overall policies directed by the museum board. At times, the Museum Foundation receives a request to host an exhibition previously mounted elsewhere – for instance in the Netherlands. Mostly this concerns Suriname-related subjects, as with the exhibit *The Heritage of Slavery* (2007). Sometimes, the subject is less obviously connected to Suriname, like the exhibition on Anne Frank

(2002). Additionally, the Department of Education creates a local division so the subject speaks to the Suriname guests and schoolchildren. In the case of Anne Frank, how were the Jewish people related to Suriname, in the far past, but also during World War II? The country became very important to the US aircraft industry because of its huge amounts of high-grade bauxite. If no exhibit is available from abroad, or is suitable for schools, the museum creates an exhibition in house, for example, the exhibitions *Telecommunications* in 2000 or *Susanna du Plessis, a Cruel Slave Mistress* (2003; this latter was comparable to an exhibit mounted in Jamaica on Annie Palmer from Montego Bay).

The museum is located in the capital of Suriname, Paramaribo. This means that most schools can reach the museum by bus, since the majority of the Suriname population lives in the coastal area. Still, the costs of transport are by far the biggest barrier to school visits. To accommodate schools, the museum has decided to charge only half the usual children's ticket price for students. Still, distance means there is no equal opportunity for visiting the museum. A number of Amerindians (the indigenous people) and Maroons (descendants of runaway slaves) live in villages scattered deep in the interior. The schools from the interior all provide primary education, but most can only reach the capital by boat and bus. The journey is very costly, and as a result few schools from the interior make field trips to the capital. To reach out to these children, we provide travelling exhibitions from time to time. According to Appiah, museums have an obligation to make collections more widely available, not just in the metropolis but elsewhere through travelling displays, publications and the World Wide Web (Appiah 2006, 130). A small version of the Anne Frank exhibition was made, and this travelled up the Suriname River and was exhibited in several larger towns for schoolchildren to visit. Creating opportunities for all children will improve education. The museum can have its role in these developments.

A Case Study: The Heritage of Slavery

The World Museum in Rotterdam designed and built the exhibition *The Heritage of Slavery* in 2003, constructed from and based on the ideas of Felix de Rooy. A multimedia artist and filmmaker, he was born in Curaçao (the Netherlands Antilles) of Surinamese parents. His biggest wish was for this exhibition to be shown in Curaçao and Suriname, to close the triangle created during colonial times. The display travelled first to Curaçao, then to Suriname, where the exhibition was opened on 20 February 2007. The opening was conducted by Minister of Interior Affairs Michel Felisi. This was a very rare event, because he gave his speech in his mother tongue, Aukaans, and his audience consisted of guests from abroad and local people who speak Dutch and Sranan, but no Aukaans. Felisi, as a descendant of Maroons, talked about slavery and feelings of sorrow and guilt. Even though we did not understand him literally, his message was clear; we have to unite and make sure slavery does not happen again in Suriname.

The Department of Education organized in-service training days for teachers to accompany the exhibition, on 6–7 March for primary schools and on 8 March for secondary schools. The teachers received information on the exhibition and working materials to prepare their classes for a visit to the museum. They also had an opportunity to discuss the subject with De Rooy. *The Heritage of Slavery* is an exhibition on slavery, the abolition and the lasting effects of that institution on people in the present. This exhibition is housed at the annex of the Suriname Museum, with a large area well equipped for receiving schools; already many schools have visited it.

During holidays, teachers from the densely forested interior have an opportunity to visit the capital. The Department of Education took the opportunity to invite them to the museum and to instruct them on the exhibition over Easter vacation in April 2007. Out of seventy schools in the interior, thirty were represented at the teachers' training conference. This was the first time the museum had organized an event especially for teachers from the interior, but the enthusiasm compelled us to make it a yearly event. The teachers received a DVD with a number of movies to be shown to the school students in the villages. (Mostly it is the chief captain or head teacher who owns the equipment, powered by generator, to show these movies.) In addition, the schools received instructions and questionnaires on the movies for the children to fill out. Even though this is not the same as a visit to the exhibition, these children get some exposure to the exhibition and a chance to learn about their heritage by this means. Unfortunately, because of the financial and technical barriers, distance learning via personal computers is, in Suriname, not yet an option to get education to the schools in scarcely populated areas that are difficult to reach. We expect this will improve in the future, with better availability of solar power and telecom technology in rural areas.

To be able to provide the best service possible, the Department of Education has designed an evaluation form that is presented to the visiting schools. Most teachers and children react very positively to the programmes designed, but a structured response to the questions evaluating the visits can lead to better services. This evaluation has been introduced only recently, so just the figures for 2007 on the exhibition *The Heritage of Slavery* are available. The schools started visiting from 9 March, and we counted up till 6 April, the start of the Easter break. In all, 1,345 children visited and twenty-two forms were filled out. The results are presented here:

- Two teachers learned about the exhibition by "Museumstof", two by radio, two by television, four by newspaper and nine by invitations to teachers in service.
- Eight attended the teachers' in-service training, while eleven did not receive the invitation.
- Eighteen were able to use the information before coming to the museum. (These figures may differ from the previous question because not all teachers attended the in-service programme; we invited one from every school.)
- Fifteen people were satisfied with the content of the information provided to prepare the class visit. Five were not, because they did not have it available.
- Seventeen out of twenty-two schools came to the museum by bus.
- Eighteen teachers were well satisfied with the reception at the museum. The others wanted a complete guided tour instead of worksheets for the children to fill out.
- Thirteen schools were very satisfied with the level of the worksheet, three schools thought it too easy, and three too difficult.

Overall, most of the pupils and teachers were tremendously satisfied with the exhibition.

Only one responded negatively. Nineteen out of twenty-two teachers said they would spend time to evaluate the visit and have more lessons on the subject after returning to the classroom.

Regular commentary stated that half of the visiting teachers would like a guided tour. Not surprisingly, this is very much in line with the results of Bilodeau's report on museum education in the Caribbean (Bilodeau 2005).

The Future

Museums in the Caribbean are in a difficult position. Because of colonial history, the museums are set up as collections of things past. Layout, objectives, presentation of collections and policy were bound to change over time, because of independence and nationalistic interpretations. Change depends on a number of factors, ideological and financial. However, Suriname education evolves rather slowly. For museum education this is not different. A number of plans have been designed for the future. Implementation, of course, depends on the importance the museum is given in the process of nation building and cultural education by the Ministry of Education. Additionally, the way people experience history and objects has changed. Exhibitions should ideally be projects in which content, expertise and transfer of knowledge are combined (De Vries 2004). It would be ideal if cultural field trips were incorporated yearly in the official school curriculum. More teachers should be involved in the development of school programmes for the museum. With the increase in accessibility to personal computers, more background information can be provided through exhibitions and lessons on the Internet.

The Suriname Museum is planning to build an exhibition in house that permanently shows the history of Suriname and its inhabitants from prehistoric times onward. At the end of 2005 such a display was partly implemented for the groups of Amerindians: *Suriname before Columbus*. The history of the fortress itself can also be visualized. At the moment a room in the fort is being prepared for showing original books, engravings, watercolours and dioramas. All these planned exhibitions will be accompanied by educational materials for schoolchildren at several levels to grasp their history in a concrete manner. By evaluating visits (from forms filled out by teachers or the guest book by visitors, local and from abroad), the museum can strive for a more visitor-oriented approach to display its collection in order to be a tribute to Suriname history and its cultures and people.

Conclusion

The department of education in a museum often serves as a kind of "marketing" department. In an ideal world, such a department would not be necessary. Everyone should have a sense of self-learning and basic knowledge in looking at and appreciating objects of cultural, historic or aesthetic value. However, this would require a certain "grammar" of art, by which children are taught the arts in the same way as they are taught a language (Holman 1980, 25). Of course this would need a well-developed and extensive overall national school programme in arts and culture, in which children from an early age can drink in their heritage in a natural way.

In looking for ties to your identity, you first need to learn your own history. Knowledge derives mostly from education. We all have our own history as a group, but as inhabitants of Suriname we also have a national identity. What glues us together as a people? We need to present in a clear way our common values and morals. However, a museum is not the place to spread nationalism: it is a forum to search for facts and knowledge. One has to accept that the spiritual base of our society is diverse, including such things as religion and ethnic background. It is not the sole objective of a museum to provide a theoretical and historical framework but also arguably to strive to develop social cohesion. A museum has to be a place of research and preservation but also of presenting the past in an interactive way. The population's gaps in historical knowledge may lead to misunderstandings. Knowing one's history can help to smooth out current tensions and help to achieve mutual understanding. The museum can be a starting point to create a cultural discourse between the different inhabitants of a country and the rest of the world. It can transfer ideas into concrete displays and promote interdisciplinary cooperation. The department of education has to try to reach as many people as possible, through the evaluation of the audience and reactions to the exhibitions. By working on its network and applying the best marketing strategies, these goals can be met. By creating an optimal learning environment, the museum will have satisfied visitors, young and old.

People are the creators of the future but also the product of history. Appiah states that the treasures of the world are made by people like him, through the exercise of skills and imagination. Appiah is a writer and philosopher, not a creator of treasures. But all people, including children, have the potential to be artists. If they learn and accept this notion, they will certainly be more appreciative of the world's heritage stored and displayed in museums.

Acknowledgements

I am grateful to Dr Laddy van Putten, director of the Suriname Museum Foundation, and Dr Jerome Egger, chair of the Department of History at the Teachers Training Institute (IOL), for constructive criticism and additional remarks to improve this text.

References

Anderson, Benedict. 1991. *Imagined Communities: Reflections on the Origin and Spread of Nationalism*. London: Verso.

Appiah, Kwame Anthony. 2006. *Cosmopolitanism: Ethics in a World of Strangers*. New York: W.W. Norton.

Archeologische Dienst. 1988. *Tussen leren en vormen: Evaluatie van het scholenbezoek aan de expositie "Suriname in de archeologie"*. Paramaribo, Suriname: Ministerie van Onderwijs, Wetenschappen en Cultuur.

Bettenhausen, Marije. 2006. "Sabi yu rutu" Ken je verleden. Internship report, Suriname Museum, Paramaribo.

Bilodeau, N. 2005. "Children in the Caribbean Museums Project: Report of Studies Conducted". Commonwealth Association of Museums and Barbados Museum Historical Society, Bridgetown, Barbados.

Campaign for Learning through Museums and Galleries (CLMG). 2006. "Culture Shock: Tolerance, Respect, Understanding . . . and Museums". http://partnershipandparticipation.files.wordpress.com/2011/10/c s-main.pdf

Cummins, Alissandra. 2004. "Caribbean Museums and National Identity". *History Workshop Journal* 58: 224–45.

Donawa, Wendy. 1993. "From Digs to Dolls: The Pedagogical Design of the Barbados Museum's Children's Gallery". *Journal of the Barbados Museum and Historical Society* 41: 59–73.

Ganzeboom, H., and F. Haanstra. 1989. *Museum en publiek*. Rijswijk, Netherlands: Directoraat-Generaal Culturele Zaken.

Holman, Bert. 1980. *Opvattingen over het educatieve werk van musea*. Amsterdam: Kohnstamm Instituut.

Hooper-Greenhill, Eilean. 1991. *Writing a Museum Education Policy*. Leicester: University of Leicester Press.

Kolb, D.A. 1984. Experiential Learning: Experience as the Source of Learning and Development. Englewood Cliffs, NJ: Prentice-Hall.

Ministerie van Onderwijs en Volksontwikkeling, Curriculumontwikkeling. 2004. "Wij en ons verleden: De geschiedenis van ons volk voor de vierde klas van het basisonderwijs".

Ministerie van Onderwijs en Volksontwikkeling, Directoraat Cultuur. 2007. "Intergraal cultuurbeleid".

Mitrasingh, Benjamin. 2005. "Een initiatief voor een Museumkrant". *De Ware Tijdi* (Suriname). 21 June.

Mitrasingh, Benjamin, and C. Badal. 2002. *Een nationaal onderzoek voor een cultuurbeleid in Suriname*. Paramaribo, Suriname: UNESCO Project 00 SUR 602.

Putten, Laddy van, and L. Ferrier. 1999. "50 Years Stichting Surinaams Museum (Suriname Museum Foundation) 1947–29 April 1997". *Archiv für Völkerkunde* 50. http://www.surinaamsmuseum.net.

Russell, Terry. 1994. "The Enquiring Visitor: Usable Learning Theory for Museum Contexts". *Journal of Education in Museums* 15. http://www.gem.org.uk/resources/russell.html.

Salter, Pauline. 1998. "Evaluating Children's Learning Experiences". *GEM News* 69. http://www.gem.org.uk/pubs/news/salter1998.html

Sectie Geschiedenis Hogeschool Interstudie. 1988. "Eindrapport educatie en cultuur". Nijmegen.

Stedman, John G. 1796. *Narrative of a Five Year Expedition against the Revolted Negroes of Suriname*. London.

Van Wengen, G. 1992. "Educatie in de museale sector". In *Handboek management kunst en cultuur*, edited by J. Smiers and G. Hagoort, 3–38. Alphen aan de Rijn: Samson Stafleu.

Venetiaan, Ronald. 1990. Speech at the opening of the exhibition *Art from Our Own Collection*. In *Mededelingen van de Stichting Surinaams Museum* 45 (May): 9–10.

Vries Alex de. 2004. "Cultureel erfgoed is van iedereen en van niemand: Peter van Mensch in gesprek met Susan Legîne". In *Cultureel Goed! Underground Theory*, edited by Jan Brand and Alex de Vries, 47–62. Arnhem, Netherlands: Stichting InterArt.

10.

"CAN U ASSIST ME?"
Help Needed with Students' Use of Standard English

KELVIN QUINTYNE

> My name is ... and i have a real problem. I have seriously fallen behing in this class because I have not ben able to attend. i want to complete this course and from the look at the syllabus i am way behind. I collect all class notes but i need to know what i must do in terms of assignments to catch up. Can u assist me?

I RECEIVED THIS E-MAIL IN October 2006 from a student I have yet to meet, who erroneously thought that he was registered officially for one of my classes. The language used here is referred to by many names, among them *e-English* or *Cyber-English* (Al-Sa'di and Hamdan 2005), *Netspeak, Textspeak* (Crystal 2003), *txt* or *Internet English* (Carrington 2005), and is acknowledged as a non-standard written dialect of English rather than merely slang. Through this dialect's greater flexibility in grammar and orthography, users of computer-mediated communication (CMC) technology have found the freedom to express themselves and communicate in writing in ways which do not conform to the conventions of standard written English. This rhetorical licence, or in David Crystal's words, "language play" (2003, xvi), empowers users to be more creative in how they express themselves and communicate with others in certain informal contexts, regardless of the writers' age, sex, race, nationality or even proficiency in the use of Standard English.

While I believe that its inherent freedoms should be celebrated through use in informal contexts, I was disturbed by the use of e-English in this case because the writer was presenting himself to me for the first time: this e-mail could be considered essentially a form of business correspondence, for which a more formal version of English would have been appropriate. Most of my students do not use e-English in their assignments or to communicate with me electronically, especially intentionally, but the minority who do is large enough for me to consider it a problem to be taken seriously.

The Foundation Language Programme at the University of the West Indies

Dennis R. Craig notes that the "Use of English" programmes at the University of the West Indies and the University of Guyana, which have been offered at these institutions for many years and which address students' problems with using Standard English, came out of a realization that various non-standard English dialects, English-based Creoles and in some cases even French-based Creoles, were affecting students' proficiency in writing Standard English (1997). These problems were evident despite the fact that Standard English had been the language of instruction used with these students throughout their academic careers. The current situation is that the University of the West Indies requires undergraduate students in every faculty, on every campus and at every non-campus centre, to take compulsory foundation courses in English language (formerly the "Use of English" courses). The Foundation Language Programme within the university offers compulsory level 1 courses, each one designed to focus on a particular kind (or particular kinds) of writing for students in specific faculties. Students are advised to take these courses within their first year of enrolment so that they are better prepared for further academic writing at higher levels and even writing for the world of work.

Such courses are important in teaching students the appropriate use of English and can and should highlight the boundaries within which the freedoms afforded within e-English should operate. However, formal instruction alone is insufficient to get students to apply the knowledge and skills they should be acquiring to their daily lives. A culture that supports what is taught in such courses is necessary if lasting improvements in students' use of Standard English are to be made. Although universities and other tertiary-level institutions have limited influence over the culture of the wider community, I argue in this chapter that they can develop a culture within their walls in which Standard English is required and enforced for formal written communication – even for non-English courses – and for carrying on other business outside the classroom. In such a culture, students are likely to work harder to improve their mastery of English and to pay greater attention to the occasion, audience and their purpose for writing. However, if students' use of e-English in inappropriate contexts is to be addressed, the features of this dialect and the context out of which it developed must be understood, in order to differentiate it from what might often be considered as nothing more than poor spelling and use of grammar.

THE STRUCTURE OF E-ENGLISH

Rami Al-Sa'di and Jihad Hamdan (2005, 416–17) list the following as common truncation methods used in e-English (I have inserted some relevant examples seen in my students' e-mail and text messages):

- replacing a word or a syllable within a polysyllabic word with a homophonous letter or number (*neway* for *anyway*, *2day* for *today*);
- omitting all or most of the vowels in a word if the remaining consonants still render the word recognizable (*txt* for *text*);
- omitting vowels and consonants in a word if the remaining vowels and consonants still render the word recognizable (*crckt* for *cricket*, *bsktbll* for *basketball*);
- replacing a word with a single letter (*u* for *you*);
- dropping the *g* in *-ing* constructions (*gettin* for *getting*);
- replacing the word with its shorter colloquial or slang form (*dint* for *didn't*);
- spelling a word phonetically (*wudve* for *would've*, *cud* for *could*).

In addition to these truncation techniques, there are other orthographic differences between e-English and standard written English. Al-Sa'di and Hamdan (2005) point out that capitalization of proper names and at the beginning of sentences is rare, although sometimes whole sentences may be capitalized for emphasis, to show emotion (particularly anger) to denote shouting or some other reason. This e-mail sent to one of my colleagues in 2007 is a good example of e-English, containing many of the features just described:

> Hi, this is . . . a student in your rhetoric foundation course. Im just wondering if you have any copies of the mechanism example sheet with the blood capillary thing. If you do, cud u email me a copy plz? thnx, if not, no problem.

Two words use a combination of truncation methods in this e-mail: *plz* and *thnx* omit the vowels and use phonetic spelling for the consonant endings.

Another common feature of e-English is the lack of punctuation. In the previous example only one apostrophe is missing (*Im* instead of *I'm*), but the rest of the e-mail contains standard punctuation. Here is an example of one that uses minimal punctuation:

> hi mr. quintyne dont mean to be a bother however i would like to know if when i am doing the assignment i can write some of the uses of the cricket bat which would include various cricket shots please respond as soon as possible thank you.

Although most of the punctuation is missing, this e-mail is still easy to read. Sometimes little or no punctuation can make reading more difficult, especially when reading long passages, but even so, with a bit of rereading, the meaning is usually clear, provided the grammatical structure is similar to that of Standard English, as is the case with this example. However, meaning can be obscured if the grammatical structures are similar to non-standard spoken dialects or Creoles and the audience is unfamiliar with it, or if the writer's basic grammar is poor.

Causes and Effects of e-English Usage

Having looked at the features of e-English, this section will consider why students are using this dialect even for formal correspondence. Naomi S. Baron believes that e-English, when used by teenagers, helps to construct a sense of identity in the same way that slang does when used in conversation (2005, 30). Since many young university students use this dialect when corresponding with older people, who mostly never, the reason for its use is unlikely to be the same as that for its use by US teenagers. Roughly half of my students who admitted to using e-English claimed to find it more convenient to write texts to people that way because their cellular phones lacked a qwerty keyboard. However, it would be erroneous to assume that "txting" by Caribbean university students using e-English is simply a matter of convenience in light of the technology used. These students most likely sent the correspondence cited above using a computer rather than a cellular phone, which would have improved the efficiency in typing a message in Standard English had they chosen to do so. It is far more likely that the usage of e-English for such correspondence reflects the writers' failure to recognize that both formal and informal contexts exist within computer-mediated communication, necessitating the use of different varieties of written English to suit the situation.

It must also be noted that the use of e-English does not automatically mean that the register is casual. Like the first e-mail presented in this paper, I received an e-mail from another student in 2008 whom I have never met face to face, in which the register is formal although e-English was used:

> Good afternoon Mr. Quintyne
> i have been trying to access this online test since thursday 14, november but up to now i have not been able to do so.
> i would appreciate your kind response to this important matter.
> Regards.

The lack of capitalization within the body of the e-mail is obviously intentional since capitalization is used in the salutation and the complimentary close. The use of e-English in such cases demonstrates ignorance, not only of the full range of levels of formality in CMC as with any other medium of communication, but, more fundamentally, of the link between form and content in the generation of meaning. It highlights that university students still need to be taught that the language itself is normally interpreted, consciously or unconsciously, as part of the overall message, and that this is so for communication in any medium. The writer's language is interpreted as a sign of his or her attitude towards the occasion and the audience, which then influences the audience's attitude towards the writer and his or her intentions.

Still, some instructors do prefer to have a considerable degree of informality with their students and might not object to students using e-English to communicate with them outside the classroom. For such instructors an e-mail such as the following would not seem out of place:

> hey ms. . . . i finished my intro n added another point to my outline and I would like to hear ur comments. The intro is under the outline.

However, for the colleague who received this e-mail, both the dialect and the tone *did* seem out of place, because the student had wrongly assumed that this form of the communication allowed a high degree of familiarity.

So far, I am unaware of any cases in which students use e-English for peer critiques of each other's work within the foundation language courses, whether done within class time or not. However, if instructors encourage students to be informal when corresponding outside of class, I would argue that consideration should be given to allowing students to use e-English only insofar as it supports the notion that CMC is by nature informal to some degree. If students carry this habit of inappropriate informality into the world of work, it may cause embarrassment for them and for the institutions from which they graduate. For many students educational institutions are the only places where they have opportunities to write formal correspondence before entering the workforce. This is why I believe that it is necessary to create a culture both inside and outside of the classroom that encourages students to use Standard English correctly.

Although I have detected occasional use of e-English in assignments, the most common instances involving writing *u* for *you*, these cases are normally evidence of a lack of proofreading rather than the student's lack of awareness that such language is inappropriate. I have seen only one instance in which a group of students used e-English intentionally and effectively for a coursework assignment. In a course dealing with technical, scientific and business writing, a group of my students submitted a report recommending that the Cave Hill Guild of Students host a free concert called "Free Ur Mind": they argued that such language would be more appealing to the younger students who would likely make up the majority of patrons.

As suggested earlier, regular use of e-English has affected students' approach to formal writing in the classroom. Because e-English is often used in forums like instant messaging and chat rooms that simulate oral conversation in their immediacy of response from a normally familiar audience, many students are resistant to using a structured writing process even for take-home coursework (Al-Sa'di and Hamdan 2005, 410). Also contributing to their approach is the habit of multitasking while instant messaging, chatting online or sending e-mail, which means that the writer's attention is often split. This is why introducing students, especially new ones, to a formal, structured writing process involving planning, drafting and revising, as done within the Foundation English Language Writing Programme at the University of the West Indies, is so important: it forces students to manage their time in order to acquire good writing habits for formal situations involving careful use of language for a more critical audience.

Peter Roberts explains that "learning to read involves acquiring patience to concentrate, the habit of actively looking for hidden meanings and retracing one's steps to find anything missed in the first attempt" (Roberts 1998, 179). These qualities are also important in learning to write, since critical reading is the cornerstone of effective writing, particularly in formal academic and business contexts. Approaches to information gathering and other aspects of prewriting aside, many students are weak in critiquing their own and others' work during the revision stage because they lack critical reading skills. Many students' assessments of the work of others are either unhelpful or misleading. Of course it is unreasonable to suggest that continued participation in CMC forums is solely to blame for this, but if informal CMC is fast becoming students' most regular writing experience, it would be a mistake not to consider this as a contributing factor.

In addition, most students are unaccustomed to drafting and revising their work in a structured way, and in the beginning some believe it to be impractical. Such exercises are an important, compulsory part of our foundation writing courses at the University of the West Indies, and, normally, by the end of the course most students realise the benefits of these stages of the writing process in improving their writing skills, particularly since these stages require, in part, critical analysis of the effectiveness of their communication skills. This is not to say that these stages are performed well by everyone, only that their perceptions of their value are usually changed.

Conclusion

As a relatively new dialect in its own right, e-English deserves attention and critical analysis as much as the various other dialects and Creoles that play important roles in the lives of Caribbean students and the wider Caribbean community. It allows for a particular kind of informality and for poetic licence in prose writing. However, it must be used judiciously. Since many Caribbean students exhibit incompetence in deciphering which language variety is appropriate for different types of formal written communication in spite of years of primary and secondary instruction, it is important that every effort be made at tertiary level, particularly at university level, to correct this. Much is already being done within the available writing courses, but writing instructors need help from other members of academic staff and even administrative staff with whom students correspond in developing a culture which fosters the use of Standard English for formal situations.

References

Al-Sa'di, Rami A., and Jihad M. Hamdan. 2005. "'Synchronous Online Chat' English: Computer Mediated Communication". *World Englishes* 24 (4): 409–24.

Baron, Naomi S. 2005. "Instant Messaging and the Future of Language". *Communications of the ACM* 48 (7): 29–31.

Carrington, Victoria. 2005. "Txting: The End of Civilization (Again)". *Cambridge Journal of Education* 35 (2): 161–75.

Craig, Dennis R. 1997. "The English of West Indian University Students". In *Englishes around the World*, vol. 2, edited by Edgar W. Schneider, 11–24. Amsterdam: John Benjamins.

Crystal, David. 2003. "The Joy of Text". *New Statesman* 16 (774): xvi–xvii.

Roberts, Peter. 1998. *West Indians and Their Language*. Cambridge: Cambridge University Press.

11.

LANGUAGE, IDENTITY AND FREEDOM
A Creole Perspective

HAZEL SIMMONS-McDONALD

IT MAY SEEM MORE difficult to argue a case for a relationship between language and freedom than for language and identity, because the latter concepts have been associated in philosophical discussions about the self and because identity and language play a role in defining the self. Discussions about freedom usually focus on issues such as freedom of thought, freedom of the press, freedom of religion and so on, but one rarely encounters essays about freedom and language. However, careful thought would lead us to understand that language must have played an important role in the lives of slaves on plantations, in circumscribing notions of personal and collective freedom, even as it does in certain contexts in modern times – though perhaps to a lesser extent – in shaping the destinies of speakers of Creole language varieties.

The Creole perspective embraces more than just the language varieties so designated. It circumscribes notions of self and identity, of what Ernest Pépin and Rafaël Confiant refer to as the "heterogeneous reality" of the Caribbean experience (1998, 98). Using the term *Créolité*, which corresponds to the English term *creolization*, and focusing on the literary dimension of this process, they envision the states of Créolité as a process "to re-vision language, narrative aesthetics, orchestration of events and places from a plural conception of identity". They propose that from these, "paths traced by the ingenious and subtle architecture born out of the Creole spirit are reasserted" (99). This chapter is concerned not so much with the aspect of Créolité or creolization; rather, it will briefly explore some of the issues related to this concept in relation to identity, before focusing more specifically on issues related to Creole language, particularly with French Creole in the St Lucian context. It argues that within this context the power and domination that were manifested in the colonial experience – and which were maintained by successive neocolonial regimes – served through restriction of the domains of use of French Creole to exert influence over its functions and determined its status relative to other languages in that sociolinguistic space, thereby limiting the freedoms of the speakers of the language.

French Creole (Kwéyòl): Its Origin and Status

Most are well aware that the existence of Creoles is not limited to the Caribbean. They exist in other parts of the world, particularly those with a shared history of slavery and colonization (Condé 1998, 101). The varieties of Creole depend on the languages that were spoken by the groups who came into contact through slavery or colonization, so that we can speak, for example, of English-lexicon Creoles, French-lexicon Creoles and others. There is a high degree of mutual intelligibility among the French Creole varieties that are spoken in the Caribbean and which are collectively referred to as the Antillean variety of French Creoles. These varieties developed out of contact between the colonizing group and the African slaves who were brought to work on the plantations. Robert Le Page and Andrée Tabouret-Keller refer to Kwéyòl – the name given to the variety spoken in St Lucia – as "a black creole Patois brought mainly from Martinique, to a less extent from St Vincent, Grenada and Guadeloupe or taking shape locally on St Lucian plantations" (1985, 59).

This patois, Kwéyòl, was the vernacular used in many "conservative, remote, small mountain settlements" (Le Page and Tabouret-Keller 1985, 59). Although the island changed hands no fewer than fourteen times from the early 1600s until it was finally ceded to the British in 1803, the French had occupied the island for a sufficiently long period to have influenced language development patterns on the island. James Rawley (1981) reported that most of the slaves who were shipped to St Lucia in the eighteenth century had been shipped through Martinique from Senegal or Gambia or the Guinea ports (cited by Le Page and Tabouret-Keller 1985, 60–61).

Of particular importance in explaining the retention of Kwéyòl as a vernacular in St Lucian society long after the French ceded the island to the British is that a "population link" with Martinique persisted "long after the administrative link had been severed, as a source of maintained family connections and influences, as a source of both open and surreptitious immigration, and as an entrepôt for slaves and trade" (Le Page and Tabouret-Keller 1985, 61).

The latter connection no longer exists, and the other influences have lessened over time, but there are still connections between the islands through trade, tourism and also family connections. Scholars have mapped out factors that have favoured the retention of Creole and factors that dilute it within the society. Le Page and Tabouret-Keller, for example, claim that both Roman Catholicism and French Creole patois contributed to "a creole oral culture and a pantheon which could accommodate both African and French aspects [and which] united most people in the island to the exclusion of the urban, Anglican and Barbadian dominated administrators who had replaced their French opposite numbers for good by 1803" (ibid.). But a bilingual community was also developing through the administrative link with Barbados which was maintained and which was "a continuing factor in shaping the nature of the urban creole English of Castries which today serves as a model for rural dwellers who wish to identify with their urban fellow St. Lucians" (ibid.).

Under British governance, English was established as the official language and French Creole was prohibited particularly in schools, where children were sometimes punished for using it. Pierre Vérin reports that in the schools "Patois is forbidden, and several postulates are pumped into the scholar's head: 'Patois is not a language, Patois cannot be written, Patois has no grammar it is only broken French, to speak Patois displays inferiority' and so forth" (1958, 164). Mervyn Alleyne reports that the "creole is primarily the vehicle for expressing the more elemental and vulgar aspects of life. It is the language of abuse and insult; it is used to relate jokes, particularly smutty and obscene ones; to complain about the harshness of life" (1961, 8).

These negative perceptions about Kwéyòl and the ascription to it of labels such as "inferior" and "inadequate", as well as continued efforts to suppress it through its exclusion from official domains, relegated it to a subordinate status relative to English in St Lucian society. Alleyne notes the lack of logic in such attitudes to Kwéyòl: "The stigma that is attached to the French creole, as it is called in St. Lucia, is completely unjustified. What we have here is a deprecation by the colonizer which leads to the self-deprecation by the colonized, so that St. Lucians themselves look at their language with a great deal of contempt" (1976, 37).

Despite the efforts to suppress it, Kwéyòl has persisted, and though not as widely spoken as it once was and while having undergone change through continued contact with English, St Lucians now seek to promote its use to a wider range of domains through official recognition of a "French Creole culture and identity".

As Maryse Condé (1998) and scholars of Creole linguistics have pointed out, Creole emerged through contact between groups that spoke different languages. Condé says, "It was a means of communication to be understood by both masters and slaves." As such, "it can be seen as the first example of the Caribbean syncretic culture". She goes on to say, "When Creole became widespread in each island, at its outset, it was not perceived as a unique linguistic creation, but rather as a distortion, a perversion of the model of the European colonizer's language" (1998, 102).

It is this basic misconception that pidgins and Creoles were solely generated by slaves because of their inability to learn or use the colonizer's language that has distorted views of these languages and their speakers. Both groups, because of the exigencies of communicating in a situation in which the languages were not mutually intelligible, created linguistic forms that permitted dialogue. They were engaging in the kind of creativity that human beings have exhibited with respect to language and about which Chomsky writes extensively in his early works, for example, in *Aspects of the Theory of Syntax* (1965). The issue, then, is not one of inferiority of form of the Creole variety but rather the extent to which the political and sociological contexts permitted the development of that variety by allowing its speakers the freedom to explore its use in the very contexts of education that would have served as a catalyst for the intellectualization of the language.

Recent evidence will show that even limited extension of the domains of Kwéyòl by permitting it to be used in parliament, and particularly for the delivery of a significant portion of the governor's speech, has focused attention on its written form, on the more formal and complex structures and modes of expression that are not always or normally observed in oral communication. Further, the claims that it is not a language because it lacks a grammar have been dismissed through scholarly contributions, such as the comprehensive description of the grammar of and the creation of an orthography for Kwéyòl (Carrington 1984; Louisy and Turmel-John 1983). This has paved the way for standard representation of the language in writing and for the development of literacy in it.

The policy of excluding Kwéyòl from most domains except the private over the last century served to limit the referential adequacy of the language, which might otherwise have expanded normally in a context in which it could have been used for educational purposes. It is therefore not the inherent qualities of a language that necessarily dictate its capabilities; it is rather the political positioning, the relegation of status and the validation of one language versus another that results in the devaluation of one variety in relation to another, as in the case of Kwéyòl in St Lucia.

Keith Whinnom concedes, "Though languages obviously differ greatly in their referential adequacy, it can be argued that this is not an inherent inadequacy and that it can easily be repaired. It is certainly true that referential inadequacy can be repaired with astonishing speed" (1971, 108). He gives the example of Sr Francisco Bernís who "single-handed and at one fell swoop repaired the referential adequacy of Spanish with regard to bird names" (109). But Whinnom expresses reservations with regard to pidgins and Creoles. While he goes on to allow that a pidgin or a Creole or what he calls a "primitive language" (although he does not give a definition of the latter) can repair its referential inadequacy when this is required for the purpose of "naming objects" and while he also allows that a Creole can be used for "literature" because literature and "most especially lyric poetry can be produced in languages adequate for day-to-day intercourse", he suggests that they would be "quite inadequate for literary criticism (or linguistics)" (109). Confiant's novels in French Creole and Carolyn Cooper's (2003) rendering of a professorial lecture using Jamaican refute this claim. Extending his argument, Whinnom claims that one feature of Creoles that "appears to be seriously impaired by pidginization is the capacity for word-coinage from within the resources of the language". He specifically cites the generation of abstract terms by the combination of concrete words as an area in which he claims that pidgins and Creoles are deficient and concludes that "there may be some reason to suspect that the creole-speaker is handicapped by his language. . . . I feel that someone should venture the suggestion that modern linguists may have been dangerously sentimental about creole languages, which, with only a few notable exceptions, constitute in most communities a distinct handicap to the social mobility of the individual and may also constitute a handicap to the creole-speaker's personal intellectual development" (1971, 110). One would need to point out that if there have been "notable exceptions", that is, cases in which Creole languages have not been "a distinct handicap to the social mobility of the individual" nor to "the creole-speaker's personal intellectual development", then there must be factors other than those relating to the language itself that have led to such an outcome. I propose that it is contexts of domination and the exercise of power, typified, for example, by the colonial experience, that create a situation in which speakers become "handicapped". Typically in such contexts, one language is promoted while the other is restricted in terms of domains of use and function, and the restricted language is also denigrated. Exclusive speakers of the language accept these ascriptions to the language that they speak, extend them to their own persons and buy in to the prevailing belief that these attributes are true and valid. These beliefs result in the handicap that becomes manifested in a certain loss of freedom by denying speakers of the Creole access to the means of intellectualizing this language through the education system – the very context from which the language is excluded but in which it is most needed.

KWÉYÒLNESS AND ISSUES OF IDENTITY

The matter of language and identity in the St Lucian context is a particularly interesting if ambiguous one. St Lucians have been reported to be ambivalent about Kwéyòl. On the one hand, Alleyne (1976) commented on the "self-deprecation" by the colonizer which led St Lucians to view their language with "contempt". Yet, he noted further that, on the other hand, St Lucians "express great affection and a great deal of loyalty to the mass language. So that you have a great deal of ambivalence, which is again typical of colonized people: conflict between the imposed set of values from outside and a more native set of values" (Alleyne 1976, 37–38). Other studies on the attitudes of St Lucians towards their language, for example, Marcella Alexander (1993) and Dena Liebermann (1975), reported that although St Lucians admitted that Kwéyòl was "more expressive" than English in casual communication, that it was "better" for jokes and for the recounting of stories and anecdotes, they considered it less useful than English for the conduct of serious business and rejected the suggestion that it could be used for purposes of education. In a study with teachers in training, Hazel Simmons-McDonald (2006a) reported a shift from these earlier results to greater acceptance of Kwéyòl as well as an admission that it helps the child who speaks Kwéyòl exclusively on entry to school to understand the processes being undertaken. Some teachers admitted to using Kwéyòl for these purposes in a limited way, but ironically the majority of subjects in the sample claimed not to be able to speak Kwéyòl.

Changes in patterns of language use in St Lucia have been interpreted by some to reflect a tendency towards homogeneity which, according to Didacus Jules, for example, "erodes the differentiating character" of culture (1998, 3). He notes that St Lucians have become more "cosmopolitan in their outlook, taste and aspirations". As noted earlier, both Alexander (1993) and Liebermann (1975) reported ambivalence among St Lucians towards their language, with the results showing a more or less sharp demarcation between preference for use of Kwéyòl in private domains as opposed to its formal usage in some contexts where it was considered to be more appropriate and acceptable. Greater and more public acceptance of French Creole culture indicates that St Lucians accept as central to their identity the French Creole language as well as the norms of what Jules (1998, 2) refers to as "Kwéyòlness". He explains it as follows:

> Kwéyòl culture must be that sum total of our way of life that is distinctive in its Kwéyòlness. It was once a totality that defined us – it was how we worked and played, our waking reality and our dream state, the things that we made, how we made them and the ways that we used them; the foods that we ate and the manner in which we prepared them; the habits that we cultivated and the common sense that they became. It was the way of life that was the product of our history and geography and it continues to be the language that we speak in common understanding with 13 million other Kwéyòl speakers worldwide.

Jules's view is essentially synchronic because it focuses on a way of life that was dominant during a particular period across every stratum of society. It was a period in which values, beliefs and behaviours were shared by the majority in the community. Kwéyòl was also widely spoken by the majority, and the French Creole traditions were more widely known and celebrated. These traditions have been and continue to be eroded by the hegemonic effects of foreign cultural domination as well as the hegemony of an English-only policy in education. Kwéyòl continues to suffer the effects of English linguistic imperialism, as do many Creoles and other indigenous languages the world over. This concept of Kwéyòlness is similar if not identical to the concept of Créolité or creolness that has occupied Caribbean scholars and writers.

Wilson Harris observes that the term *creoleness* is peculiar, as it may sustain "a conservative if not reactionary purist logic" (Harris 1998, 26). Yet, he goes on to assert that "creoleness signifies. . . a cross-cultural nemesis capable of becoming a saving nemesis", the latter implying "recuperative powers and vision". Pépin and Confiant assert that Créolité stems from the "fertile ground" of a "multicultural heritage (which) yields a polycentric approach in which the question of identity generates a mosaic identity affirmed by idioms, languages, places, systems of thoughts, histories fertilizing one another and untying the predictable" (1998, 97–98). Embracing the notion of creoleness is seen as a force for forging a particular identity and for achieving liberation from the hegemony of the colonial language. Yet an exploration of the concept reveals deep tensions. On the one hand, writers, scholars and the majority of the population have achieved a mastery of the colonial idiom and, as Bill Ashcroft, Gareth Griffiths and Helen Tiffin (1989) have shown, writers have used that mastery to "deconstruct" the colonial language of power through the use of vernacular languages, either minimally or extensively in their texts. Condé (1998, 102–3) lists many specific examples of texts that attempt such deconstruction. She argues that by embedding Creole in texts, some writers seek "by their very presence the words injected the marginalized and despised culture into the heart of the dominant one and in so doing, destroyed the latter's hegemony" (Condé 1998, 103).

The relatively recent publication of an orthography for Kwéyòl in St Lucia has not allowed for the production of full-length works such as those found in the Martiniquan context – in the work of Confiant, for example. Yet, writers such as Derek Walcott and Roderick Walcott did inject Creole into their texts, thus embracing the duality of the cultural experience of St Lucian society. The paradox in that context lies primarily, on the one hand, in the wide acceptance of a language that meets the communicative purposes of its speakers, through which their cultural traditions are expressed and which is evidenced in the efforts to revive and reclaim that language and preserve the cultural traditions through more formal avenues of national festive celebrations. On the other hand, official policy, and perhaps political expediency, fails to recognize the value of the language and the role it is required to play in the liberation of the many for whom it is still a first language. Such liberation is one of the mind and of how language is perceived, and it is essential for the full freedom of those who speak the suppressed language.

LANGUAGE AND FREEDOM

The island of St Lucia has undergone significant language shift from the beginning of the twentieth century when the majority of St Lucians were monolingual Kwéyòl speakers. Figures recorded for the census taken in 1911 showed that 58.58 per cent of the population spoke Kwéyòl exclusively, 5.4 per cent were monolingual English speakers and 30.91 per cent were bilinguals; 5.04 per cent spoke other languages. By 1921 the figures for exclusive Kwéyòl speakers had decreased to 56.53 per cent, and the figures also showed a decrease for exclusive English speakers to 4.09 per cent, while bilinguals increased to 33.45 per cent. In 1946, the last year in which records on language distribution are available, the figures for monolingual Kwéyòl speakers had decreased further to 43.32 per cent, monolingual English speakers had decreased to 0.22 per cent, but the number of bilinguals had increased to 54.16 per cent. These trends show the shift to a bilingual situation that has had implications for the education and development of the people of the island. But the decrease in monolingual English speakers is interesting, because it suggests a use of English that is not considered to be somehow "standard". Other works, for example, Alleyne (1961), Carrington (1984), Isaac (1986), Le Page and Tabouret-Keller (1985), and Simmons-McDonald (1988), have reported on the emergence of an English lexicon, the St Lucian English lexicon variety, which is now widely used on the island. Yet by prescribing the use of one language exclusively for purposes of education among other public uses, this policy has served to marginalize a significant number of speakers from full participation in the development and intellectual life of the state.

As Condé points out, "The control of language is one of the primary aspects of colonial oppression – the dependency of the periphery upon the center. Language is a site of power: who names controls. The politically and economically alienated colonized are first colonized linguistically. In their attempt to gain freedom and self-determination, the colonized must put an end to the pre-eminence of the colonial language" (1998, 102). But the power for achieving such freedom and self-determination can only be realized in instances where the Creole speaker has access to literacy. Even the minor acts of deconstruction to which reference was made earlier can only be realized if the speaker has access to literacy in both the languages in question, that is, Kwéyòl and English.

The use of an English-only policy in education with students who on entry to schools do not speak English and where programmes do not exist to enable the Creole speaker to acquire that English serves to diminish the possibility for literacy in any of the languages in question and to introduce a restriction on the cognitive development of the learner. Whinnom's assertion that Creole is a handicap to speakers of that language is only manifested in the educational practices that are enforced and the outcomes that are realized from these practices. One must eschew the notion that such limitation is inherent in language.

Studies conducted in situations similar to that of St Lucia have indicated that deleterious effects result when the first or native language of the learner is suppressed. Dorothy Eichorn and Harold Jones (1952) reported that children who grew up in communities where the language of the school was not that of the home suffered adverse cognitive effects. Anne Anastasi and Fernando Cordova (1953) conducted a study of Puerto Rican children in New York. They discussed the question as to whether bilingualism constitutes a handicap and concluded that this depended on the way in which the two languages were learned. They used the term *linguistic bifurcation* to refer to a situation in which one language develops in one set of situations and the other in another set. They claimed that it was not the "interference between the two languages as much as the restriction in the learning of each to certain areas that leads to handicap" (Anastasi and Cordova 1953). They indicated that in such contexts the "extent of the child's vocabulary as well as other aspects of his linguistic development will be inferior in both languages". More recent studies conducted in a variety of contexts have supported these early findings. For example, Ellen Bialystok (1991) reported that the metalinguistic development of learners is enhanced by the acquisition of two or more languages. Jim Cummins reported that studies he reviewed in 1991 showed that if the conceptual foundation of a child's first language was well developed, the child would be more likely to develop "similarly high levels of conceptual abilities" in a second language (1994, 38). Jeff Siegel reviewed research in which stigmatized varieties were used in the classroom, and he concluded that the findings showed that "appropriate teaching methodology incorporating students' vernaculars may actually help them acquire the standard" (1999, 721). In a more focused study (1997), Siegel reported on a programme that he had examined which used Tok Pisin to develop literacy in preschool children who were native speakers of Tok Pisin. He indicated that the use of the pidgin resulted in greater gains for the native speakers of the pidgin than for children who had not been exposed to programmes in which the pidgin had been used. He concluded that the use of the pidgin had not been a hindrance in the children's acquisition of literacy.

In a study with native speakers of French Creole, Simmons-McDonald (2006b) reported on a pilot study which was done to test the effects of using Kwéyòl as a language of instruction in St Lucia. The results of that study showed that instruction in Kwéyòl did not hinder the literacy development of the learners. Simmons-McDonald noted, "In fact, in this study, the use of Kwéyòl actually seemed to help the development of reading ability in English" (Simmons-McDonald 2006b, 142). She noted further that the students in the study developed fluency in reading texts "at least one grade level higher than their levels at the start of the study. At the start all the students had been listed as being at risk and they had only limited word recognition abilities at kindergarten level." She explained further, "One student's gains in reading in both languages exceeded expectations and, by the end of the study he was able to read texts at Grade 3 level, that is, two grades higher than at the start of the study, and he went on to sit the Common Entrance Examination and gain a place in a secondary school" (Simmons-McDonald 2006b, 142). These studies all indicate the possibilities for academic success for native speakers of pidgins and Creoles. And it is such successes that help to initiate the process of liberation and the freedom of the individual to operate outside the restricted functional areas assigned to native speakers of Kwéyòl.

The case of St Lucia has been exacerbated by the fact that the education system has not provided exposure to the first language in which the child has fluency. Access to literacy through Kwéyòl as well as communication in it is discouraged in the classroom, so that the situation of subtractive bilingualism, in which the English is not learned fluently for oral communicative or school purposes, is the outcome for most speakers of Kwéyòl. Carrington (1984) presented a figure of 64 per cent functional literacy for children in St Lucia (mostly speakers of Kwéyòl) at the end of primary school. There is no concrete evidence from Minimum Standards Tests or the Common Entrance Examination results to suggest an increase in functional literacy since Carrington published his results in 1984. This leads one to question the purpose and function of schooling and the issue of language as a liberating influence in the lives of people.

If indeed education can be a vehicle for social mobility and if in bilingual contexts education is restricted to one language, namely, that imposed by a policy established in a colonial situation, and if further the native language is stigmatized and excluded from the purview of schooling, then the exclusive speakers of Kwéyòl have an almost insurmountable task in acquiring the prized language, while advancement of their own language is stymied. The studies referred to earlier would suggest strongly that it is nothing inherent in the native speaker's language per se that leads to the handicap, as Whinnom would seem to suggest. Additional evidence from countries like the Seychelles, in which referential inadequacy of the French Creole lexicon was addressed once a decision was made that the language be included in education, provides counter-evidence to Whinnom's view. In the Seychellois context, the repair was not restricted to the naming of objects but to coinage of abstract terms – several of which were internally generated. The issue, therefore, is not one of language "inferiority" but rather of the manipulation of social and political situations to suppress the extension of the use of Creoles for a wider range of functions and purposes. Mervyn Alleyne and Paul Garvin (1982) refer to a process of "intellectualisation of the creole" which transpires when young speakers of Creoles are given the opportunity to use their language for purposes of literacy in academic contexts. This process leads to additive bilingualism and allows the use of the Creole for all the purposes that the official language might be used for.

It is only by allowing freedom of participation in the valued context of education by speakers of Kwéyòl that the issue of "handicap" can be addressed fully. Much evidence already shows that such handicap is not a property inherent in the language, but it results if negative attributes are ascribed to the language, if it is severely restricted in its domains and if, as a consequence, its speakers are restricted from full and productive participation in the enterprise of education. It is only when there is liberation in this area that language can become the catalyst for the full freedom of the individual. This can be effected through a change of policy in education, and it is only then that education, through the acceptance and functional use of the language of the people, can become a "saving nemesis", to use Harris's term, and through it the "recuperative powers and vision" of which he speaks be realized.

References

Alexander, Marcella. 1993. "An Exploration of Language Attitudes in a Selective St Lucian Community: Focus on St Lucian French Creole and English". Caribbean Studies paper, University of the West Indies, Cave Hill.

Alleyne, Mervyn. 1961. "Language and Society in St. Lucia". Caribbean Studies 1 (1): 1–10.

———. 1976. "Linguistic Aspects of Communication in the West Indies". In Language and Communication, edited by Marlene Cuthbert, 29–42. Bridgetown: Cedar Press for Faculty of Arts and General Studies, University of the West Indies.

Alleyne, Mervyn, and Paul Garvin. 1982. "Standard Language Theory with Special Reference to Creole Languages". In Theoretical Issues in Caribbean Linguistics, edited by M. Alleyne, 19–35. Kingston: Language Laboratory, University of the West Indies.

Anastasi, Anne, and Fernando Cordova. 1953. "Some Effects of Bilingualism upon the Intelligence Test Performance of Puerto Rican Children in New York City". *Journal of Educational Psychology* 44 (1): 1–19.

Ashcroft, Bill, Gareth Griffiths and Helen Tiffin. 1989. *The Empire Writes Back: Theory and Practice in Post-Colonial Literatures*. London: Routledge.

Bialystok, Ellen, ed. 1991. *Language Processing in Bilingual Children*. Cambridge: Cambridge University Press.

Carrington, Lawrence. 1984. *St Lucian Creole: A Descriptive Analysis of Its Phonology and Morpho-syntax*. Hamburg: Helmut Buske Verlag.

Chomsky, Noam. 1965. *Aspects of the Theory of Syntax*. Cambridge, MA: MIT Press.

Condé, Maryse. 1998. "Créolité without Creole Language?" In *Caribbean Creolization*, edited by Kathleen Balutansky and Marie-Agnès Sourieau, 101–9. Kingston: University of the West Indies Press.

Cooper, Carolyn. 2003. "Professing Slackness: Language, Authority and Power within the Academy and Without". Inaugural professorial lecture, University of the West Indies, Mona, Jamaica, 25 September.

Cummins, Jim. 1994. "Knowledge, Power and Identity in Teaching English as a Second Language". In *Educating Second Language Children: The Whole Child, the Whole Curriculum, the Whole Community*, edited by F. Genese, 33–58. Cambridge: Cambridge University Press.

Eichorn, Dorothy, and Harold Jones. 1952. "Bilingualism". *Review of Educational Research* 22 (5): 421–38.

Harris, Wilson. 1998. "Creoleness". In *Caribbean Creolization*, edited by Kathleen Balutansky and Marie-Agnès Sourieau, 23–35. Kingston: University of the West Indies Press.

Isaac, Martha. 1986. "French Creole Interference in the Written English of St. Lucian Secondary School Students". MPhil thesis, University of the West Indies, Cave Hill.

Jules, Didacus. 1998. "Kwéyòl Culture: Differentiation in a Globalized Context". Feature address given at the International Symposium on Creole Cultures. Roseau, Dominica, October.

Le Page, Robert, and Andrée Tabouret-Keller. 1985. *Acts of Identity: Creole-based Approaches to Language and Ethnicity*. Cambridge: Cambridge University Press.

Liebermann, Dena. 1975. "Language Attitudes in St. Lucia". *Journal of Cross Cultural Psychology* 6: 471–81.

Louisy, Pearlette, and P. Turmel-John. 1983. *A Handbook for Writing Creole*. Special Series 1. Castries: Research of St Lucia.

Pépin, Ernest, and Rafaël Confiant. 1998. "The Stakes of Créolité". In *Caribbean Creolization*, edited by Kathleen Balutansky and Marie-Agnès Sourieau, 96–100. Kingston: University of the West Indies Press.

Rawley, James A. 1981. *The Trans-Atlantic Slave Trade*. New York: W.W. Norton.

Siegel, Jeff. 1997. "Using a Pidgin Language in Formal Education: Help or Hindrance?" *Applied Linguistics* 18: 86–100.

———. 1999. "Stigmatized and Standardized Varieties in the Classroom: Interference or Separation?" *TESOL Quarterly* 33 (4): 701–28.

Simmons-McDonald, Hazel. 1988. "The Learning of English Negatives by Speakers of St. Lucian French Creole". PhD diss. Stanford University, California.

———. 2006a. "Attitudes of Teachers to St. Lucian Language Varieties". *Caribbean Journal of Education* 28 (1): 51–84.

———. 2006b. "Vernacular Instruction and Bi-literacy Development in French Creole Speakers". In *Exploring the Boundaries of Caribbean Creole Languages*, edited by Hazel Simmons-McDonald and Ian Robertson, 118–46. Kingston: University of the West Indies Press.

Vérin, Pierre M. 1958. "The Rivalry of French Creole and English in the British West Indies". *De West Indische Gids* 38: 163–67.

Whinnom, Keith. 1971. "Linguistic Hybridization and the Special Case of Pidgins and Creoles". In *Pidginization and Creolization of Languages*, edited by Dell Hymes, 91–116. Cambridge: Cambridge University Press.

PART 4
GENDER

12.

REPRESENTATIONS OF GENDER AND SEXUALITY IN (JAMAICAN) DANCEHALL POPULAR CULTURE

The Search for a Method

AGOSTINHO M.N. PINNOCK

THIS CHAPTER SEEKS TO ADDRESS the development of an appropriately oriented and indigenously authored Caribbean research method or process in the contemporary academy, specifically as it relates to exploring the phenomenon of Jamaican dancehall popular culture. It argues that a clearly articulated framework within which the multiple intersected and intersecting experiences of Caribbean people may be foregrounded and validated simultaneously achieves their psychic and academic wholeness. This is especially important in terms of "centring" the research subject in relation to the process of knowledge production. Research canons which promote positivistic methods with their largely European origins impose an alien and alienating set of experiences on non-white, non-European researchers on account of the unique historical relationship – academic and otherwise – of the Caribbean region with Europe. The Caribbean, as well as other places and spaces with similar histories, is thus located within these (research) practices as Other, that is, in terms of traditional restrictions of the concept of objectivity.

Here, strict research protocols enforce conformity to near clinical rigidities of notions of replication and verification and severely reduce the role of the researcher in relation to the research process. Evidently ethnocentric, in terms of the promotion of certain ideas originating within the context of the hegemonic discourses of the Western academy, these antiseptic approaches (re)produce social and political inequities, in both the society and the academy. The role and interventions of researchers are limited on the premise that their active involvement in the research process contaminates the knowledge produced. The biases inherent in this process are clear. Only certain schools of thought are privileged on account of these lenses which invalidate indigenous subjectivities and foreground them as incomprehensible. This obvious quantitative hegemony promotes a one-sided view of social reality, which actively undermines the potential uses of multiple methods of exploration in addressing untraditional types as well as sources of knowledge.

Linda Tuhiwai Smith (2005) refers to Lester Rigney's argument in favour of the development of what he calls the "indigenist method". According to Rigney, appropriately evaluating discourse warrants the use of multiple techniques and methods which afford movements between traditionally underexplored subjectivities and mainstream academic practice. Here, the line between the researcher and the research process itself is perceived as being fundamentally more fractured than is often considered in the standard empiricist method which argues in favour of allowing the *data* to "speak for itself". In fact, in the Jamaican context where elements of popular culture are often imbricated in dancehall as a cultural phenomenon expressed primarily as music and fashion (Pinnock 2007), there is a way in which the dancehall artiste also operates as a form of social/ethnographic researcher. It may be argued, accordingly, that a primary part of the work of dancehall (musicians) is, itself, an ethnographic expedition, that is, in terms of how social and political realities are framed in the musical discourses of the various artistes who work in the field. Researching this phenomenon necessarily ensures asking the following questions: What is the link between the social researcher who researches dancehall and the dancehall musician who articulates its political and other concerns, both as entertainment and lived reality? Can dancehall be understood through the divorced and, presumably, uncontaminated lenses of the traditional academy where the roles of researcher and the research process are clearly delineated?

I ask the latter question in large measure because, in the approximately five years in which I have been engaged in my own explorations of the phenomena of dancehall, and Jamaican popular culture more generally, I have often encountered immense hurdles in terms of resisting induction into dancehall and popular culture. The two are similar and, in fact, it may well be argued that dancehall is an expression of the other and vice versa. Carolyn Cooper

(2004b) argues for instance that dancehall is "Jamaican culture at large". In this way, she attempts to capture some of the contradictions between the roles of cultural researcher and the cultural phenomenon itself, as they are imbricated in each other. In these instances, I have found that there have not been easy distinctions between the research community and the researcher. Often, I was "mistaken" for a "party regular" at times when I interacted with the partygoers at a central (New) Kingston dancehall hotspot as well as in online (chat and dating) communities, in which a significant portion of the interviews for this study were conducted. I also discovered, in the process, that, with the near intoxicating quality of the music and the seductive ambience of the particular environments, it was hard to resist being sucked in by the process. Before long, the lines were blurred, and I was one of them and they part of me. To attempt to distinguish between the researcher and the research process in such a context, therefore, proved futile and forced me to consider the implications of the notion of the observer/researcher as being removed and separated from the process under review, otherwise regarded as (scientific) academic detachment. In the words of one participant: "dancing to these songs (in the club) your heart could stop! . . . It is that exciting!" (Pinnock 2007).

For my own purposes, I also discovered that long and involved conversations with colleagues as well as continuous note-taking, especially after attending a dancehall event and going online, otherwise known in localized terms as "deconstruction", were necessary for disentangling myself from the study community as well as the phenomenon itself. This was also important in terms of looking clearly at the reasons that those in attendance at some of these events responded to me in certain ways. I was to discover, therefore, that the body (mine included) is continuously (re)constructed and deconstructed in the dancehall, as well as within the wider reaches of popular culture, as a site for articulating notions related to (Jamaican) citizenship, rights of sovereignty, race, class and identity, among others.

Both my lack of height and slender build constantly placed me at risk of being pushed out of the way in crowded settings, whereas others who were much taller and bigger were asked permission to move out of the way. That I was perceived as "uptown" and, admittedly, also Other in terms of the multiple and conflicting readings of both my body and presence in such places afforded me a unique vantage point from which to gain many and important insights into the processes of cultural formation, performance and elucidation. My movement, then, from distant academic observer to "nativized" participant itself became a traumatic part of the research process/experience. I discovered that the closer I got to the research subjects and the subject community, the further away I moved from my original peers in the middle class and the wider academic community.

I also discovered in my lived/research experiences, that my own body often became part of the research process. As other bodies rubbed (up) against mine with much regularity, it became apparent that this experience was part of the standard expectations I developed (in this context). Here, men, mostly, (though they were women as well) would often engage me in what I considered these sexualized practices, which I, initially, found very disturbing. This was primarily because we were in an environment that advertised itself as staunchly anti-homosexual. However, I was then to learn through observations as well as further interactions with the study community that the issue of sexual distinctions did not so much matter at this level as it did when gender is performed as a signifier of sexual preference(s) in the wider community. By which I mean, there seemed little concern with the (actual) sexual identities of the men in such a packed, sweaty entertainment environment. By all appearances, what mattered more was the almost necessary contact of bodies.

Sexuality performed as gender, however, was a matter of importance only when people, men mostly, were felt to cross over some invisible taboo lines which governed cultural performances of masculinity (Butler 1999, 1993), not only inside the particular club environment but also, and mostly, outside of it. In fact, I never in the extent of my experiences in these entertainment venues witnessed the persecution of any man on the premise that he was homosexual, despite the obvious and questionable physical interactions which occurred in these spaces. I also noted that the deejay would routinely play various types of anti-homosexual songs at certain points in the "juggling" (music selection). Accordingly, it forced me to consider that those men who were beaten by angry anti-homosexual mobs (according to recent newspaper reports) or, more generally, that those homosexuals who were considered legitimate targets according to very popular urban legends in Jamaica, were singled out not because of their sexuality but because they were considered far too flamboyant in their homosexual behaviour. This was often read as an offensive display of homosexual desires, which clearly signified their preference for same-gender sexual gratification and made them targets of public disaffection.

This, however, did not mean that those within the safety of a packed club environment were not themselves engaging in same-gender sexual dealings.

Rather, men in these clubs were often perceived as being more "discrete" in terms of how they expressed such desires. It was very disconcerting for me to see men exchange telephone numbers in darkened corners and whisper into each other's ears. Consequently, I was shocked to learn that these types of practices existed in "straight settings". This was based on my research hypothesis which claimed that (Jamaican) nationalism embodied as gender identity was performed differently by different audiences of men, particularly those who operated under labels such as "gay", "straight" and "bisexual". The knowledge which I garnered in these environments, accordingly, was far more important in terms of defining the parameters of my enquiries into nationalism as a signifier of gender (identity) in Jamaican popular culture and dancehall, in which regard, sexuality and sexual expressions became important barometers in defining this process. The multiple constructions of the male body in these various entertainment settings, therefore, meant that the layered constructions of gender identity in Jamaican popular culture occasioned all types of contested and, at times, contradictory experiences. My initial theories, therefore, of a clearly marked set of distinctions between different groups of men defined in terms of sexual orientation – gays and straights – was fundamentally challenged.

While undertaking this research, I attended both types of events – parties conducted specifically for men who identified themselves as gay, as well as so-called straight parties. Usually, in the latter, there would be familiar faces seen at the former and vice versa. In fact, it was not at all unusual for "straight" friends to accompany their gay acquaintances to parties conducted for these audiences. It was said, in instances where such men and women were identified whether in conversation or in a more general introduction at the door, that they had come "to see what was going on [in these places]". While the extent of the interactions in gay parties was not the same as in "straight" club settings, there was still a noticcable interest in sexual hook-ups. Interestingly, it was in the "straight club scenes" that I felt more "hit on" by other men than in "alternative club" environments. This, however, may well have to do with the fact that I made it my business to stand as much to myself and observe the activities which occurred in this environment. That I often stood by myself perhaps made me an obvious target.

In fact, it became apparent that the issue of sexual orientation never seemed a matter for debate in respect of men who defined themselves as gay, straight or even bisexual – a popular category, I was to later discover, in my many conversations throughout this study. In terms of looking at how these ideas became embedded in (Jamaican) popular culture, I turned to online communities, including websites such as www.go-Jamaica.com and www.Adam 4Adam.com. These attracted entire communities of men who called themselves "bisexuals", or "bi" or "bi-curious". The term *straight-acting* immediately jumped out at me as a popular reference to (gender) identity in these communities. Often profiles define sexual tastes and interests in terms of heterosexual practices by denouncing men said to be effeminate through labels such as "no fems, fats or people with issues". By this it was meant that men who acted like women were fat (read: unattractive), while men who did not know whether they were gay, straight or bisexual, as well as those with unresolved feelings of guilt about their sexuality, were not considered ideal partners. Bisexual men, for instance, were interested in other bisexuals who, apparently, "know how to act like a man", as some profiles read. It is interesting to note, therefore, that within these online communities of Jamaican men who operated under labels outside of those considered heterosexual, they defined themselves first as men and everything else afterwards. Whether a man was sexually active and regardless of whom he slept with, he was still a man – first, last and always. In the words of two online interviewees:

> Online Speaker One: I want a man who will be a gentleman in the streets and a *bitch* in the sheets.
>
> Online Speaker Two: Man mus' act like *man*! Not a woman. If I wanted a woman I could get that [woman, elsewhere].

In this regard, it is important also to highlight that it was important for me to enter these communities as a participant, as this was the only means of gaining access to this type of information. Additionally, as there were not that many other opportunities to engage gay and bisexual men in settings other than those in which they revealed their sexualities in this way, it was important to visit online communities in order to observe the methods of self-definition as it related to the performance of gender identity. Sexual activity among men, though governed by strict rules of an adherence to masculinity, became a defining characteristic in terms of constructing gender.

Of note, then, is the fact that there seemed very little distinction regarding the definitions of masculinity within these communities and the larger, more publicly accessible "heterosexual zones" of entertainment. Here, men defined their authority in terms of sexual liaisons as well as the seriousness of purpose with which these relationships were pursued. Men who were considered "flakes" or "femmes", meaning those with unresolved issues about their sexual identities, as well as men who were "too girly" (to use the expressions of one other correspondent) were not ideal partners. In fact, one profile read: "people with issues should not have profiles. No pic[ture] = [equals] no response", by which it was implied that those who did not have pictures in their profiles were still afraid of defining themselves as gay and therefore were not ready for sexual intimacy with other men sharing these interests.

Effectively, then, sex is the defining principle by which a man is declared ab/normal. After all, a line from an Elephant Man song seems most appropriate in terms of capturing the sense in which sex defines masculinity in Jamaica and Jamaican popular culture. According to "Ele", as he is sometimes called, *"nuff man a live ah nuh fuck nuh pum-pum! Dem nah fuck nuh pum-pum!"* (Many men are living and are not having sex (with a woman, that is!), without sex [repeated for emphasis!]). At one level, Elephant Man's mocking of this state of affairs suggests the clear need for men to have sexual activity with women and, apparently also, lots of it as a defining part of their gender identity as legitimate (Jamaican) men. There is also, though, an implied awareness that while some men are celibate, others (in the group) are engaged in same-gender sexual relations. Either way, sexual activity is the basis for defining masculinity in Jamaica.

In such instances, men should not in any way appear to contravene the accepted social (and moral) codes for masculine behaviour. It may well be argued, therefore, that with respect to dancehall's definition of the terms of the nationalist ethos of Jamaican society, there is an unrepentant celebration of a rampant male (hetero)sexuality. Notably, men defined under the rubric of alternate sexualities defined themselves in similar ways, using the heterosexual matrix as the standard against which their own identities as Jamaican nationals are measured, at the very least among those within the ambit of popular culture, whether in terms of attending dancehall clubs or visiting the online community.

There is also a very notable valorization of the female body in terms of the constructions of appropriate gender identity among Jamaican men, regardless of sexual preferences and gendered performances. According to newspaper columnist Melville Cooke, in an article entitled "'Hiding' Homos":

> From what I have observed, as much as Jamaicans who are not gay express rage about man to man homosexuality being so unjust and not knowing who to trust, it is mostly gay *pride* that really offends to the point of breaking into action instead of chatter. Male homosexuals are expected to be even a little ashamed of their sexual orientation (or disorientation), to the point where they do not publicly attempt to elevate it to a position of equality with heterosexuality. . . . It is more than a bit of straight-up hypocrisy, actually, a situation of "I know that you are homosexual, you know I know, I know you know I know, but as long as we both keep up the pretence of ignorance everything is alright". (Cooke 2007; emphasis added)

Here, the celebrations of the female body as the site through which normative masculine attitudes and identities are constructed are obvious. Men who are perceived as having subverted these requirements are demonized, ostracized and even terrorized (Fanon 1967) for bringing into jeopardy the unspoken, though very important, rituals of masculinity in this regard. Their presumed flight from "the masculine", therefore, echoed traditional feminist rhetoric regarding the (so-called) mandatory expectations and requirements of heterosexuality, in which the presumption of heterosexuality is standard practice (Warner 1993; Rich 1980). Therefore, men considered to embody the contradictions inherent in the official narratives of identity, as premised on the notion of a homogenized national identity (Cooper 2004b), become the benchmark of difference in society. Ironically, they are hated as a required part of the cultural scripts of performing masculinity in Jamaican society and popular culture.

It is reasonable to argue, then, that Jamaican men who do not clearly embody characteristics defined as normative are considered alien beings in a society whose understanding of itself is fundamentally premised on notions about a definable and immediately recognized masculinity (Forbes 2005). In this regard, it may also be argued that a certain type of essentialist construction of masculinity exists in Jamaican culture, in terms of ideas about "uptown", brown (ness), education and heterosexuality. Ironically, however, these rituals (of the masculine) are never explained directly. Consequently, subverting "masculine rituals" and aesthetics are considered, in the main, a subversion of the myth of a homogenous (national) gender identity in which all men participate as well as from which they appropriate their own versions of identity. Accordingly, only those with the economic means as well as political clout (read: "uptown/brown people") are able to do this uninterrupted, in this context. All others are considered pretenders and are treated in this way.

It is also important to highlight that the knowledge which I gained/produced in this context could not have been developed without actual participation in the various dancehall events and online communities and chat sessions in and around which these various meanings of the masculine were (re)created. It should also be noted that these online chat communities reinterpret the idea of the "female" to refer to a signifier of "femaleness" in sexual relations between men. "Effeminacy" is usually considered an undesired and undesirable public display (of male homosexual inclinations) on the part of men who engage in sexual dealings with each other, whereas the sexualized role of the "bottom" (the receiving partner) or, at least, "verse/bottom" (alternating partners who mainly receive) are read as "boi-pussies" (anus/vaginas) to be "topped" (the penetrating partner) by "real men" (straight acting/heteronormative). The roles of man and woman (in the sex act) are reconfigured in this discourse as part of sex act (ions) of men engaged in sexual relations with each other (Cooper 1995).

The extent to which such processes impacted my understanding of myself in relationship to these discourses of (gender) identity, articulated through the corporeal, emphasized my own search for a more "nativized"/"indigenist" method of research (Tuhiwai Smith 2005). This proved absolutely important in terms of exploring the body dynamics of Jamaican/dancehall/popular culture in the context of the performance of nationalism as gender – both online and in the actual spaces of the dancehall. In this regard, I was both researcher and research subject.

While my personal involvement in these ethnographic experiences has shaped my understanding of the phenomena about which I write here, it has also meant the unintentional subversion of the empiricist method of exploration. My initial theories about the extent to which dancehall (re)scripts discourses of "the (Jamaican) nation" could not have been appropriately understood outside of the context of my own experiences and body. Consequently, the process of achieving objectivity, with its emphasis on verification and replication, was challenged. My experiences, in other words, could only be verified and replicated by recounting the research process, as articulated through the actual moments in which I lived them. Certainly, I could re-enact through verbal strategies as well as staged performances (Alexander 2005) the types of (research) experiences of which I had been privileged to have been part at the various research sites without ever really going back to those actual moments. The moral force of my conclusions was no less valid, therefore, on account of my inability to replicate and verify such findings. This means, inter alia, that each individual (Jamaican) experiences "the nation" in terms of its performance as gender in dancehall and online in uniquely different ways.

In fact, my experiences as an ethnographic researcher in dancehall and popular culture, in this regard, give credence to the progressive standpoint theory as articulated by Digby (1998). Here, Digby critiques the concept of experience. According to him, the province of experience is a valid space within which to make certain important assertions about particular social phenomena, such as giving birth to a baby. He, however, refuses to accept that those who do not, or cannot, have the same exact experience are unable to make valuable insights into discussions around which such "evidences" are used to marshal support. Said differently, while I operated primarily in the capacity of social researcher in the foregoing, there was no denying the validity of my own standpoint in relation to the phenomenon under review – dancehall as space/culture articulated by "ghetto politics"/ideology, primarily. As a matter of fact, there were several times in which I was caught up in the dancing and showmanship as well as the online chat identities and sessions during the various moments around which meanings (of masculinity) were (re)produced and subsequently (re)negotiated.

I was, in other words, as much imbricated in the "experience" of dancehall as the experience was in me. This twinned relationship made referencing my experiences to others within the academy fundamentally very challenging. I was criticized for not conducting "real research"; using "anecdotal evidences" and even "hearsay" in some instances, especially where I related elements of discussions I either heard or participated in. I was asked, several times, to "justify" my methods with an "appropriate" rationale. The continued second guessing of my (initial) observations which, ultimately, informed the larger process of my research project continued with the insistence that my research questions had to be revisited and the research itself conducted against this premise. This, effectively, meant that I would have wasted my time earlier, expending critical resources to attend these events as well as in online chat sessions observing, exploring and living in the moment(s) of the research, as indicated above.

My obvious "inability", then, to address these concerns "appropriately" (that is, without much effort at self-control) has, in part, led to the writing of this chapter as one of the several ways in which social/ethnographic experiences may be had and interpreted in the process of myth and meaning making in society (Alexander 2005). It also foregrounds the importance of theorizing knowledge production in a Caribbean (research) context that obviously requires the interventions of strategies and methods not as yet configured in the academy. This is in large part because the epistemological approaches used to apprehend knowledge in the Caribbean have, generally, not been sufficiently democratized to allow new, innovative and non-traditional approaches to the exploration of phenomena. This is especially where the body also becomes part of the dynamic of the research process, in terms of understanding discourses about identity, sexuality and gender.

The extent to which criticisms such as these have been used in the academy to undermine the validity of claims made both by me and others about observations of dancehall and popular culture questions the integrity of such research. They speak to a clear bias in terms of, presumably, "more formal" methods and highlight the limited research horizons within which the contemporary academy operates in the Caribbean. The hierarchic structures upon which Caribbean academy and research practices are structured are also clearly articulated. Only certain actors are allowed space and, even so, only when the works explored achieve some semblance of similarity to the prevailing ideological status quo. The need to configure lenses which go beyond constructing "the native" (Fanon 1967) as Other must be celebrated and affirmed, accordingly, as a way of appropriately capturing and articulating "alternative approaches" which explore untraditional subjectivities, as part of the valid and multiple research experiences to be had in such an environment.

The idea that there is only one way of accessing social (and political) reality fosters a context in which new and emerging knowledge is not adequately represented or, for that matter, recognized within the formal, middle-class academy. The complex range of considerations involved in the definitions and negotiations of the Caribbean research topography, therefore, suggest the urgent need to review and rethink the types of gatekeeping approaches used to mediate this particular social/political environment. More than the need for the creation of "safe spaces" in the Caribbean academy for new thoughts and ideas, there is also a critical need to nurture and encourage environments in which the proverbial "new blood" may flow through the veins of the academy. It is imperative that social research processes which give voice as well as credence to positive (note not positivistic!) methods of enquiry be entrenched. These aid in making obvious, as well as overturning, the tyranny of Eurocentric canonical practices and simultaneously elevate "indigenous consciousnesses"/methods as a uniquely merited site of exploration. In so doing, neophytes as well as established intellectuals are afforded new platforms on which to organize a sustainable philosophy of research both within the region and outside.

Before moving further, it is important that I also highlight my ideological affinities with postmodern/feminist intellectual methods of inquiry. These argue, inter alia, that social reality is a constructed process which articulates the views and considerations of those who hold power in society (Harewood 2006; Hutcheon 1989; Butler 1999, 1993; Rabinow 1984) as a means of securing those interests. Ruling-class ideologies, in turn, construct within them the inbuilt prejudices and assumed hegemony and positions of authority of society's power brokers. Foucault (Rabinow 1984) argues that "power-knowledge" is produced by those who rule (over others) in society. Knowledge, in this instance, serves the explicit purposes of constructing and preserving the ruling class' status, ideology and culture as normal. Their "power-knowledge" becomes the template for (all) others to follow.

The realities in the Caribbean are no less affected by Foucault's theorizing of knowledge production and articulation, as indicated above. The politics of colonial hermeneutical methods inherited in the Caribbean have historically promoted epistemologies of power which define the contours of Caribbean intellectual theorizing. The methods involved in the production, articulation and reinforcement of knowledge have, over time, promoted a bias in favour of largely positivistic research frameworks and methods which have privileged the concept of objectivity over other (cultural) subjectivities. Here "power-knowledge" not only ordains what is considered legitimate sources of intellectual expression and preoccupation but also, in many ways, suggests and even reinforces/enforces methods of research for exploring these phenomena.

Notably, however, this does not mean that there have not previously been "untraditional methods of exploration" as well as "untraditional knowledge" explored in Caribbean intellectual spaces. Rather, it is to underline the fact that such enterprises are fundamentally handicapped by the monopolization of Caribbean intellectual resources in favour of more formal, quantitative methods as well as the reality that "alternative"/indigenous knowledges are marginalized in such a context. In view of this marginalization, Cooper's (1995) theorizing of the scribal/oral split in the postcolonial Caribbean environment over a decade ago, as well as before (and after), seems particularly relevant in the contemporary mode of the academy.

In fact, in a recent review of attitudes towards a statue created by Jamaican sculptor Laura Facey-Cooper in celebration of Jamaican emancipation and independence, contradictorily entitled *None But Ourselves Can Free Our Minds*, Cooper contends Jamaican aesthetic *and intellectual* sensibilities are "enslaved in stereotype" (Cooper 2004b). Here, she traces the connections between a colonial ruling-class imagination which constructed (enslaved) Africans as animalistic beings devoid of human emotions and intelligence and the images crafted by a white Jamaican artist to reference the importance of Jamaica's emancipation from British rule two hundred years ago. Needless to say, at the time, a range of (conflicting) opinions was raised indirectly on the subject of Jamaican nationalism and, more importantly, on the question of the location of the (black) body in the emancipation discourse of Jamaican/Caribbean society.

The penis on the male statue was, it seemed, (unduly) criticized for its prepossessing width and length in relation to the rest of the statue – a pair, as it were, of (naked) ex-slaves looking up to the heavens (notably, without eyes), possibly in search of the freedom which obviously eluded them in a previous dispensation (Cooper 2004b). Notably, however, if viewed in totality the statue's proportions seem consistent with the rest of its various parts. The "eye-level" criticisms in this instance, then, seem consistent with the inherited academic traditions about perceiving social reality in the Caribbean whereby only that which can be seen immediately (at eye level, as it were!) as well as replicated in future are deemed as fundamentally valid in relation to social phenomena. It also speaks to other cultural attitudes as it relates to the en/gendering of dress as a political representation of gender identity in the wider reaches of "nation discourse", or popular culture (Pinnock 2007). Historically, clothes occupied a singular importance in the lives of the Jamaican people (Pinnock 2007; Buckridge 2004). Their importance as beings of self-worth and value were, inter alia, signified by and through the wearing of clothes. Nakedness, while obviously sexualized and responded to in different ways, at different levels, occupies a contradictory space in popular culture. Women can participate publicly in various states of un/dress (Pinnock 2007; Cooper 2004a, 2004b, 1995), while men do not have the same opportunities without, of course, incurring the wrath of others. There is a way, then, in which the attitudes expressed concerning the statues upon their unveiling in 2004 at the entrance to the newly constructed Emancipation Park in New Kingston, Jamaica, captured some of these concerns.

The contradictions are obvious, in that there is no acknowledgement of what Foucault (Rabinow 1984) claims is the need for the reclamation of the (full) *body politic* in the formulation and generation of knowledge produced in society. Foucault (1978), who also contends that everything is political, sees as precisely an act of political disenfranchisement the continuous constructions of knowledge in society around certain indices of power. Here, some elements of the society are excluded in the production and valorization of formal, written knowledge. In Foucault's view, as well as the view of other scholars such as postmodern critic Linda Hutcheon (1998) and philosopher Jean François Lyotard (Rice and Waugh 1989), "the real" as we know it, is a constructed process. It is an inherited episteme/tradition whose reality, *as well as integrity*, are dependent on the extent to which certain historical forces in society have fostered and, therefore, sought to ensure its creation, materialization, articulation and reinforcement over time. In this way, then, certain traditions – intellectual and otherwise, are normalized as a regularized part of discourse creation, formation and promulgation.

Here, the manifestation of the discursive universe follows in line with the political order whose views are also on the ascendancy. Social reality is, thus, (re)presented as a process of celebrating the rule of the powerful (Agozino 2007; Foucault, in Rabinow 1984). In fact, Agozino insightfully contends that "the study of social relations is not the study of unconscious matter with no self-interests and vested interests in politicized global societies" (2007, 5). He is decidedly critical of positivistic methods, in particular those which reduce social reality to unidimensional or, to use his word, "unilinear" realities which presume as well as promote the myth of a universal homogeneity (Barriteau 2007). In which regard, Agozino contends that Caribbean social research traditions, specifically in the vein of criminology, are particularly flawed if they do not take a more valid account of the social and other relations of *true* Caribbean realities. In other words, the intellectual epistemes inherited from Europe and imposed (up)on what he calls "Third World" societies, do significantly more harm than good in terms of reducing the scourge of criminality in the Caribbean and other places. In fact, in Agozino's view, some of these very methods are themselves criminal and (only) serve to enshrine the means by which more criminals are created in places like the Caribbean and elsewhere in the "Third World".

Accordingly, (Caribbean) social reality is problematized as a matter way beyond the scope of (limited) Eurocentric methods of enquiry, which promote the one-sided view of the power elite's demand for respect (Agozino 2007). Such imperialistic rationalizations of social phenomena, then, clearly articulate the agendas of ruling class elites in Caribbean societies with vested interests in maintaining racial and racist attitudes inherited as part of the colonial system of myth making and meaning creation (Alexander 2005) in the Caribbean and its academy. Analysing representations of the (black male) body in this type of culture brings with it certain innate limitations, as indicated above in the case of the Emancipation monument in Jamaica.

The intention here is not to define Facey-Cooper's statue as a racist representation of the Jamaican body politic epigraphed in the Emancipation monument: "None But Ourselves Can Free Our Minds". Rather, it is to highlight that Facey-Cooper – a white Jamaican artist – herself seems vested in the privileged perceptions of the postcolonial ruling class elite imagination. This is to the extent that her representation of the freedom of the black Jamaican body (politic) is referenced in a way that elicited strong (negative) public reactions. The point is that even to the extent that the statues themselves are looking (towards freedom) without eyes would indicate Facey-Cooper's removal, at some level, from the "soul of black folk" (DuBois 1989).

This seeming essentializing, while disturbing in that it does not fit into my acknowledged postmodern (intellectual) leanings, is necessary in this instance in that it clearly foregrounds the contradictions of race, class and gender, including sexuality, in Jamaican society. This is to the extent that the views of those "above" (read: the power elite) do not appear in synch with those "below" (read, in this instance: dancehall), at the very least *at eye level*. The separation of the "soul" of the struggle from the struggle itself, that is, in terms of the reading of the emancipation statues in Jamaica, then, has serious political and other implications. In another instance, in Barbados, it "eerily" suggests what are generally considered the (distant and hegemonic) attitudes of white Bajans towards slavery in that society.

Similarly, class, race and racial politics in Jamaican society mediate the extent to which those at the helm, usually of European extraction, may be inclined to see the rest of the society as equals, that is, to the extent that their contributions may be meaningfully incorporated into the imagery used to define both their status and identity in the official discourses of the society. Cooper's (2004b) assessment of the nature of Jamaican society, in this regard, as "enslaved in stereotype" is particularly instructive here, especially as it relates to how similar attitudes mediate the relationships between the academy and social phenomena. That there seems little appreciation for the awareness that culture does not operate only at the rarefied level of the visual arts, specifically as it relates to the Jamaican emancipation statues as a literalized and frozen (in time) explication of the politics of the black body in Jamaican culture and society, would also suggest that exploring cultures (of the body) beyond these restrictions does not fit into official projects of the academy in Jamaica and the Caribbean.

This clearly highlights the need for a widening as well as an overturning of the tyrannical superiority complexes which govern gatekeeping attitudes in the Caribbean and its academy. "Until all are free, then none is free", as indicated by Jamaican national hero and elder statesman Marcus Mosiah Garvey, at least a century earlier. This is a necessary part of the process of subverting the intellectual myopia which beset anti-colonial nationalist societies like those in the Caribbean (Scott 2004), which must, therefore, begin with a re-evaluation of notions of canonicity in terms of (appropriate) research methodologies in the Caribbean.

David Scott (2004) is convinced, and perhaps rightfully so, that currently the Caribbean academy is experiencing the onset of a malaise as it relates to meaningful (political and other) changes. The idealism of the post-independence era has been stunted, and in its place near despotic regimes have been created by some of the very leaders who were at the vanguard of the movement to replace colonial rule with indigenous Caribbean leadership and authority. The restrictive appropriations of power in the Caribbean are also to be experienced within the halls of the academy, one of the initial bedrocks of support for the then newly founded independence movements.

Surely, however, this is not the case in all instances. Yet the fact that an area such as dancehall as well as the body, itself a source of numerous sexual and other fantasies and pleasures as well as intellectual preoccupations, have not been sufficiently interrogated in the Caribbean academy is testament to the urgent need to widen the resources used to engage such explorations. In addition to this, there is an important need to expand the horizons of research in which such projects may be executed. De/constructing the politics of the black body in Jamaican and Caribbean culture, then, is the equivalent of also narrating into consciousness the collective as well as individual experiences of those within the nation (Tuhiwai Smith 2005), whose identities are often overlooked in the pursuit of the sanitized politics, slogans and representations of officialdom. These are part and parcel of how "nation discourse" is embodied as gender performance within the "nation space".

The "inconvenience" of subjectivity, therefore, gets marginalized as inappropriate and unsuitable as a space of intellectual consideration, in large part because there is no appropriate frame of reference which would, necessarily, support such projects. This is in urgent need of correction as a matter of principle, especially considering the Caribbean's own placement in the larger globalized intellectual arena of world scholarship. Certainly, we are more than just performing artistes and athletes, more than just expressive culture as an indication of our connections to an often (overly) romanticized African past. We are also a people with a full range of heterogeneous, complex and complicated experiences which, unfortunately, are not always foregrounded in official narratives of identity about the region. It is incumbent upon the academy, therefore, to seek the equalization of this vision through engendering support for as well as the creation, nurturance and sustenance of indigenous methods of enquiry which elevate the "native" as more than just a (black) body of disarticulated and often negative (sexual) desires.

Conclusion

Current research, publication and funding opportunities in the Caribbean must be widened as part of the necessary process of engendering and developing a reputable action-oriented research culture and tradition in the region. In so doing, emphasis will be placed on centring Caribbean subjects and subjectivities as legitimate areas of academic enquiry, specifically those that do not readily coincide with conventional approaches. Orthodox positions which attempt to undermine the confidence of untraditional research projects in terms of enforced claims of "authenticity" and conformity in the Caribbean are not only challenged but other knowledges are also foregrounded as important. This is a crucial part of balancing theoretical considerations alongside real-life matters.

Expanding the frames of reference used to analyse as well as to allocate support for research projects which focus on other areas of Caribbean life such as popular culture is a fundamental imperative in building support for a new and truly emancipated research tradition in the region. This is important, as often the roles of the researcher and the research process itself are not distinguished, though this is generally unacknowledged. Popular culture is thus, generally, considered a frivolous activity from which real meaning cannot, rationally, be made. Consequently, there is a definite need to create research chairs for these fields of enquiry as well as to provide funding to graduate students and other such researchers engaged in the excavation, articulation and elevation of new discourses of Caribbean consciousness.

Tuition and other related fees also need to be waived in many instances, as these often present real obstacles to accelerating the research process. This is especially so for students who do not undertake research projects on a full-time basis or who cannot afford to do so and, therefore, must juggle these alongside other substantive and necessary work commitments. The sense of alienation engendered as a consequence, through lack of understanding of and support for research projects of this kind by the academy needs to be corrected. Policy-makers must recognize the importance of research as a necessary tool to shaping appropriate development models tailored to suit Caribbean realities. This is especially the case in areas such as popular culture and other sites of Caribbean academic endeavour which can and, often, do shine needed light on gaps between society's superstructure and those who operate at its base level. There is a clear and urgent need for rethinking, re-evaluating and reconceptualizing research practices and tradition in the Caribbean academy.

References

Agozino, Biko. 2007. "Power: An African Fractal Theory of Chaos, Crime, Violence and Healing". Paper presented at the eighth annual SALISES conference, "Crisis, Chaos, and Change: Caribbean Development in the 21st Century", Trinidad and Tobago, 26–28 March.

Alexander, Bryant Keith. 2005. "Performance Ethnography: The Re-enacting and Inciting of Culture". In *The Sage Handbook of Qualitative Research*, edited by Norman K. Denzin and Yvonna S. Lincoln, 411–41. 3rd ed. London: Sage.

Barriteau, V. Eudine. 2007. "Theoretical Strengths and Relevance of Black Feminist Scholarship: A Caribbean Feminist Perspective". Paper presented at the eighth annual SALISES conference, "Crisis, Chaos, and Change: Caribbean Development in the 21st Century", Trinidad and Tobago, 26–28 March.

Buckridge, Steeve. 2004. *The Language of Dress: Resistance and Accommodation in Jamaica, 1760–1890*. Kingston: University of the West Indies Press.

Butler, Judith. 1993. *Bodies That Matter*. New York: Routledge.

———. 1999. *Gender Trouble*. New York: Routledge.

Cooke, Melville. 2007. "'Hiding' Homos", *Gleaner* (Kingston, Jamaica), 12 April.

Cooper, Carolyn. 1995. *Noises in the Blood: Orality, Gender and the "Vulgar" Body of Jamaican Popular Culture*. Durham, NC: Duke University Press.

———. 2004a. "Enslaved in Stereotype: Race and Representation in Post-Independence Jamaica". *Interventions* 6 (1): 1–17.

———. 2004b. *Sound Clash: Jamaican Dance Hall Culture at Large*. London: Palgrave Macmillan.

Digby, Tom. 1998. Introduction to *Men Doing Feminism*, edited by Tom Digby, 1–14. New York: Routledge.

DuBois, W.E.B. 1989. *The Souls of Black Folk*. Modified from 1989 Bantam Classic text, Charlottesville: UVA Electronic Text Center. etext.lib.virginia.edu/toc/modeng/public/DubSoul.html.

Fanon, Franz. 1967. *The Wretched of the Earth*. Harmondsworth, UK: Penguin.

Forbes, Curdella. 2005. *From Nation to Diaspora: Samuel Selvon, George Lamming and the Cultural Performance of Gender*. Kingston: University of the West Indies Press.

Foucault, Michel. 1978. *A History of Sexuality*. New York: Pantheon Books.

Harewood, Susan. 2006. "Transnational Soca Performances, Gendered Re-narrations of Caribbean Nationalism". *Social and Economic Studies* 55 (1–2): 25–48.

Hutcheon, Linda. 1989. *The Politics of Postmodernism*. New York. Routledge.

Pinnock, Agostinho. 2007. "At the Ideological Crossroads: Interrogating (Jamaican) Masculinities in Contemporary Urban Culture through Historical Discourse". Paper presented at the eighth annual SALISES conference, "Crisis, Chaos, and Change: Caribbean Development in the 21st Century", Trinidad and Tobago, 26–28 March.

Rabinow, Paul, ed. 1984. *The Foucault Reader: An Introduction to Foucault's Thought*. London: Penguin.

Rice, Phillip, and Patricia Waugh, eds. 1989. *Modern Literary Theory: A Reader*. 4th ed. New York: Oxford University Press.

Rich, Adrienne. 1980. "Compulsory Heterosexuality and Lesbian Existence". *Signs: Journal of Women in Culture and Society* 5: 631–60.

Scott, David. 2004. *Conscripts of Modernity: The Tragedy of Colonial Enlightenment*. London: Duke University Press.

Tuhiwai Smith, Linda. 2005. "On Tricky Ground". In *The Sage Handbook of Qualitative Research*, edited by Norman K. Denzin and Yvonna S. Lincoln, 86–107. 3rd ed. London: Sage.

Warner, Michael, ed. 1993. *Fear of a Queer Planet*. Minneapolis: University of Minnesota Press.

13.

THE TWENTY-FIRST-CENTURY CARIBBEAN WOMAN'S QUESTION
What Is the Meaning of Freedom?

APRIL BERNARD

IN BELIZE, ON CHRISTMAS DAY in 2006, after returning home from work at the hospital as a nurse, thirty-two-year-old Karel Idolly Gabourel began preparing food for her family. An argument ensued with her husband (who had been drinking heavily) over the cutting of their Christmas ham. The disagreement resulted in Karel being fatally stabbed by her husband in front of the couple's three sons – aged respectively twelve, ten and nine years.

In addition to Karel Gabourel, Anna Maria Magdaleno Basto and Keisha Sutherland were also brutally murdered by their partners in Belize, all within three weeks of each other between 16 December 2006 and 2 January 2007 (Milligan 2006; "Wife Murdered by Her Mate on Christmas Day!", *Amandala* [Georgetown], 28 December 2006; "Ganzie on the Run", *Amandala*, 5 January 2007). Karel, Anna Maria, and Keisha represent women across the Caribbean who stay with their abusive partners and face the possibility of death every day. Some may say these women could have left, obtained a restraining order or otherwise found a way to defend themselves, but instead apparently they freely chose to stay in oppressive circumstances with their abusers. However, upon taking a closer look into their context, we must ask, did these women, and do those like them, choose *freely* to stay in such situations?

In Barbados, Ariel (not her real name), a sixteen-year-old young woman, was featured in cell phone videos performing oral sex and engaging in various forms of intercourse. Evidence suggests that incidents such as these that start out as "just kicks" may involve the overt or covert use of narcotics to reduce sexual inhibitions (*Nation*, 3 February 2007). In the case of this sixteen-year-old and others like her, what started out as "just kicks" resulted in the appearance of pictures and sex videos of her on the Internet. Should incidents in which young women engage in sex for the camera be considered individual voluntary acts of sexual *freedom*, expressions of *neoliberation* and simply unencumbered *choices* that are boldly selected by a new generation of Caribbean women?

In Jamaica, Seraphina (not her real name), a thirty-eight-year-old mother of three, stated that the combination of irregular, low-paying jobs and the absence of support from her children's fathers drove her into "the business" of performing live sex on stage. Female performers can earn more than US$500 in one night from engaging in sex shows (*Sunday Gleaner*, 18 June 2006). Seraphina admitted she would never want any of her children to follow in her footsteps: the reason she was doing the shows was to offer her children a better life and educational opportunities that had not been available to her (*Gleaner*, 18 June 2006).

The third of the seven United Nations Millennium Development Goals has been a focal point for promoting gender equality and empowering women: to eliminate gender disparity in primary, secondary, and tertiary levels of education no later than 2015. Goal 3 is closely intertwined with the other seven goals because gender equity in education is intended to provide leverage to combat labour discrimination, lack of access to reproductive and health services, inequality within the household, violence against women and the barriers against women's political participation. According to a 2005 report from the UN Economic Commission for Latin America and the Caribbean, most governments in the region acknowledged significant but uneven achievements toward gender equity (ECLAC 2005, 1–12). Advances have been made in the areas of educational attainment, employment and health care, yet the challenge of entrenched gender ideologies that circumscribe women's existence remain. Clearly, the extent to which traditional gender ideologies and social constructs restrict the full expression of men is also an area that warrants further exploration.

Caribbean women have made great strides in recent years regarding educational attainment relative to men. The higher enrolment and completion rates of females compared to males at primary, secondary, and tertiary levels of education are becoming a predominant trend throughout the region. Despite these advances, educational attainment has not translated into comparable levels of employment among women relative to men. Women are more likely than men in the region to be unemployed or underemployed and to be single heads of households. In addition to having no or lower-paying jobs when compared to men, Caribbean women are more likely to live in poverty and for longer durations. While male marginalization and poor academic achievement relative to females have become topics for debate in the region, the feminization of poverty remains a justifiable area of concern (*Nation*, 9 March 2008).

Women in the Caribbean, whether married or single, often possess the substantial responsibility of being both the primary caregiver and breadwinner in their households. Surely, this dual responsibility was not the intended benefit of equal opportunity. Similarly, unemployment, underemployment and the legacy of poverty for a disproportionate number of women cannot be perceived as an exercise of rights.

In 2005, the Inter-Parliamentary Union's annual release of the world classification of women in national parliaments indicated that, of the 187 nations surveyed, only Guyana, Grenada and Suriname among English-speaking Caribbean states were in the top thirty. These three nations outperformed both the United States and Britain on the scale. Of these three Caribbean nations, only Guyana met the international Convention on the Elimination of All Forms of Discrimination against Women standards of having women hold 30 per cent of the seats in parliament (Guyana 30.8 per cent, Grenada 26.7 per cent and Suriname 25.5 per cent); it ranked 17th among all nations surveyed. Barbados placed 77th in the world (14 per cent), and Dominica, where Dame Eugenia Charles served as the nation's prime minister for more than a decade, ranked 80th (12.9 per cent). Jamaica ranked 88th in the world (11.7 per cent), Belize was 117th, with only two women out of thirty parliamentarians (6.7 per cent), while St Kitts–Nevis came in at 138th and was among eleven nations across the globe with no women in parliament (IPU 2005). In the most recent figures available (November 2011), the region appears to have gone backwards, as only Trinidad and Tobago (26th) was ranked in the top thirty, with women forming only 28.6 per cent of parliamentarians in that country (IPU 2011).

While the Caribbean is at the forefront of efforts to eliminate gender barriers, given that women represent more than half of the registered voters in the region, how do we explain why they hold a relatively small minority of the seats in local parliaments? Should this fact be considered a reflection of their preference for male candidates over those that are female? Are women freely choosing to refrain from exercising their right to fully participate in the political process? Whether just for kicks or as a matter of survival, the apparent willingness (or acquiescence) of women – whether individually or collectively – to be abused, exploited, underrepresented and oppressed warrants a closer look into the relationship between social constructs, contexts and the degree of freedom women have to make efficacious choices.

How we answer questions about women like Karel, Anna Maria, Keisha, Ariel and Seraphina, those who live in poverty, those who are both caregiver and breadwinner, those who are unemployed, underemployed or poorly educated, those who raise their children alone, and those who do not fully participate in the political process, depends upon how we define the concept of freedom. This chapter argues that a skewed definition of freedom has resulted in uneven achievements toward gender equality and equity in the Caribbean region. This subjective definition of freedom reinforces patriarchal social constructs that contribute to the persistent subjugation of women in the region.

For women in the Caribbean, oppression can be defined as subjective freedom, rendered absolute (Jackson 2001). In this analysis of what oppresses women, we must begin by defining freedom. The twenty-first-century Caribbean woman's question is not what oppresses her, but rather, what is the meaning of true freedom? This question is asked with the assumption that if we cannot point to someone who is oppressing Caribbean women, then perhaps our definition of freedom is the antagonist. By rendering absolute a subjective definition of freedom that circumscribes and binds my existence and that of other women, then I must also assess the extent to which the oppressor is I.

Freedom and the Duality of Social Construction

The meaning of freedom is reflected in the social, political and economic environment through policy, practice, human relationships and expressions of self. Our individual and collective definitions of freedom are an indication of embedded social constructs that give rise to gender ideologies and shape the public and private lives of women and men. What has yet to be mended in the lives of women in the private realm of domesticity and sexual relations festers in the public social, economic and political arenas (Barriteau 2006).

Nancy Hirschmann in "Toward a Feminist Theory of Freedom" (1996) provides a framework from which to assess the concept of freedom that can be applied to the Caribbean context. Hirschmann contemplates the implications of masculinist and feminist definitions of freedom based upon the concepts of negative and positive liberty. Isaiah Berlin (1969) divides the concept of freedom along the lines of "negative" and "positive" liberty. Negative liberty defines freedom as the absence of constraints or the non-restriction of options and *opportunities* for action. Positive liberty defines freedom as the congruence between one's will or true self and the ability to *exercise* their full capacities (Berlin 1969, 118–72).

The significant difference between negative and positive liberty lies in the definition of *the Self* and *the Other* as sources of barriers to freedom. Negative liberty points to the presence of external barriers or the Other as constraints to action, and positive liberty identifies the existence of internal barriers or Self as the cause of one's oppression. In the former case, other people, either directly or indirectly, intentionally or unintentionally, constrain or restrict one's opportunities for action and freedom. In the latter, one's personal fears, addictions and compulsions stifle true expressions of self and the exercise of will; these inhibitions restrict action and suppress freedom.

This notion of the Other when applied to the "male perspective" of the theory of negative liberty is similar to the concept of the Other in traditional existential feminist theory in which man is defined as the Subject and women are viewed as the Other, insignificant and an impediment, and whose existence is only defined in relation to man. While existentialist feminism encourages women to acknowledge notions of men as Other rather than Subject, negative liberty accepts a reality that any entity external to Self could be considered a barrier to freedom.

NEGATIVE LIBERTY

Based upon the theory of negative liberty, the self is the Subject, and is viewed as the source of one's desires. The Self functions as a personal guide to freedom. In a context governed by individual autonomy and the absence of external constraints or the Other (including the state), one is *free* to make choices and take action. Expressions of individual freedom are expansive, diverse and innovative, yet modernity and morality are together tenuously bound by the subjective limits of "collective selves". Based upon this theory, women, like men, are equally and innately separate, individualistic, unconnected, rights-oriented and even antagonistic (Hirschmann 1996, 50). As free agents women and men have the right to choose among the array of options to which all are equally entitled, and in doing so they define their own limits, their own freedom and their own oppression.

POSITIVE LIBERTY

The theory of positive liberty implies a self that is constantly conflicted by the incongruence between perceived personal limitations and free will. In a context limited by self-perceptions, one requires the intervention of the Other to focus desires, reveal true capacities and guide action toward freedom. In contrast to the concept of the Other in the theory of negative liberty, here the Other functions as a dominant force of equilibrium that seeks to shape and be shaped by the consciousness of Self.

Expressions of freedom are the result of intervention from the Other to help resolve internal conflict within the Self. While expressions of freedom may be subjectively restricted by perceptions of self, in this case, modernity and morality are intricately bound by the limits of "self within the collective" (Hirschmann 1996, 50). Based upon the theory of positive liberty, women, like men, can perceive themselves as innately connected, communitarian, selfless, and concerned with responsibility and care (ibid.). They are free to choose among the array of options deemed appropriate by the Other, and in doing so together women, men and *the Other* define their own limits, their own freedom, and their own oppression.

The theory of negative liberty underscores some of the ideals of liberal feminism such as individualism, rights and entitlements in the pursuit of freedom. Positive liberty provides a theory leading toward freedom through the transcendence beyond the inhibitions of the inner self or psyche and could be ascribed to the psychoanalytic feminist tradition. The theories of negative and positive liberty inform women's expressions of freedom or lack thereof, yet both approaches to defining freedom are gender biased.

According to Carol Gilligan (1982), the theory of negative liberty displays a masculinist bias. The ideals heralded by liberal feminists are the same as those that reinforce structures that support an oppressive environment for women.

Since the 1960s, the international women's movement has reduced obstacles that prevent women from actively engaging in the market. Caribbean women, when compared to previous generations, have enhanced legal rights, choice and entitlements regarding reproductive health, opportunities for education and employment, and protection from domestic violence and sexual harassment. These advances can be considered among the many achievements of the international women's movement, yet these gains for women can also be attributed to the promotion of a concept of freedom based upon the theory of negative liberty. The fundamental ideals of individualism and entitlements that form the basis for negative liberty also support capitalist mythology.

Capitalist mythology is based upon ideology that promotes individual freedom, personal autonomy and notions that persons who are poor lack a Protestant work ethic and related virtues, are lazy, undeserving, unintelligent and to blame for their own plight. Rhetoric that assumes all individuals have the freedom to maximize their material interests and possess the personal autonomy to earn and spend as they choose is faulty. Freedom and autonomy are relative based upon social status – class, citizenship, and other classifications that structure society. Neoliberalism is supported by rhetoric that asserts that reducing the size and scope of the state can empower people, revitalize local life and promote economic self-reliance. Such neoliberal approaches point to the lack of understanding about the interdependent contributions of public and private entities and relationships to poverty. The results of capitalist mythology are fragmented, inflexible and non-responsive poverty reduction schemes that at best provide a crude safety net as a means to meet the needs of the poor, the majority of whom are women (Wineman 1984; Marris and Rein 1982; Piven and Cloward 1993).

The theory of negative liberty ignores the complexity of the Caribbean woman's reality as she negotiates expressions of self within the sphere of opportunities available to her in the public and private domains, based upon her gender, social status and other classifications used to structure society. Historically laws, customs and social norms have been *imposed* upon women. Women's opportunities, choices, actions and behaviours have been inequitably sanctioned and restricted by entities outside of herself. Rather than acknowledging the persistent classism and gender ideologies that limit women's self-expression within public and private spheres, the theory of negative liberty implies that women who fail to exercise their freedom to attain "the good life" have no one to blame but themselves.

The ideals of community and care espoused by the theory of positive liberty have historical significance for the concerns of women (Gilligan 1982), yet while not masculinist in essence, the theory is gender biased. The relationship between the Other and the Self in the theory of positive liberty is one in which the Other has sovereign power to shape and guide expressions of Self. The Other in this case is powerful and the Self is powerless. This relationship between Other and Self is theoretically similar to the relationship between master and slave. This relationship is replicated in social contexts fostered by traditional gender ideologies that view women as being powerless, defective and dependent and that determine the significance of their existence relative to men. Similar to the way in which the ideology of capitalist mythology assumes poverty is a result of pathology, the theory of positive liberty poses that a lack of freedom is based upon internal barriers to progress.

When applied to women, the theory of positive liberty implies that a woman's worth is defined by her environment. The social context defines how women are *allowed* to act, think, desire, prefer and conceive of themselves and others. Women, in turn, through their behaviour, act to reinforce the same social context that restricts them. If the social context is one that has the norms, customs, and language of patriarchy at its core, then the subjugation of women in public and private domains as well as women's internalized perceived deficiencies work together to oppress and suppress their ability to exercise free will.

The theory of positive liberty fails to recognize the hegemony of patriarchy and its role in influencing the social context and its impact on women. The gender bias of the theory of positive liberty becomes evident when one acknowledges the influence of a patriarchal context in shaping individual and collective historical, social, political and economic relationships. The patriarchal context at once affects and is affected by women's desires, preferences, beliefs, values, intimate aspects of being (including sexuality) and their way of defining the world. Women's self-expression within the norms, customs and language of a patriarchal context reinforces their own subjugation and perpetuates the cycle of oppression. The theory of positive liberty fails to acknowledge the duality of social construction in a patriarchal context and falls short of providing a meaningful definition of freedom for women in the Caribbean.

An Alternative Theory of Freedom

The acquisition of language, ritual and community that redefines, reconceptualizes and fosters congruence between the inner self and outer environment is a prerequisite for creating an alternative approach to freedom for women. Men and women function as both objects and subjects in a system of control (Havel 1987). Along with men, women have helped to create the oppressive conditions of the patriarchal context in which they live. To transcend the internal and external limitations of patriarchy, men and women must consciously and collectively create new conditions.

To intentionally reconstruct a definition of true freedom for women that is not limited by patriarchal language and norms, a new paradigm is proposed. This new paradigm confronts the myths of patriarchy by realizing that male superiority and female inferiority are socially constructed and consequently illusions. This new paradigm requires the transcendence of both men and women toward their true Self in a mutually liberating context. The creation of an alternative context is dependent upon women's relationships with women and women's relationships with men as a means to define freedom.

The relational or communitarian context is based upon the development of an individual and collective history of social, economic and political mutual liberation that would replace patriarchy. Women's self-expression within the norms, customs and language of a relational or communitarian context would reinforce their liberation and that of others, and perpetuate a cycle of freedom. The proposed theory of relational liberty differs from negative and positive liberty in that it fosters freedom *with* as opposed to freedom *to* or freedom *from* respectively. Entitlements, personal autonomy, separation and individual action become secondary to responsibility, community, connectedness and collective reflection. A transcended inner self or psyche evolves to become a transcended society in which both men and women support each other's full capacity to contribute to the collective well-being.

Under this new paradigm, true freedom for the twenty-first-century Caribbean woman would be defined by three elements: (1) a transcended Self, (2) mutually affirming relationships among women, and (3) the absence of social, economic and political dominance in relationships between men and women. The transcendence encompasses a distinction between women's intrinsic and extrinsic orientation. If each woman can be classified as a point within the universe of all women, then at any given moment in time, each woman provides a unique expression of both feminism and femininity.

Women with an extrinsic orientation toward expressing Self are disposed to use feminism or their femininity for their own ends; their desires, preferences, will and behaviours are expressed because they serve other "ultimate" or "primary" interests. Women with an intrinsic orientation toward expressing Self *live* their feminism or femininity. Extrinsic or utilitarian orientation is the use of feminism and femininity as means to obtain security, status and self-gratification (Allport and Ross 1967). Intrinsic orientation is the motivation primarily by needs linked to transcendence, universal purpose, reciprocation and collective responsibility.

This new paradigm diverges from perspectives that interpret intrinsic and extrinsic orientation as dichotomous and fixed states of being. Rather than discrete categories or polar opposites on a continuum of feminist orientation, this new paradigm recognizes that each woman's expression of self is dynamic and at any given moment in time embodies a unique combination of extrinsic and intrinsic qualities. Progress toward transcendence is achieved as women increase their ability to attain and sustain an intrinsic orientation, so that they are at once continually *crafting and living* an actualized expression of their femininity and feminism. Women's ability to sustain an intrinsic orientation is dependent upon their will to engage in the processes of incessant self-reflection and meaningful discourse within a collective that mutually affirms the intrinsic qualities in all women.

The Caribbean woman's transcendence of self beyond the social construction of patriarchy requires an intrinsic orientation toward feminism and femininity that at once values, affirms, celebrates and seeks a deeper understanding of womanhood. This understanding deepens through self-reflection and is dependent upon the quality of women's relationships with women and with men.

Based upon the proposed theory of relational liberty, women's relationships with women are characterized by mutual support and intentional consciousness that affirms the value of women's activities, forms of expression and micro-, mezzo- and macro-level social, economic and political contributions. The quality of women's relationships with men are distinguished by the collective will to confront and remove social, economic and political forces that create oppressive restrictions or barriers to opportunities for action, circumscribe internal will, create inhibitions and prevent both men and women from exercising their full capacities.

The relational context becomes one that is neither masculinist- nor feminist-centred but rather self-actualizing and communal. The discourse that gives meaning to this alternative context is neither patriarchal nor masculinist but transcending. Notions of hegemony, suppression, oppression and victimization by the Other are replaced by mutual liberation ideology. The connections and interdependence rather than differences and separations between emotion and intellect, the public and the private, and masculine and feminine will be explored, described, rearticulated, reformulated and created anew based upon the concept of a collectively free society.

To redress the history of gender inequality and patriarchy, affirming the role of women as the drivers of the process of conceptualizing their true freedom by working together and with men to reshape oppressive gender ideologies is imperative. This reconceptualization process is achieved by creating safe spaces or contexts at the micro-, mezzo-, and macro-levels of society that foster counterdiscourse and social relations that ultimately perpetuate and facilitate their own existence.

Freedom, like the concepts of equity and equality, is a guiding principle rather than an outcome or absolute end that can be achieved. This new context and discourse will need to be assessed with new ways of measuring progress for women. The masculinist conception of freedom asks women, are you free? and assesses their opportunities for and exercise of action as a means to measure progress. This new paradigm asks women, how free are you? only after asking them for the relevant criteria from which to measure their degree of freedom.

Is this new paradigm possible? An alternative to the oppressive patriarchal context is a requirement for development in the Caribbean. In the global context, the places where human development is pronounced are also locations where policies impacting the public and private lives of women have most fully mended the wounds resulting from traditional gender ideologies that favour patriarchy. Political scientist Pippa Norris, in her book *Rising Tide*, uses cross-national data to show how gender issues correlate with development (Norris and Inglehart 2003). Countries such as Canada, West Germany, Sweden and Finland that rank among the highest in the world in achieving progress toward gender equality also have relatively low rates of crime, infant mortality, teenage pregnancy and single-parent families.

What oppresses Caribbean women in the twenty-first century is the failure of women and men alike to radically dispute patriarchal sovereignty in ways that go beyond limited conceptions of negative and positive liberty. Legal rights, choice, entitlements and psychotherapy are not enough to combat persistent oppression. This new paradigm suggests meaningful relationships, community and collective action are needed to eliminate oppression and initiate movement toward mutual liberty. The creation of a relational or communitarian context and discourse is a requirement for responsive and sustainable development in the Caribbean.

Race and the New Paradigm of Freedom

Caribbean women, like women of colour around the world, experience oppression based upon their gender and race. To ignore the race factor in a discussion on theories of freedom for Caribbean women would be negligent. Audre Lorde (1984) argues that women's oppression knows no ethnic or racial boundaries, and feminist theorizing that ignores the experience of black women encourages its own demise. Because this discussion focuses on the experiences of women in a Caribbean context, one cannot dismiss the importance of race as an additional contributor to their oppression.

Scholars of slavery in the British colonies describe how the bodies of African women were used to provide male slaveholders with the rhetorical justification to set aside their traditional gender ideologies in terms of race; black women were viewed by colonists as commodities and valued solely for production and reproduction purposes (Beckles 1989, 1999; Morgan 2004). Historically, black women have been exploited as a means to build wealth for others. Since the institution of the plantocracy, black women were, and continue to be, oppressed not only because they were women, but also because they were black.

Similar to the ways in which women must go beyond the confines of patriarchy to discover language, customs, religion and tradition that affirms their experience, they must also challenge the limits that a historically racist context places on their potential to impact global development. In the new paradigm, the discourse and context that emerges to affirm their womanhood must also affirm their African heritage, acknowledge the persecution their ancestors suffered and celebrate their ancestors' contributions to global development and their legacy of resilience.

A black feminist manifesto calls for anti-racist and anti-sexist politics, and encourages black women to struggle with white women against sexism and with black men against racism. When applied to the global context, the new paradigm of true freedom for Caribbean women adopts this black feminist manifesto. Patricia Mohammed (2003) adds the element of culture to the manifesto for the new paradigm and insists that the significance of the experience of women of Amerindian and East Indian descent in the Caribbean cannot be ignored as definitions of feminism and femininity are shaped and revised. The dynamic discourse created by Caribbean women to affirm their womanhood and their Afro-Caribbean and diverse cultural heritage holds the potential to empower them to work with and lead others regionally and globally in the struggle against patriarchy and racism.

THE IFEMINIST CRITIQUE

Criticism of the new paradigm of freedom for Caribbean woman may be derived from various perspectives, particularly individualist feminism or Ifeminism. Similar to the theory of negative liberty, Ifeminism upholds the ideals of individual freedom and personal autonomy and asserts that women make choices as individuals, not collectively. While a community of women may believe that women should not stay in abusive relationships, engage in pornography or decline to exercise their right to participate in the political process, those are paths individual women are free to choose.

Ifeminists apply the principle of "a woman's body, a woman's right" (McElroy 2002, 5) and believe that all individuals have a right to their own body and should exercise their capacities to maximize their own welfare. Ifeminism promotes the perspective that pornography and prostitution are merely choices, and liberation for both men and women can be achieved through participation in the free market (McElroy 2002, 14–15). Michele Alexandre (2006) describes the method of body protest as a means for women to revolt against patriarchy by engaging in suggestive or sexually explicit dance, dress or performance that is intended to challenge socially imposed restrictions on women's bodies and sexual expression. Pornography and prostitution would be considered extensions of the body protest or Ifeminist movement.

Pornography and prostitution present an area of disagreement between radical feminists and Ifeminists. Radical feminist theory views pornography and prostitution not as an exercise of free choice but as indicators of exploitation and victimization of women that occurs in male-dominated or patriarchal society. The new paradigm of freedom for Caribbean women counters Ifeminism by supporting and furthering the radical feminist argument. Because of male dominance, in a patriarchal context every opportunity for women to exercise choice holds exploitive potential. Even in the absence of coercion and despite the rewards of a liberal market, pornography and prostitution are viewed as exploitive because of the oppressive nature of the patriarchal context in which they function. A new paradigm is needed that enables women to exercise choice, maximize their capacities, establish tradition and contribute to the well-being of the collective through the creation of counterdiscourse, relationships and communities that are devoid of patriarchy.

Conclusion

The results of a 2007 annual global survey of freedom conducted by Freedom House, a US-based human rights organization, listed Barbados as one of the most free countries in the Western Hemisphere. The survey criteria were holding free and fair elections, opening up opportunities for women, anti-corruption efforts, tackling violent crime, observing the law and allowing the courts to function independently, and having a free and vibrant press. While Barbados received the highest classification from Freedom House, the findings also indicated that domestic violence in Barbados has yet to receive priority attention and remains a concern that needs to be addressed. How free are Barbados and other Caribbean nations for women who are domestically abused, sexually exploited or harassed, living in poverty, non-participants in the political process and single-handedly both caregiver and breadwinner?

In October 2005, Joycelin Massiah gave the Sir Arthur Lewis Institute of Social and Economic Studies Public Policy lecture at the University of the West Indies, Cave Hill: "Ten Years After Beijing: What More Do Caribbean Women Want?" In her discussion, Massiah provided the blueprint for the new paradigm of freedom for Caribbean women. According to Massiah, "True freedom for Caribbean women is characterized by equitable relationships. Such a relationship is one of equals, where each party has equal rights and obligations, each person has respect and wants the best for the other, and where understanding the other's point of view is essential. These are the ingredients for a good and equitable relationship" (Massiah 2006, 77).

True freedom for Caribbean women includes affirming, flexible and responsive social, economic, cultural and political institutions, structures and environments: "Women want to see the institutions of education, religion, the law and the media reviewed and assessed. They want old institutions reconstructed and new ones created; they want to see administrative tools and structures refined; they want ongoing data and relevant research; they want to see institutions which are efficient, effective and free of gender bias" (Massiah 2006, 77). True freedom for Caribbean women calls them to engage in individual and collective action, to exercise their rights responsibly and to function as "the vanguard of the journey in the quest for gender justice, for a genuine ethics of care for people, and for closure of that gap between liberal rhetoric and illiberal reality" (ibid.).

Is this new paradigm possible? The reality of a developed society requires freedom that is not bound by patriarchy (Ban 2007). The rhetoric of liberty for women must be grounded in the affirmation and the truth of their individual and collective experience and in their intrinsic quest for transcendence. To find liberation, Caribbean women must seek community and acknowledge differences among and between themselves and men. To find true freedom, not only must women go beyond using the master's tools to dismantle the master's house (Lorde 1984), they must begin with a critical look at the tools used to construct or deconstruct their place of abode. True freedom calls.

Acknowledgements

A modified version of this paper appeared in the *Journal of Eastern Caribbean Studies* 33, no. 3 (September 2008): 1–23.

References

Alexandre, Michele. 2006. "Dance Halls, Masquerades, Body Protest and the Law: The Female Body as a Redemptive Tool against Trinidad's Gender-Biased Laws". *Duke Journal of Gender Law and Policy* 13 (Spring): 177–202.

Allport, Gordon, and J. Michael Ross. 1967. "Personal Religious Orientation and Prejudice". *Journal of Personality and Social Psychology* 5 (4): 434–43.

Ban, Ki-moon. 2007. UN Message of the Secretary General on International Women's Day, 8 March. http://www.un.org/events/women/iwd/2007/sg-message.shtml.

Barriteau, V. Eudine. 2006. "Thirty Years towards Equality: How Many More? The Mandate of the Bureau of Gender Affairs in Promoting Gender Justice in the Barbadian State". Centre for Gender and Development Studies, University of the West Indies, Cave Hill, Barbados.

Beckles, Hilary. 1989. *Natural Rebels: A Social History of Enslaved Black Women in Barbados*. London: Zed Books.

———. 1999. *Centering Woman: Gender Discourses in Caribbean Slave Society*. Kingston: Ian Randle.

Berlin, Isaiah. 1969. *Four Essays on Liberty*. New York: Oxford University Press.

de Beauvoir, Simone. 1953. *The Second Sex*, edited by H.M. Parshley. New York: Knopf.

Economic Commission for Latin America and the Caribbean (ECLAC). 2005. "Gender and the Millennium Development Goals". *Gender Dialogue* 17: 1–12.

Freedom House. 2007. *Freedom in the World*. http://www.freedomhouse.org/report/freedom-world/2007/barbados.

Gilligan, Carol. 1982. *In a Different Voice: Psychological Theory and Women's Development*. Cambridge, MA: Harvard University Press.

Havel, Vaclav. 1987. *Living in Truth*. London: Faber and Faber.

Hirschmann, Nancy. 1996. "Toward a Feminist Theory of Freedom". *Political Theory* 24 (1): 46–67.

International Parliamentary Union (IPU). 2005. "Women in National Parliaments. Situation as of 31 December 2005". http://www.ipu.org/wmn-e/arc/classif311205.htm.

———. 2011. "Women in National Parliaments". http://www.ipu.org/wmn-e/classif.htm.

Jackson, F.L. 2001. "Freedom and the Tie That Binds: Marriage as an Ethical Institution". *Animus* 6. http://www2.swgc.mun.ca/animus/vol6.html.

Lorde, Audre. 1984. *Sister/outsider*. New York: Crossing Press.

Marris, Peter, and Martin Rein. 1982. *Dilemmas of Social Reform*. Chicago: University of Chicago Press.

Massiah, Joycelin. 2006. "Ten Years after Beijing: What More Do Caribbean Women Want?" *Journal of Eastern Caribbean Studies* 31 (1): 55–79.

McElroy, Wendy, ed. 2002. *Liberty for Women: Freedom and Feminism in the Twenty-first Century*. Chicago: Independent Institute.

Milligan, Keisha. 2006. "O.W. Nurse Stabbed Dead by Addict Husband". *Amandala*, 19 December 2006.

Mohammed, Patricia. 2003. "A Symbiotic Visiting Relationship: Caribbean Feminist Historiography and Caribbean Feminist Theory". *Confronting Power Theorizing Gender: Interdisciplinary Perspectives in the Caribbean*. Kingston: University of the West Indies Press.

Morgan, Jennifer. 2004. *Laboring Women: Reproduction and Gender in New World Slavery*. Philadelphia: University of Pennsylvania Press.

Norris, Pippa, and Ronald Inglehart. 2003. *Rising Tide: Gender Equality and Cultural Change around the World*. New York: Cambridge University Press.

Piven, Francis, and Richard Cloward. 1993. *Regulating the Poor: the Functions of Public Welfare*. New York: Vintage.

Taylor, Charles. 1979. "What's Wrong with Negative Liberty?" In *The Idea of Freedom: Essays in Honour of Isaiah Berlin*, edited by Alan Ryan, 175–93. New York: Oxford University Press.

Wineman, Steven. 1984. *The Politics of Human Services: Radical Alternatives to the Welfare State*. Boston: South End Press.

CONTRIBUTORS

ALAN COBLEY is Professor of South African and Comparative History, Department of History and Philosophy, at the University of the West Indies, Cave Hill, Barbados, and Pro Vice Chancellor and Chair, Board for Undergraduate Studies, at the University of the West Indies.

VICTOR C. SIMPSON is Senior Lecturer in Spanish Literature, Department of Language, Linguistics and Literature, and Deputy Dean (Outreach), Faculty of Humanities and Education, at the University of the West Indies, Cave Hill, Barbados.

AGNEL BARRON is an instructor in the Foundation Language Programme, Faculty of Humanities and Education at the University of the West Indies, Cave Hill, Barbados.

APRIL BERNARD is Assistant Professor in Criminal Justice and Affiliate Faculty, Women and Gender Studies, Chicago State University.

BRIDGET BRERETON is Professor Emerita of History at the University of the West Indies, St Augustine, Trinidad and Tobago.

SANDRA GIFT is Senior Programme Officer, Quality Assurance Unit, at the University of the West Indies, St Augustine, Trinidad and Tobago.

ENA HARRIS is Assistant Professor of English, Bard High School Early College Network, Newark, New Jersey.

OBA KENYATTA OMOWALE KITEME is a member of the National Joint Action Committee, Port of Spain, Trinidad and Tobago.

HILDE NEUS VAN DER PUTTEN works with the Suriname Museum Foundation in Paramaribo, Suriname.

EDITH PÉREZ SISTO is Professor of Caribbean Literature, Universidad Simón Bolívar, Caracas, Venezuela.

AGOSTINHO M.N. PINNOCK is a doctoral student in the Caribbean Institute of Media and Communications at the University of the West Indies, Mona, Jamaica.

KELVIN QUINTYNE is an instructor in the Foundation Language Programme at the University of the West Indies, Cave Hill, Barbados.

KIRWIN R. SHAFFER is Assistant Professor of Latin American Studies and Coordinator of Global Studies, Penn State University–Berks/LeHigh Valley, Pennsylvania.

HAZEL SIMMONS-McDONALD is Professor of Applied Linguistics at the University of the West Indies, Cave Hill, Barbados, and Pro Vice Chancellor and Principal at theUniversity of the West Indies, Open Campus.

JEROME TEELUCKSINGH is Lecturer, Department of History, at the University of the West Indies, St Augustine, Trinidad and Tobago.

www.ingramcontent.com/pod-product-compliance
Lightning Source LLC
Chambersburg PA
CBHW021827300426
44114CB00009BA/356